THE MENTAL GAME
OF BASEBALL

THE MENTAL GAME OF BASEBALL

A Guide to Peak Performance

Third Edition

H. A. DORFMAN
and
KARL KUEHL

Diamond Communications
An Imprint of
ROWMAN & LITTLEFIELD PUBLISHING GROUP
Lanham • South Bend • New York • Oxford

published by
DIAMOND COMMUNICATIONS
An Imprint of the
Rowman & Littlefield Publishing Group
4501 Forbes B'lvd - Suite 200
Lanham, Maryland 20706

Distributed by National Book Network

The Library of Congress catalogued the previous edition as follows:

Dorfman, H. A. (Harvey A.), 1935-
    The mental game of baseball : a guide to peak performance / H. A.
Dorfman and Karl Kuehl. —2nd ed., rev. ad updated.
        p. cm.
    1. Baseball—Psychological aspects. I. Kuehl, Karl, 1937- II. Title.
GV867.6.D67 1994
796.35701'9—dc20   94-34355
                                                                  CIP

ISBN 1-888698-54-3 (pbk. : alk. paper)

To all who tolerated our persistence, and there were many; to all who encouraged it, and there were more; to all who shared with us their knowledge and experience, through the printed word and word of mouth; to all who love this game of baseball — and to the vigorous pursuit of excellence, we dedicate this book.

About the Authors

Harvey A. Dorfman's background has been in education as a teacher, counselor, coach, and consultant. He has a Master's Degree in Communications/Psychology and is most knowledgeable about baseball and the factors necessary for success in the game. He was employed from 1984 through 1993 as the A's full-time instructor/counselor and from 1994 through 1997 with the Florida Marlins. He joined the Tampa Bay Devil Rays in the same capacity in 1998. In 1999 he became full-time sport psychology consultant for the Scott Boras Corporation. He lectures extensively on sports psychology, management and leadership training, and personal development. He has, as well, been a consultant to the Vancouver Canucks and the New York Islanders of the NHL, and to a number of major universities. In addition, he has experience as a newspaper columnist and freelance journalist, writing for *The New York Times, Boston Globe,* and *Miami Herald,* among others.

Since co-authoring *The Mental Game of Baseball*, Dorfman has written two other books for Diamond Communications—*The Mental ABCs of Pitching: A Handbook for Performance Enhancement* and *The Mental Keys to Hitting: A Handbook of Strategies for Performance Enhancement*. He is currently working on his fourth book, *Coaching the Mental Game*, which will be released in the Fall of 2003.

Karl Kuehl, a native of California, has had a *distinguished* career of more than 35 years in baseball as a player, scout, major league coach, major league manager, minor league player-manager at the age of 21, and director of player personnel. Serving in these various capacities, and in his current role as special advisor to the Cleveland Indians' general manager, Kuehl knows first-hand the importance of the mental aspects of the game. As the minor league director from 1983 to 1991, he was instrumental in applying that knowledge and in making the A's farm system one of the finest and most progressive in baseball.

The illustrations in *The Mental Game of Baseball* are by Sharmy Buechner Altschuler, of Cambridge, Massachusetts.

CONTENTS

The theory of baseball is as simple as that of any field sport in vogue, and herein lies one of its attractive features; and yet, to play the game up to its highest point of excellence requires as great a degree of mental ability . . . as any known game of ball.

From *The Game of Baseball*
By Henry Chadwick, 1868

FOREWORD

In the winter of 1991, I finally met the guy who wrote the most help-ful baseball book I'd ever read. I, along with several of my team-mates, referred to *The Mental Game of Baseball* as the "Baseball Bible." I discovered the book at a point in my playing career when I had begun to realize that the difference between mediocrity and great-ness was governed by what was between the ears.

As a pitcher I'm now absolutely convinced that pitching a poor game or dominating a game shouldn't be attributed exclusively to a pitcher's "stuff." A pitcher who can simplify his thoughts to one pitch, one mo-ment in time—and execute that pitch—will be far more successful than one who cannot, irrespective of what kind of "stuff" he has that game.

The Mental Game of Baseball is clearly written and simplified enough for the reader to learn, as I did, about those mechanisms of the mind that can either inhibit or help him to develop appropriate thinking patterns. After reading the book, I began to formulate seemingly simple game plans. Plans that worked. My game plan today is based on the many enlightening and practical ideas included in *The Mental Game of Baseball*.

This book, and Harvey Dorfman, have helped me cultivate the right perspective—even about matters beyond baseball. I do know that my career turned around when I was introduced to both. I wish they had been available to me sooner.

I guess I first found this book in 1990, a year after it was originally published. It's been with me ever since. I reluctantly picked up the 2nd Edition in 1995, because my original copy was marked, referenced and dog-eared to serve my immediate interests—and needs. It's been a valuable resource for me, as I've indicated. And, as mentioned, I've seen the book in the lockers of many of my teammates over the years.

Now, the 3rd Edition is here. And Harvey asked me to write a Foreword. Essentially, there's only one thing more to say now that hasn't already been said about this classic baseball book: the content will always be up-to-date—relevant. By that I mean that the universal themes, issues and strategies haven't changed and won't change over the years. That's why this book will continue to be the great reference that it has been.

The only things that change are the names of the players. But it's absurd (and not feasible, Harvey tells me) to re-write the book every time a new edition is put out, just to bring the names of contemporary players into the text. The points are always applicable, that I know—no matter who the players are. The ideas are never outdated, no matter what season is being played. Ty Cobb said as much in the 1920's!

Let me give an example. In the 1st Edition, Rusty Staub (still a prominent figure in New York, my city of choice) was used as a model for how to take effective batting practice. In the 2nd Edition, Tony Gwynn was added as a more contemporary example. Now Tony Gwynn has retired. Should the editors throw Alex Rodriguez' names in there in order to 'update' it? Alex broke the record for most home runs by a shortstop in the history of the game in 2001. But it's not necessary to add his name to the list of hitters who take impeccable b.p. Or Edgar Martinez. Or Mike Piazza. Because it's the *behavior* of great hitters that is the constant—the thread that runs through the approach of *all* outstanding players. It seems to me that it's less important to know the *who* than it is to know the *what-to-do*. This book continues to provide such direction.

Another example. The earlier editions have a couple of terrific anecdotes about Tom Seaver, illustrating how important commitment and preparation are to performance. Tom (another New York fixture) is now in the broadcast booth. But Roger Clemens, Jamie Moyer, Barry Bonds, and any other number of names could now be used. (I'd like to believe mine would be appropriate, as well.) What matters most is what people *do* to maximize their mental game. To learn what is required, to recognize the obstacles and pitfalls, to understand how to integrate the right strategies into the appropriate actions during competition. That's all between the covers of this book. Has been, still is, always will be.

If you read the sports section of the newspapers, you'll read all about who performs well these days—and why. Last winter, outfielder Darren Lewis talked about missing Barry Bonds at the gym for their regular 7 a.m. off-season workout. As it turned out, Bonds had to deal with a personal matter at 9 a.m., and rather than delay the workout, he went to the gym before dawn, and before Lewis arrived. After Lewis learned about the circumstance, he remarked that Bonds is "one of the hardest-working athletes I've ever been around. He's got a tremendous work ethic . . . That's why he's still in such great shape." That ethic, Bonds acknowledges, is directly linked to his performance.

It is one of the attributes of great players, and *The Mental Game of Baseball* reveals and emphasizes those constants, even as the names of the players may change.

Of course, the book applies to more than baseball. Its topics and guidance refer to many of life's pursuits. A fully actualized person needs to understand the principles of responsibility. These are clearly offered in a chapter that very specifically covers that subject. Mental discipline has broader application than to the world of sport. That is also made clear to every reader, as is the definition of 'attitude'—and how one can change it from not-so-good to good.

O. K. That's what I have to say. But I asked a Mets teammate of mine, a guy who's been called "an over-achiever," to jot down a few words for me about this book. I know he used to carry it around wherever he went. The player's name is Joe McEwing. This is what *he* had to say:

"Through *The Mental Game of Baseball*, I've been opened up to a whole new world. It gave me a mental approach to the game and to life that I never had before. I spent six years in the minor leagues going to the ballpark every day without a mental plan or approach. Harvey and the book inspired me and guided me to become mentally stronger with simple approaches that turned my career around."

Sound familiar? Many big league players have said essentially the same thing.

Joe concluded, "This book gives you guidelines to follow, to help you to develop your own mental plan and get you on the path to becoming a better player, and most of all, a better person."

Five years from now, some other guy will be writing this Foreword. But the context of the book will remain the same. At least I hope so.

One last thing. Over the years, Harvey and Karl have used self-evaluation sheets that many players have been enthusiastic about. When the self-scoring has been high, the performances tended to be very good. These forms have been added to the back of the book. They can be found in the Appendix.

Al Leiter
New York Mets
2002

INTRODUCTION

This is a baseball book. Whatever else it may also be, its form and substance, its focus and application, concern baseball and how to recognize and master the mental requirements of the game. Books have been written on hitting, pitching, fielding, and baserunning. But this book is about thinking and feeling and how they affect specific performance. It looks at negative influences on that performance, such as improper goals, pressures, lack of concentration and confidence, pain and a variety of attitudes that create anxiety. It also teaches positive techniques that help to improve performance: proper breathing, visualization, focus and control, to name a few.

Ty Cobb, one of the great achievers in the history of major league baseball, believed that "what's above the [player's] shoulders is more important than what's below." Outfielder Jim Wohlford's major league accomplishments in no way approached Cobb's, but his belief, if not his wording, is as profound as Cobb's. "Baseball," Wohlford said, "is ninety percent mental half the time." Speaking in the 1920s and the 1980s respectively, Cobb and Wohlford were essentially repeating what Henry Chadwick had said in 1868. It is what managers, coaches, and instructors of every sport at every level now recognize — mental factors are highly significant to athletic performance. It is understood that it takes a great deal of physical skill to have any hope of high achievement in sport. Yet, the higher the level of skill and competition athletes reach, the more they themselves identify mental factors as having a positive and/or negative bearing on their performance.

If that is the case, an obvious question arises: What percentage of time does a coach or instructor spend teaching mental skills and strategies and working on winning the mental game? Studies by sports psychologists indicate the most common figure to be somewhere near 10%. Many baseball coaches and instructors explain that they are expert only in the physical elements of the game. Though they're often heard shouting such directions as "Hang tough!" or "Be ready!" or "Keep your eye on the ball!" they have seldom been able to tell their players how to be tough, or what's required in order to be ready and see the ball well. The players are left to their own devices, most often without realizing how much their thoughts influence their preparation — and their performance. And even if they did recognize it, they still are not quite sure what to do about it.

The fact is that mental skills needed for maximum performance can be acquired in the same manner as physical skills. Both kinds of skills should be worked on at the same time. Many athletes have indicated that, because they worked on physical skills exclusively, they were forced to learn their mental lessons the hard way — through trial and error. Some don't ever learn.

The very best athletes have the very best instincts: their natural, "unlearned" senses are sharp and functional. So are their minds. They are complete and exceptional athletes. But educators and baseball men agree that instincts can be sharpened, suggesting, therefore, that players can learn to develop better instincts.

Many of the players who have the best physical equipment can eventually develop their mental skills on their own. Darryl Strawberry, for example, has had the time to do so. His abilities compensated for acute weaknesses in approach to performance during his early years as a professional. Less able players are not that fortunate and, having faced too many trials and committed far too many errors, they never develop to their full potential. With proper help, they might have done so; the good athletes would become better ones; the best would more quickly and more often be at their best. A major aim of this book is to help players find the limit of their potential, and, having found it, play to it consistently.

This book includes anecdotes and insights provided by major and minor league baseball players, many of whom, sooner or later, discovered the importance of mastering the mental game in order to play baseball as it should be played. These players reveal their own discoveries. Threaded through the fabric of their individual problems, solutions, and resolutions is a common design.

This is a book in two sections. One examines and reveals mental preparations and pitfalls; the other develops some fundamental mental approaches—what we call "winning mind games"—that can help a player reach maximum physical performance.

Mind games are recurring thoughts, existing attitudes, self-appraisal and criticism, approaches and concerns. So often, as Shakespeare well knew, they include "horrible imaginings."

Mind games can be positive or negative. They can help a player to be a winner or they can cause him to be a loser. They directly and certainly affect his performance.

They are inevitable. We all play mind games. Everyone who has ever played competitive baseball—from Little League on up—has played mind games before the actual ball game was started, played them during the game (between pitches, between innings, between at-bats), and played them after the game. Too often (most often?) what was in or on our mind hurt performance rather than helped it.

This book aims to help. People often are reluctant to express their thoughts to others, thinking some of their thoughts to be foolish. Baseball players are no exception, but when they discover that others share their thoughts, they learn that such thoughts are "normal." They learn to share them more easily.

Major leaguers are becoming increasingly interested in sharing their mind games. Ozzie Smith, Greg Maddux, Tony Gwynn, Wade Boggs, and a growing number of others spend much of their time on that part of their game. Professional players, generally, seem more receptive to psychological change than to physical change. They change their mind more often than they change their batting stance or pitching delivery.

The Mental Game of Baseball will allow baseball players and fans a glimpse into the minds of some of the game's outstanding performers. Problems will be examined, though not always solved.

The coach may be stimulated to find out more about his players' thinking and to encourage them to consider how that thinking might be altered and what might be done differently as a result. And the individual player can use this book to improve both mental approach and physical performance and to gain a self-awareness necessary for development as a self-directed, confident performer — and person.

H.A. Dorfman
Karl Kuehl

For three years he had daydreamed of how he would be a scintillating high-school baseball star and how he would hit a home run with the bases full. And look at the way he had folded up in a pinch. Yes, after kidding himself about his destiny, and having the nerve to think that he would be a star like Ty Cobb or Eddie Collins, he was a miserable failure. Whenever he was in a tight situation, he was a bust, a flat tire. He didn't have what it takes. He was eighteen years old, and he was no good. He lacked something—nerve, confidence. In a pinch, it was always the same. He lost his confidence. When he didn't have time, a few seconds in which to think, it was different. That was why he was better in football and basketball than he was in baseball. In baseball when you batted, there were those few seconds and fractions of a second between pitches, when your mind undid you. In football and basketball, you didn't have the time to think as you did in baseball. That made the difference. And it was in just that period of a very few important seconds that he was no good. Yes, even though he was considered one of the best athletes in school, he was never really going to be any good.

About the character, Danny O'Neill
In *Father and Son*
By James T. Farrell
Copyright 1940

Part One

1
WHERE DOES IT START?

Approach major league players, managers, and coaches and ask them what distinguishes the best players from the rest. They'll usually point to their heads. They believe that anyone good enough to make it to the big league possesses impressive physical tools. But it's the mental toolbox that holds the difference between an ordinary player and a great one.

Hall of Fame pitching great Tom Seaver was strong in that conviction. "The difference between the physical abilities of the players in the major leagues is not that great, and, something going hand in hand with that, the difference between the teams is not that great. So what it comes down to is that the dividing factor between the team that wins and the one that loses is the mental attitude, the effort they give, the mental alertness that keeps them from making mental mistakes. The concentration and the dedication—the intangibles—are the deciding factors, I think, between who won and who lost. I firmly believe that. I really do," Seaver said.

This belief, of course, extends beyond baseball circles. But baseball has been slow in making sure that the intangibles receive proper attention. Baseball experts have paid more attention to theory than application. This is changing, however slowly.

The general field of sports psychology has grown dramatically in recent years. The U.S. Olympic Committee, recognizing the success of the Soviet Union and East Germany, has begun mental conditioning programs for American athletes. Though we are only "rookies" compared to the Eastern-bloc countries, we are learning and gaining experience rapidly.

Michael Maloney, a clinical sports psychologist formerly at Penn State and currently at U.C. Santa Barbara, believes that, at a high performance level, "the difference between two athletes is 20% physical and 80% mental." At lower levels, the percentages are significant enough to convince those involved in sport to pay more direct and appropriate attention to mental conditioning.

Baseball, being the traditional and ritualistic American game it is, has been slow to develop systematic methods to help players develop the best possible mental habits. Until very recently, players have had only themselves as resources in their search for solutions to most of their performance problems. Former major league third baseman Doug DeCinces is a striking example of a player fortunate enough to have gotten essential outside help. It probably saved his career.

DeCinces had struggled in the shadow of Brooks Robinson, a Hall of Famer now and the man DeCinces replaced at third base for the Baltimore Orioles. DeCinces had weak performances for the 1976 and 1977 seasons, having felt what he described as Robinson's "gnawing presence." The 1978 season started terribly, despite the fact that Robinson had retired the previous September. His presence was still in DeCinces' mind, the effect being that DeCinces hit .226 and made 12 errors in the first 57 games.

A friend recommended that the player undergo counseling. DeCinces visited a psychiatrist who worked with athletes. The counselor, Skip Connor, worked on relaxing the third baseman, taking DeCinces' "mind off details, letting his body do the work."

Simply stated, but not always simply enacted. It takes work, but DeCinces was a conscientious and able student. "It was a question of confidence and relaxation," he said, just as simply as Connor.

At the same time, DeCinces stated his belief that "baseball is 80% mental," and that every team should have a professional therapist. "Baseball players are viewed as so masculine, so virile, so above all problems. It's not true. Every player is a human being. Some-

Doug DeCinces felt Brooks Robinson's "gnawing presence."

DeCinces' Second Half Stats—1978			
AVG.	HR	RBIs	SLUG. PCT.
.324	20	64	.611

One error in the last 72 games.

times the strain and mental problems are too much. I don't feel a manager can always be expected to find out what makes a player tick."

Doug DeCinces ticked effectively in the second half of that 1978 season — and loud enough to impress those around him, including Brooks Robinson. "I have never seen a player turn it around the way Doug did in the last half of (that) season," Robinson said.

We can safely say that Doug DeCinces did not suddenly realize a change in his physical ability. The amazing increase in efficiency was based on psychological control. He was winning his mind games.

The key, then, is for a player to regulate his mental performance as he regulates his physical performance. He must learn the strategies and skills required for controlling himself and his situation in the ball game. He must handle worry and anxiety, often based on the pressures of performing; he must take responsibility for that performance; he must approach his game with commitment, concentration, and confidence. As we said, this is not an easy task, but it's a necessary one, assuming a player's goal is to do the best he is physically able to do.

That's where mental training starts: with that assumption, with that goal.

2
ESTABLISHING PROPER GOALS
The Proper Start

The motivation to work on the mental part of baseball has to be carried forward. Goal-setting helps do that. It makes the player's purpose clear and gives direction. The successful player sets goals in order to stimulate himself to act in a way to achieve his objectives. He focuses his attention and energies. In other words, the more aware he is of what he wants, the more likely he is to do what is necessary to get it.

When selected properly, goals become a player's most important tool. Studies indicate that specific performance goals have a very real and positive effect on many complex coordination tasks. (See Bryan Cratty, *Movement Behavior and Motor Learning*) A person who is encouraged to "just do your best" usually doesn't. He doesn't clarify what his best might be; he doesn't extend himself to find out. Setting personal goals is essential for gaining control of potential, of success — of self.

The performance goals a player sets — what he thinks he can do, based on his ability and degree of confidence — usually become his personal standard of acceptance. For this reason, it's very important for the player to set realistic, reachable goals. Non-attainable goals lead to discouragement, frustration, and loss of motivation. On the other hand, goals should not be too easily attainable. They should challenge the player, pushing him toward his limits.

The player should evaluate his performance daily, determining whether or not he is making progress. His goals must be adjustable— able to be set high or lower. But they shouldn't be changed too hastily. Success is not usually immediate and other factors such as effort are involved. "How much effort am I putting forth?" That question should be carefully and honestly considered before a goal is revised by a player.

First baseman Bob Watson, after 19 years in the big leagues, retired at the end of the 1984 season with a lifetime batting average just under .300. Currently the General Manager for the Houston Astros, Watson had been a batting instructor with the Atlanta Braves and Oakland A's. He always tried to accelerate his students' progress by passing on to them some of the lessons which he wishes he had learned earlier. He recalled, as an example, how limited his attitude was toward goals early in his career, even as a major leaguer. He gave credit to a veteran outfielder, Tommy Davis, for teaching him to change that attitude, while both players were Houston teammates.

Said Watson; "I'd go into a game with a goal of getting two hits. That would look good in tomorrow's box score, I would think. One hit, at least. Well, if I got hits the first two times up, I coasted for the rest of the game, unless there was a crucial situation. If not, I didn't pay the best attention. I learned later that I gave away all those at-bats. Tommy told me that if he got a hit the first at-bat, his goal changed to three hits; if he got hits the first two times, he wanted four. I learned from him that every at-bat counted; I learned not to be satisfied with a goal easily reached."

Aside from such daily goals—game goals—players set long-range goals. A hitter might aim at batting .320, for example. If at mid-season he is hitting .240, it would serve the player to change his season's goal to a more realistic figure. Unattainable goals create pressure because they can make even a good performance unsatisfactory. That hitter won't feel any sense of accomplishment, even on a good day because of the overall frustration of reaching for the unreachable. Either he should change his goal to a more realistic season's average (.280?) or start fresh by setting a goal of .330 (assuming the .320 at the season's beginning was an attainable goal) for the second-half performance.

"Result goals" (i.e. 20 wins, 100 RBIs, .290 batting avg.) whether long or short range, are measurable and can therefore aid the player in honest self-evaluation. That is why revision of goals is so important. The goals should *encourage* the player to work hard and be rewarded for his efforts. They keep him aware of what he wants to achieve and what choices he has. Excellence is largely dependent upon knowing what should be accomplished, how it should be accomplished, and how much the player believes in his ability to accomplish what he desires.

This point is best illustrated by the example of former tennis star Virginia Wade, who, prior to her magnificent victory at Wimbledon in 1977, had suffered from what she called "post-competition feeling(s) of emptiness." Before a tournament that year, Ms. Wade made a determined and single-minded effort to change her "basic self." She had always "wished" to win the Wimbledon final, but had never "actively wanted it."

There is a big difference between the two attitudes and she identified it for herself. "If you waste time wishing, you can't be alert to any of the practical solutions marching by you," Ms. Wade said. She set about changing her behavior.

"I was more than ready to *want* Wimbledon for myself. I thought about it every day with that goal uppermost in my mind. New ideas came to me. How to do it. Why I deserved it. Soon I had a realistic picture of myself winning Wimbledon. It was not merely a dream. I knew exactly what I wanted and how to get it."

How To Get There—That's the key! If someone from another planet touches down in the middle of the Sahara Desert, looks around and says, "My goal is to get to Kokomo, Indiana," he'd better have a plan. If Kokomo is his exclusive goal and he starts walking with no other sense of direction, his chances of ever seeing Indiana are not very good. Our outerspace man must do more than just dream about getting there, as Virginia Wade realized, and as baseball players must also realize.

Process Goals

Setting a broad goal, then, is not enough. Tennis players, baseball players, and extra-terrestrials all must focus on the method—the process—of getting the desired result. For baseball players, the result goals we spoke of—statistical goals—relate to box scores and record books. Pete Rose set his sights on the record book for many years. Two-time National League MVP Dale Murphy sets season goals every spring; New York catcher Gary Carter, a frequent All-Star, is very conscious of game goals and wants to be in the Hall of Fame. Yes, long-range, intermediate-range, and short-term goals are important and useful. But they all look toward the end results. The means to those ends—the "how to get it"—are the process goals: the specific methods of getting the job done. All the best achievers—Rod Carew, Pete Rose, Don Mattingly, Roger Clemens, etc.—have known how to apply that focus, whatever their broader goals may have been.

Pete Rose knew that the only way to surpass Ty Cobb's hit record was to do what had to be done during each at bat. On each pitch his process goal was "See the ball, hit the ball." That was his immediate goal, his constant focus, his self-command—time after time, after time. He made it simple. He made it functional. He made it past Ty Cobb.

Tom Seaver won more than 300 games. In 1970, he set a goal of winning 30 games. This was not entirely unrealistic in light of his known ability, but he pushed himself unreasonably, pitching with only three days rest in August of that season.

"If you're going to be effective," he told author Devaney in *The Perfect Game,* "you can't rush things. You can't be greedy. You can't go out and beat everybody in the world pitching every other day."

You can't allow yourself to forget that you possess the goal; the goal should not possess you.

Two years later, Seaver acknowledged that he had learned as much about goal-setting as he had about pitching. ". . . I know that just as I am refining my pitching, I am refining the pleasure I get from it. A victory used to give me pleasure, then a well-pitched inning, and now I get satisfaction from just one or two pitches a game. I get in a situation where I have to apply all I know, mentally, physically, on just one pitch."

And so it should be: One pitch at a time! Seaver got great satisfaction, he said, "in knowing that for one specific moment (he could) achieve perfection."

These specific moments — on the mound, in the batter's box, in the field, on the base path — hold the immediate goals of every outstanding player. They are the goals of execution: Action goals.

Action goals confine the player's thoughts.

Action goals direct his focus.

Action goals leave no room for distractions that interfere with top performance.

Action goals help the player assert as much control over his situation as possible, and if the controls are the right ones, the player is much more likely to reach his broader goals.

Focus and Control

These are the essential elements in great ballplayers' approach to their game — controlling their game results from proper focusing, which is a result of properly set goals.

As mentioned, focus should be on specific performance and behavior. This includes the action of the body and the action of the mind.

"My goal is to hit the breaking pitch better."

"My goal is to get a better jump on balls hit over my head."

"My goal is to pitch more effectively on the inside of the plate."

"My goal is to relax more while at bat."

"My goal is to concentrate better on the game situation before the batter hits the ball to me."

Self-Improvement

These "right" goals are the building blocks for improvement. Practice time is the right time for the player to form the foundation for success. Games provide the opportunities to test for structural soundness. Necessary adjustments must then be made.

Judgment of success is thereby focused on the player's own specific approaches and actions, not on statistical results or victories and losses.

The focus on self-improvement also transfers the concern from the opponent to the performer. It will come from the belief that the player is responsible to himself and for himself — for what *he* does, not what his opponent does.

The focus will dictate the language of self-improvement, which is the language of self-control; of positivism, not negativism; of relaxation, not anxiety. How the player talks to himself determines how he thinks. How he thinks determines how he plays.

Positive and Negative Goals

Goals are actually directed toward the reduction of anxiety in players. (That's why it's so important that they are attainable.) They motivate, as we know, and they guide the player in a desired direction so he can increase the probability of success. This, in turn, should relieve whatever anxiety he feels. Yet poorly constructed goals are also motivators, though not good ones. They can be the cause of anxiety and increase the probability not of success, but of failure. The right kind of goal-setting is the first of many mind games to be won.

Wanted: Quality Thoughts

A physical performance is the outcome of a thought. Players cannot ignore the mental activity that precedes these workings of the body. We'll reiterate: the mental message will dictate the physical action and help determine its quality. A negative thought is not a quality thought and it doesn't lead to quality action.

When it's said that people are creatures of habit, the statement usually refers to physical habit. However, we all have habits of thought as well. A thought has been learned and used so often in similar situations that it becomes automatic. It often drops from conscious awareness; we don't even realize we're employing it. The thought becomes part of a "programmed" behavior. Negative programming hinders us both as athletes and as human beings.

Negativism isn't a philosophy, it's an attitude. It's the attitude of a player whose nerves aren't as strong as he'd like them to be. Attitudes can be changed, but first they have to be recognized. It's quite common for a player to think to himself, "I don't want to boot this ground ball," or "I don't want to walk this batter." The word "don't" will not get through to the body. The word carries no functional image. The phrase "boot this ground ball" does bring forth an image. The expression of a negative goal will therefore emphasize an undesirable image—and the error or the walk is more apt to be made. The body tends to do what it hears most clearly; the mind tells the body what it sees most clearly. So, thinking about what you *don't* want to happen greatly increases the chance that it *will* happen.

Even All-Star players such as former Philadelphia Phillies third baseman Mike Schmidt and Atlanta's Dale Murphy have fallen into the trap, as have all of us who are human, when they expressed "don't goals" in the recent past.

"I don't want to strike out as much this year," (one of Murphy's 1983 goals) redefines itself as, "I don't want to strike out in this at-bat," and ultimately is translated as, "I don't want to miss this pitch." This attitude can be corrupting—for anyone. It can lead to fear of failure, to a player's belief that he will strike out. His belief becomes what is known as a self-fulfilling prophecy. The player, predicting failure, fails.

In 1983, while with the Los Angeles Dodgers, second baseman Steve Sax had a terrible time making the simple throw from his position to first base. The more time he had, the more likely the ball would miss its target by a wide margin. Disgruntled home fans who sat in the stands behind first base took to wearing protective helmets. Sax was frustrated, embarrassed, helpless—and certain his problem wasn't physical. "If anyone has a solution, let me know," he said at the time. Sax probably received more suggestions than he had bargained for, but the most common, judging from his later reaction, must have been, "Just don't think about throwing the ball away."

Of course, he had been thinking exactly that, but such advice was not helpful. Sax responded, "If someone said to you, 'Don't think about elephants in the next two minutes,' naturally you're going to think about elephants."

The image implant is "elephant," and the word "don't" cannot block out the elephant image. Sax needed to hear what he *should* do (just as Schmidt and Murphy would have been better off saying what they should do [make good contact, etc.]). Sax knew what he shouldn't do, but that wasn't enough to solve his problem because it gave him no directive for positive action.

Gary Carter recalled the 1983 All-Star game. "I was catching some of Steve's throws prior to the game, in infield practice. The second ball he threw to me at first base he air-mailed and hit some reporter. It wasn't even close to me. Then, all of a sudden, I tried to signal to him to get over the top with his throws, and every ball he threw to me was perfect.

"Then he got into the game, and the ball was hit to him by Manny Trillo and, I'm telling you, I was behind the plate and I knew he was going to throw it away. I just knew it. He hadn't kept a positive outlook. He'd said to me before, 'Hey, I'm in the major leagues, and I can't even make a throw from second base.' Now, he should have said to himself, 'Hey, I gotta be here for one reason; it's gotta be that I have the talent.' But if he lets that other stuff play on his mind, he's not going to be in the big leagues very long."

On double play throws or the quick "bang-bang" plays, Sax threw well. He didn't have time to allow his self-doubting thoughts to interfere with his body's confidence of movement.

Self-Doubt

Self-doubt can develop at any level, in any performer. A young pitcher throwing his "good stuff" is being hit hard—line drives to outer-field regions—on a given day. The thoughts come quickly: "Maybe my stuff isn't good enough; maybe I can't pitch in this league; maybe I just don't have it." That is a path into the depths of disappointment, frustration, anger, or depression. Positive motivation is lost; functional, directive goals are forgotten because the pitcher is losing confidence. He is losing a positive and realistic attitude and losing control of his game—and himself. Negativism and defeatism are in control and all that does is to increase the positive control of the opposing players and teams.

Hoping vs. Believing

"I hope" is another phrase to be avoided. Hoping you will means you don't believe you can. By hoping you won't you most likely will. Hoping they don't ("I hope they don't hit the ball to me") means you're afraid they will. Bad hopes. Awful goals. They are not truly directed toward success, but rather at a hope not to fail.

"I Gotta"

For all his understanding of the mind's role in a player's performance, his own included, Gary Carter has occasionally fallen victim to the "I Gotta Syndrome," still another link in a chain of poorly-stated goals. Though the wording doesn't sound negative, the thought behind the words certainly is. It suggests, "If I don't, I'm a failure." The sense of urgency is the clue.

Carter shares most hitters' particular dislike for the dreaded "ofers"—0-3, 0-4, or worse. He was asked how he behaved before a fourth at-bat during a game in which he has been held hitless in his first three at-bats. He admitted that he has said to himself in the batter's box, "I gotta get a hit now." He acknowledged that this tightened him up considerably, and he recognizes that being relaxed is "one of the most important things in performance." His or anyone else's.

How often had Carter gotten that hit under those conditions? "Rarely," he said, with a wry grin. "There are times when your mind plays games. A player gets himself out when he thinks like that."

The mind should always be in the game, playing along. But, we reiterate, the *quality* of the mind games will affect the quality of the body's game. Thinking that you *must* do this or *must* do that during the moment it is to be done—or even before—indicates an anxiety that will surely harm the performer and weaken his performance. The anxiety is based on a fear of failing.

He Who Makes Goals Takes Risks

To aspire to great achievement is to risk failure. Many players are reluctant to set high goals because of this risk and the fear that may go with it. Many others are brave enough to set the goals but not

"I gotta get a hit!"

brave enough to make an honest effort to achieve them. The thought of trying so hard and not succeeding can be very intimidating. The best players have had fears of inadequacy, but the best players ignore or suppress them, determined to overcome them and gain control of their thoughts, feelings, and behavior. When they do that, they exemplify a "winner's" approach.

Everyone needs to feel self-worth, but the winners are those who, though success-oriented, recognize that everyone meets with occasional failure. They understand that failure reflects on the performance, not the performer. Not the person. Never the person. A winner will simply try again and work at being more effective next time. He establishes just what he must do to make the next effort a better one. And he continues to assess his efforts and make the necessary adjustments — even if "next time" is not a successful time. Failure, as well as success, will act as a positive motivator for the winner.

Rick Sutcliffe won the National League's Cy Young Award in 1984 and was second in the 1987 voting. In 1979, he was the Rookie of the Year, pitching for the Los Angeles Dodgers. On October 3, 1981, Dodger manager Tom Lasorda informed Sutcliffe that he was being taken off the team's post-season roster. Sutcliffe felt the loss of self-esteem, and Lasorda's office felt the effect of Sutcliffe's loss of control. The young pitcher upended the manager's desk and did considerable damage to his office. He and his athletic achievements have come a long way since. His difficulties — his failure — moved him forward. Changing his mental approach became an important goal. His performance was positively affected.

Said Sutcliffe, "I don't have Nolan Ryan's fastball, and I don't have Steve Carlton's slider or Mario Soto's changeup, but when I go to the mound the one thing I usually take with me is a good attitude.

"That's something I've believed in basically the last three years ('82, '83, '84). If I work harder and believe in myself, then I will be successful."

No Goals Set, No Limits Reached

Every time Sutcliffe takes the field for a game he has an objective, something he aims to accomplish or achieve. Success is on his mind — on the mind of the 1985 Cy Young Award winner also. Dwight Gooden advises, "Just keep feeling you're the best out there. You never give in . . . you're in command."

On the other side of the spectrum is the failure-oriented player, whose self-doubts and anxieties lead him to believe that his lack of ability is responsible for his failure, that luck is responsible for his infrequent successes and that his effort is therefore useless. He protects what self-esteem he has by not trying hard. The irony is clear: by giving a half-hearted effort, he almost assures the very failure he wishes to avoid.

Yes, he desires success, but he's afraid to set goals that might lead him there. He's afraid his self-worth will continually be threatened by the further expectations others will have for his future successes and achievement.

Former big league infielder Enos Cabell once said, "I don't want to be a star, they get blamed too much." Cabell implied that stars are required to be too successful too often. Wanting to be a "star" is not a good goal to frame in the first place. Not wanting to be one is worse, in that it suggests a reluctance to be a top performer — or an excuse for not being one.

The need to achieve creates a real and understandable pressure, and one way many players try to eliminate the pressure is not to set any goals at all. In these cases, "goals are set by default," wrote Jim Newman in *Release Your Breaks*. "Whatever you think about most will function as a goal." It's not a deliberate or conscious intention. Still, when a player fails to set specific, positive, controllable goals, and instead spends time concerning himself with pressure and failure and the consequences, he has inadvertently set a goal of failing.

Goals Help, Excuses Hurt

Failure-oriented players have another protective device — the excuse. Bad bounces, bright lights, an injury, umpires, vague illnesses are common excuses. Blaming teammates' performance is another. Children most often transfer blame, and so we consider such behavior childish. But people of all ages — players at all levels — all too often employ the same tactic. Pitching for the champion Minnesota Twins, Frank Viola was the World Series MVP in 1987 and the Cy

Reprinted by permission of United Feature Syndicate, Inc.

Young Award winner in 1988. In 1981 he was 10–0 as a junior at St. John's University, and he won a 12-inning, 1–0 NCAA playoff game, defeating New York Mcts pitcher Ron Darling, who was playing for Yale. Viola was pushed to the majors in 1982 with less than two years of minor league experience.

The higher level changed his statistics and outlook. "I got hit hard, and it shook me up," Viola recalled. "I doubted myself on every pitch."

And he provided many excuses for his poor performances. In 1984, the excuses disappeared and the successes appeared. "I stopped pointing the finger at somebody (else)," said Viola. "I'm at fault when I lose, nobody else. It's part of maturing. . . . Now, I'm committed to every pitch. I'm a new man." He is now a success-oriented man with defined goals and a redefined self.

The "winner," we have said, adjusts his goals. By lowering his sights, because he knows it is a realistic thing to do, he avoids failure. The "loser" sticks to unrealistic goals that are beyond his skill level. He feels the pressure they create and allows the resulting failures to remain with him. His past assures his future — more failure. "Winners" live in the present, with new goals, when it is necessary and appropriate to create them, and with a zest to achieve them.

Golfing great Jack Nicklaus knows it is always important to keep the desire to work toward goals. "Otherwise, stop competing," he advises.

SOME FURTHER ADVICE FOR THOSE WHO CONTINUE TO COMPETE:

A) *Goals must be compatible.* The attainment of one of them should not interfere with the attainment of any other.

Viola tended to aim the blame at others.

B) *Goals should be limited in number.* Attention can then be concentrated on those few. Goals can always be added to the list, once success and further confidence are established.

C) *Goals should be prioritized.* The most important, the most immediate, should be right up at the top of that list.

D) *The list should be in writing.* Putting the goals in writing encourages the writer's personal commitment to specific and directed behavior. The writing process helps assure that the goal-setting process is thought through, rather than being casually created.

Outfielder Gary Ward struggled into June of the 1982 season, when he was playing for the Minnesota twins. He was "ready to climb the walls." He couldn't sleep at night; he considered himself "a nervous wreck" and worried that "it might be all over." Though very capable of controlling his emotions and tension, Ward did not do so until he listed that control—in writing—as one of his goals. He had a number of other goals and put them all in writing, with fine results, he thought.

Ward's Stats "Before Control"—1982

AVG.	HR	RBIs
.226	6	17

Ward's Stats for the Entire Season—1982

AVG.	HR	RBIs
.289	28	91

E) *Reread the list of goals regularly and judge behavior and performance honestly.* Gary Ward made a habit of referring to his list of goals daily. "It took me a long time to come up with them; I wasn't going to let them slip away," he explained.

F) *Remember to make the most important goal(s) relate to the job at hand.* The "how in the now."

One-pitch-at-a-time goals — "See the ball." "Throw a good low strike." And so forth. These are the goals within the player's immediate control during the ball game. These are the goals that keep the player's focus on function. They direct his mind and body. They assist him in his effort to reach maximum capability.

That effort is evident in every great player, during good streaks and bad. He knows what he wants; he knows how to go after it. No one can do more; no one should do less.

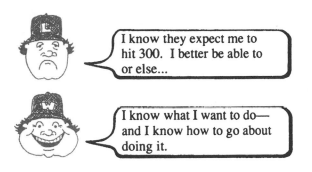

I know they expect me to hit 300. I better be able to or else...

I know what I want to do— and I know how to go about doing it.

3
EXPECTATIONS
The Wrong Goals of the Wrong People

On the final play of the historic Thanksgiving holiday football game in 1984, Boston College quarterback and Heisman Trophy winner Doug Flutie threw a spectacular 64-yard pass into the end zone for the touchdown which defeated defending national champion Miami, 47–45. Flutie was spectacular throughout the game, throughout the season, throughout his entire college career. But that one last-second throw seemed to represent to many just how great a player he truly was. Flutie recognized that the play gained immediate inclusion in the annals of sport history. He also knew there is a price to be paid for such an honor.

"I think people are going to be waiting for something," he said, "and I don't know if I have anything for them."

Flutie sensed at the time he spoke that people not only would *want* him to continue to prove his outstanding ability, they would *expect* him to do so.

How much does an athlete have to achieve to "prove" himself? Flutie had established his great ability long before THE play. To whom does the player have to "prove" himself?

The answers to these questions are closely related. First, what an athlete has to do to "prove" himself depends on who is setting the standard for his performance. Obviously, the goals we spoke of in the previous chapter are, for the most part, set by the player himself. (A coach or manager can be part of the goal-setting process, but the player and coach must be in agreement about what is realistic and helpful.) Then, who is best able to judge how performance measures up against goals? The answer should be: the player himself.

"Perform without fail what you resolve," Ben Franklin wrote, long before baseball was being played. The word we'd like to emphasize in Franklin's sound advice is "you." *You* resolve.

Goals are set by "you," the player—the individual. That's why we choose to devote an entire chapter to distinguishing between resolutions of a player and the expectations of others for that player. Those expectations can damage the player's game and his view of himself as a performer—and as a person.

Who are these others? They are parents, Little League coaches, minor league managers, teammates, fans, organizations, the media, and anyone else a player allows to determine what level of performance he must reach and when he must reach it.

Before documenting the case against "outsiders," let's look at the motivation of the "insider," the player. Literally millions of young people desire to become professional baseball players. These youngsters have fun just playing the game, when adults do not corrupt the game and the youngsters' attitude toward it. They see their fun extended through their early adult years; they see the romance of being a big league star and celebrity; they see pay for play. A typical childhood dream. An improbable goal. But the kids still have fun.

People young and old are motivated by needs. Having fun, being stimulated—aroused—is an important need. So too is the need to feel worthwhile—to feel able and successful. To feel a sense of achievement. The degree to which people share needs is different, as is the way they satisfy them. But it is generally agreed upon that we are alike in the basic nature of our needs. The need to have fun is satisfied most when we are young. There are many reasons for this, but as it relates to children playing baseball the reason is clear. The goal of the youngster changes as he becomes more involved in organized play. These days, the organization comes early. Adults are the organizers, and they have their own way of satisfying their own needs. The young players often become the means to the adults' end. Fun can easily go out of the game for all involved.

An "adult" makes his expectations known.

The player who can retain his joy for baseball is the one who has not let others' needs intrude upon his own. He is also the one most likely to perform best, and that, in turn, will help keep the fun in the game. His senses won't be dulled; his being won't be threatened. He'll be able to concentrate on what he's doing. He will be in control of himself and, as much as is possible, in control of his situation in the game. He becomes the game—and he "plays within himself,"—the phrase commonly used to describe concentrating and performing at a perfectly balanced arousal level for the individual. He is playing as if detached from the "real world" (as in a dream, in a higher state); having a "flow experience." "I think I could come to home plate, stand on my head, and still get a hit when I'm feeling like this," says Gary Carter.

Well, such states are created within the player by the player. However, the feeling can easily be (and most often is) inhibited, prevented, or intruded upon. The cause is external, but it becomes an internal problem. The player's problem. He has to push hard against the door of these pressures to keep the intruders in their place—and out of his.

The Intruders

Now we must document the case against these would-be intruders. Enough has already been written about inept and self-serving Little League coaches and inadequate parents who, in so many ways, turn the joy of recreation into a burden of anxiety. Verbal abuse and punishment are given to children who do not produce what adults around them expect.

At the higher levels of baseball the demands, the abuse, and the punishment can be just as severe. Usually, the psyches are better equipped to withstand the ordeals—at great cost, nevertheless, regardless of who the abuser might be.

Mike Schmidt was most upset about fans and what they expected of him. After 13 years of playing in Philadelphia, he was still trying to handle the booing of hometown fans. He told a writer that those fans have been his most difficult test as a player. "I can handle the strikeouts, the errors, the failures, the 1-for-20s. But sometimes, I just can't handle the boos."

Schmidt has a theory about the booing fan: "(The fan) says,

"... The environment is not conducive to playing well."

'How can that guy be making that kind of money and strike out for the third time in a row?' . . . If they boo the 76ers, the Flyers, they're gonna play worse. The boos are gonna make them feel bad and frustrate them and make them lose concentration, because the environment is not conducive to playing well," said Schmidt.

"Baseball is a subtle game, like golf. Can you see if Jack Nicklaus walked up to the tee and they announced him and everybody went 'BOOOOO!'? Could you see him hit a golf ball? Baseball is the same way—it takes touch, timing, good eyesight, concentration. The fans should be forced to be quiet when you walk up to hit. It would be easier to hit that way," Schmidt concluded.

Very true, but very unlikely to become a reality, as Schmidt knows. The "conducive environment" he spoke of must be an internal environment—for him or for any other player. The boos must not be heard. But we are getting ahead of ourselves.

The 1983 season in Montreal was a tough one for Gary Carter. He injured himself early in the year, tried to compensate physically, felt the pressure of the 1.8 million dollars the Expos were paying him for his season, was affected mentally, and had a performance that reflected his state. He remembers playing in St. Louis and being very conscious of fans' voices when he came to bat. "They would chant my batting average," Carter explained. "They'd say in unison, 'One ninety-five . . . one ninety-five . . . one ninety-five . . .' It bothered me. In fact, I hated it."

Carter hated the number he heard more than he hated the people who shouted it. Understandably, the St. Louis fans didn't mind his paltry average. They weren't expecting more from him; they were hoping for less. Carter felt the symbolic weight of the statistic they chanted, and it pressed on him more than the taunting voices of the Cardinal fans. It distracted him greatly while he was at bat.

People sitting in the stands can cause problems. So, too, can people sitting behind desks in the front offices of baseball organizations. Houston pitcher Dan Schatzeder didn't hear voices, but he thought he saw the handwriting on the wall in the Detroit front office after he was traded by the Expos to the Tigers in December 1979 for outfielder Ron LeFlore. Schatzeder, a 24-year-old pitcher that year, had been 10-5 with a 2.83 ERA for Montreal.

He remembers the season that followed the trade (11-13, 4.01 ERA) and the painful experience it was. "When I think about those struggling times, it's not a real lot of fun to relive. But it's good for me, because it helps me mentally," Schatzeder said, as preface to the reliving.

"I was coming into a new camp, trying to impress people. The people in Detroit liked LeFlore; he hit .300 (and stole 78 bases) the year before."

So Schatzeder decided that everyone connected with the Tigers expected him to win 20 games. He told himself, "I'd better win 20," and then asked himself, "How the heck am I going to do that?"

He was struggling with his delivery by that time. "Things just fell apart for me," he recalled.

What fell apart was Schatzeder's belief in his natural ability—and his ability to construct his own goals and, eventually, his self-identity. He accepted the external expectation, real or imagined, of 20 victories as the only appropriate trade-off for LeFlore's accomplishments.

"I thought they were all saying, 'You'd certainly better win 20 games and be a young phenom. If you don't you'll be a failure.' Mentally, I wasn't prepared to handle that, coming from that different environment. I had had success, but we (Montreal) had Steve Rogers, Ross Grimsley, Rudy May, and all the veterans. I was a youngster and maybe in the shadows, but I liked that. And all of a sudden I was supposed to be the ace of the staff of a team that wanted to elevate themselves through me. I just felt that much more pressure."

Schatzeder told how this pressure affected his performance. "I went from feeling the ball release out of my hand during my delivery—not even thinking what I was doing—from seeing only the catcher's glove, visualizing where the pitch is going—to thinking, 'What does the manager think of me today?' and 'I'd better not give up a home run.' I'd hear as well what was going on up there (in the stands). Somebody would be calling me a bum, and I heard that, and I couldn't get it out of my mind. All negative vibrations."

Distractions of all kinds, caused by what he perceived to be the expectations of others. Some intruders had pushed down the door and invaded the fortress of his mind. Others had been "welcomed" through an open doorway. Not much of a fortification, in either case, Schatzeder admitted.

He produced a 6–8 record, with a 6.08 ERA in 1981, and was traded by Detroit to San Francisco in 1982. He struggled there also.

His record was 1–6 in '82; the Giants had sold him back to Montreal by mid-season. Schatzeder then regained his comfort and confidence in the familiar environment. Once again he became a winning pitcher. The Expos, considering all Schatzeder had been through, had relatively modest expectations when they reacquired him. In a comfortable environment once again, he performed well above those expectations.

At the minor league level the expectations a player perceives and the pressures he feels are just as great. Some say they are greater. Whether greater or less, whether real or imagined, the expectations a player senses his organization has for him compounds the pressure he puts on himself in his desire to prove he has what it takes to be a big leaguer. Three minor leaguers serve as good examples. Two were playing in the Cincinnati farm system in 1984.

The first player, outfielder-first baseman Paul O'Neil, is now a major leaguer. In 1984, he was on the Reds' 40-man major league spring training roster. He opened the season at the Double-A level. O'Neil's early batting performance was poor. He disclosed to a newspaperman the pressure he felt, being the only player on his minor league team to have been on the major league roster.

"I thought everyone really expected me to get a hit every time I came to bat," he explained. The results, predictably, were far from anyone's reasonable expectations. Once the player became more reasonable himself, his hitting indicated that he was, indeed, a major league prospect. He had a very respectable season.

A teammate of his, a pitcher, also had an outstanding season, but he had his own particular mental hurdle to clear. A converted outfielder, this strong-armed young man overpowered opposing batters. His record was 7–1, his ERA under 1.00, when he revealed the very real problem he was having.

"The more I win," he said, "the more I think everyone expects me to never lose. I feel I've gotta keep winning next time. The pressure keeps building (between starts), and I'm having a harder and harder time getting through the first two innings. I have a fear of getting knocked out (of the game) early. Once I'm into the third or fourth inning, I settle down."

That he did survive the first two innings was a tribute to his pitching ability, his physical skill. (He walked the first three batters, then retired the next three without a run scoring the outing before he discussed his problem. On another occasion, his mind anywhere but where it should have been, he ran behind home plate to back up his catcher on a ground ball hit between first and second, with no runners on base.)

The pitcher put his pre-game and game mind to better thoughts. In his next outing, he retired the first six batters he faced — and completed another win. He was to have been the starting pitcher in the league's All-Star game, but he was promoted to Triple-A prior to the playing of the game.

The third player was a catcher in the Oakland organization. He had a history of steady, dependable performance. In June of 1984 he was unsteady.

"What do you do when you've been told all through high school, college, Class A, and Double-A that you're no (major league) prospect — and you do fine. Then, all of a sudden, they tell you they think you *are* a prospect — and you go phftt?"

The player's hand made a sharp descent as he finished his question. He had always considered himself an overachiever; now he thought of himself as an underachiever. One remark from someone in the organization's upper strata had changed the player's view of himself. That, in itself, was not bad, but his reaction was, until he put the words of that person out of his head, particularly while he was playing. Then his performance elevated itself.

Juan Nieves signed with the Milwaukee Brewers organization in 1983. He arrived in the United States from Puerto Rico under the recommendation of former major leaguer Vic Power. The 6'3" left-hander posted a career pitching record of 19-1, with a 1.05 ERA and 288 strikeouts in 196 innings at Avon Old Farms School in Avon, Connecticut. The Brewers are said to have given him $150,000 for signing.

Nieves showed early promise and poise as a professional. In his first start, in July 1983, he held the Madison Muskies (Class A) hitless in the six innings he pitched. He struck out eight, walked three. Newspapermen were there in swarms, along with the Milwaukee brass. Nieves was as impressive handling the observers as he had been in handling opposing batters.

"I wasn't playing against the media. I was playing against Madison," he said. "I just go out and do the best I can. You can hurt your-self by worrying too much about other things. I get mentally ready, but I try not to worry."

Ray Poitevint, the Brewers' director of player procurement, was there. He offered his own expectation, though qualifying it some-what. "I'm not predicting anything, but I wouldn't be surprised if he (Nieves) was in the major leagues in two or three years."

Nieves did not "worry about such things." He just pitched his way there.

When pitcher Greg Maddux left the Chicago Cubs as a free agent after his 1992 Cy Young Award season, many baseball pundits pre-dicted he would buckle under the pressure of trying to justify his lofty salary and meet the accompanying expectations. Maddux is an example of one who fortified himself against these expectations and did his job, winning another Cy Young in 1993. "Regardless of where you're pitching, regardless of what goes on before or after your game, you still have to be ready," said Maddux, who obviously was.

Third baseman Wade Boggs is not a worrier either. He is one of the finest hitters in baseball, and he is quick to attribute much of the success he's had to his mental approach to the game. Never-theless, while with the Red Sox in 1984, Boggs admitted to frustration, at worst; perplexity, at least—not with his performance, but with the performance of the media as they assessed him.

At the time, Boggs was hitting .309. The Boston press was critical. Weeks earlier, on a nighttime sports talk show, lamenting was heard over Boggs' batting "slump."

"I had a nine-game hitting streak then," Boggs noted. He couldn't restrain a wry grin. "But I wasn't having multiple-hit games as often as everybody was used to. I guess they were spoiled."

Put in other terms, Bostonians had built their expectations on the foundation of Boggs' first two years with the Red Sox, years in which he had hit .349 and .361.

Wasn't Boggs hitting less effectively during that so-called "slump?"

"No!" Boggs was quick to answer. "My average may not show it, but I'm doing everything the same as I always do. I'm seeing the ball fine; I'm concentrating well; I'm hitting the ball hard. It just goes at somebody. Most critics just look at the batting average."

Even Boggs' high batting averages the previous two years didn't satisfy everyone. It would be hard to know on what one particular

Boston Globe sports columnist and television sports reporter based his expectations. The following is extracted from the "critic's" column in the July 19, 1983 edition of the *Globe*:

> As I write this he (Boggs) is hitting .374. That's Cobb Land, Hornsby Land, and, yes, Carew Land. Every day we read about another "multiple-hit game." [When, oh when, will they ever run out of stats?] Boggs leads the league in hits. He's first in doubles. He's second (to Carew) in on-base percentage. He's among the leaders in walks and runs scored. But he didn't make the All-Star team because he wasn't deemed to be better than either George Brett or Doug DeCinces. Nobody squawked, not even his own manger. That must mean something.

To begin with, the writer apparently didn't think it meant All-Star selections are above criticism, or that Boggs, in his second big league season, should not be expected to replace Brett and DeCinces as the American League's premier third baseman. Instead, the writer concluded it meant Boggs didn't have enough power. "His RBI total (41) is so-so..."

Despite the writer's "when-will-they-ever-run-out-of-stats?" grievance, he held Boggs accountable for one unrealistic statistical expectation: a high home run total. Boggs had never hit more than five homers in his professional career. (How many hitters with power do hit for a very high average? Few. Very few.) In fact, Boggs finished the 1983 season with 74 RBIs. In six years as Baltimore's regular third baseman, Doug DeCinces had as his highest single-season total 80 RBIs, and it took him 28 home runs to do that. His batting average was .286 that year, his highest as an Oriole. What does *that* mean? Whatever a writer, or anyone else, wants it to mean.

In 1983, Boggs did lead the league in "creating runs" for his team, according to Bill James' *Baseball Abstract*. His total of 130 was one behind the major league leader, the National League's MVP, Dale Murphy. Boggs had to be quite creative, hitting five home runs to Murphy's 36.

In his "slump" year, 1984, Boggs batted .325. He hit .336 with men in scoring position, an adequate response to that same Boston writer's willingness to "wager that...rivals aren't terrified to see

Wade Boggs come up in the eighth with a man on second and two away in a tie game."

His batting championships and other achievements since then are a matter of record. Still, it's hard to know how to please some people. It's easy to know it's impossible to please them all. But it's essential to know the attempt *should not* be made. A player's list of goals should not include "pleasing others." Boggs knows— and plays according to what he knows. That is what players should expect of themselves—and to what they should aspire. What Boggs has achieved since the criticism early in his career has erased it from the public's mind, perhaps even from the mind of the "critic" himself. But had the player taken the remarks seriously, his career could have been hurt.

For example, infielder Torey Lovullo, labeled another "can't miss star" by Detroit manager Sparky Anderson, had a disastrous post-remark season and has never come close to "stardom." When pitcher Bobby Witt was traded in 1993 by Texas to Oakland in the Jose Canseco deal, Texas reporters were ecstatic. Said on, "...The guy never really performed. Witt was going to be the next somebody, but, unfortunately, he was always the next Bobby Witt." It has been said of many players; it will be said of many more.

A Classic Example

One of the most, if not the most, dramatic examples of a young player being subjected to and affected by the great expectations of the media is the case of Clint Hartung, not a household name these days. Still, Hartung's story is historical—and, more importantly, it is instructive.

Hartung had ended four years of military service in 1947 when he began spring training with the then New York Giants. In 1942 Hartung pitched with Minneapolis (American Association) and Eau Claire (Northern League). He pitched a total of 50 innings, having no won-lost record with Minneapolis and a 3-1 record with Eau Claire. He then served four years in the U.S. Army. He came to the Giant camp a shy, quiet, 6'4", 25-year-old rookie from Hondo, Texas. He was dubbed "The Hondo Hurricane" and the New York press made him a legend, not in his own time, but before it—before his first intra-squad game, at that.

The more sensational tabloid papers boosted him as a combination of Bob Feller and Babe Ruth. He would be a great pitcher, an even greater hitter. The reports on the sports pages of *The New York Times* were less exaggerated but just as frequent. Hartung was a daily story. His every move was scrutinized. The interest in him was extremely high; the expectations for him were absurdly high.

On what were these expectations based? The *Times* made it clear:

> He (Hartung) came out of the army with a record that commands respect. As a member of the Hickam Field team that won the Hawaiian service team championship, Hartung pitched and played the outfield, acquitting himself admirably on both assignments. He hurled twenty-five games and won them all, allowing but twenty rival

runs and averaging fifteen strikeouts. With a service team
that won sixty-seven games and lost but four, Hartung,
as an outfielder, hit .567 and got thirty homers.

There it was. All the media-hype was based on his performance
with an army base team. The opening spring training article had
this to report: "The object of greatest attention among rookies was
Clint Hartung . . . around whom the Giant outfield will be built.
Everybody, it seemed, wanted to see Clint."

The following day, Giant manager Mel Ott proclaimed Hartung's
hand "twice the size of mine," saying also that Hartung was "the
key man in the outfield."

Another day, and Hartung "knocked the ball over the fence" in
batting practice; other days he "hooked one over the left-field barrier," or "pounded the ball," or "dented the fences." All this against
batting practice pitching, though performed "to the admiring ex-
clamations of onlookers."

Hartung was then pictured in the paper with his admiring manager. The next day's edition included an article suggesting the "star"
from Texas was "overanxious" and his "swinging suffered accordingly." Hartung "didn't get the ball out of the batting cage in his
first turn."

This equation is a simple one: unreasonable expectations + unnatural attention = anxiety. Soon after, Ott noted a "batting weakness"—Hartung was having trouble with off-speed pitches, Ott
claimed. The manager would work with his rookie "sensation."

The most objective, realistic, and significant commentary in any
of those *Times* articles appeared one week prior to the first spring
training game. While reporting on the Giants' prospects as a team,
the writer James P. Dawson wrote: "Hartung, like so many highly
publicized athletes, has been handicapped with the weight of the
widespread publicity, but is gradually shaking off what amounts to
be a moderate mental hazard."

Moderate, indeed. Only Hartung could know that the hazard
was anything but moderate nor was he able to shake it off. His career
lasted six years. He never came close to emulating Feller or Ruth.
Or, most likely, the real Clint Hartung.

It's more than 40 years since that story began. Hartung does not
enjoy discussing the experience. He understates, but states strongly:

Hartung's Major League Record—1947-1952					

BATTING-

AVG.	AT-BATS	HITS	HR	RUNS	RBI
.238	378	90	14	42	43

PITCHING-

GAMES	INN.	WON	LOST	ERA	SO	BB
112	511.1	29	29	5.02	167	271

"There was lots of pressure from what others expected of me." And, yes, it affected his performance. Very much.

Hartung did not pitch in 1951 or 1952. In those seasons he hit .205 and .218, respectively. In no season did he have 100 or more at-bats.

There are other would-be "stars" for whom bright futures were predicted, but whose achievements were dull when compared to the glow of expectations. Lack of skill was a factor in many cases. Some of those players were not nearly as well equipped as others had thought them to be. The best mental equipment couldn't have helped them very much.

Detroit Tigers 1984 World Series hero and the National League's 1988 MVP Kirk Gibson had the tools when he signed in 1978. But Tigers manager Sparky Anderson concedes that he contributed to the delay of Gibson's development, with the cooperation of the Detroit media. Anderson drew a comparison between Gibson and Mickey Mantle. A very likely comparison, which Gibson heard — and felt. Anderson regrets those remarks.

"I was trying to draw a picture of him (Gibson)," Anderson told *Sports Illustrated* years later, after Gibson appeared to have "reached his potential" in the Series against the San Diego Padres. "He could hit the ball so far and run so fast. Well, that statement just took off. I was wrong to say it."

Fortunately, Gibson had the mental stamina to struggle through years of frustration and disappointment—through failure, as some saw it. His perseverance—and his real talent—allowed him the luxury of time. Fate allowed the situation, and millions of viewers watched him shine. More often than not, a player put in the initial position Gibson was in will fade in the firmament and disappear.

Mantle, himself, had to struggle to live up to New Yorkers' expectations for Joe DiMaggio's replacement in Yankee Stadium's center field. Bobby Murcer, Mantle's eventual replacement, lost his struggle.

A more recent illustration is former Oakland outfielder Jose Canseco, named the 1985 Minor League Player of the Year by *The Sporting News* and *Baseball America*. At the age of 20 he had batted .318 with 25 homers and 80 RBIs, despite missing three weeks with a broken thumb, while playing 58 games with the Huntsville Stars at the Double-A level (Southern League). After being promoted to Triple-A Tacoma (Pacific Coast League), Canseco batted .348 with 11 homers and 47 RBIs in 60 games. The West Coast media gave elaborate accounts of his strength, speed, and throwing arm. They wrote of the certainty of his becoming the game's next superstar. The major league media in Oakland waited eagerly for him.

Canseco arrived in September, at the end of the minor league season. He had his first major league at-bat in the role of a pinch hitter. He struck out.

The headline on a sports page of an area paper the next day read: "Canseco Fails." The nature of baseball writers' approach to their coverage and their relationships with players have certainly changed since the days of Clint Hartung. Sometimes it's for the better, sometimes it's not. But it is surely changed. We can't be as sure of the headline's intention. If it was meant to be ironic, it was also cruel. If it was meant to be serious, it was surely foolish.

Canseco struck out 14 times in his first 28 at-bats, before putting his press notices and his experience in perspective.

"You can't let it go to your head, or it will affect your play," Canseco said. "I'm not looking for stats. I'm just trying to be a consistent player. I don't know if Oakland is as excited about my stats as much as my maturity as a player and as a person."

Canseco ended up with a 1985 major league batting average of .302. He had five homers and 13 RBIs in 29 games. In 1986 he was the American League's Rookie of the Year; in 1988 the league's Most Valuable Player—the first player in baseball history to hit 40 home runs and steal 40 bases in the same season.

The pressure of expectations often comes from sources other than media and management, especially for younger players at the high school and college levels. Peer pressure is experienced early by all young people; it's certainly not exclusive to baseball players. But a distinction of some sort can be made—athletes take on peer pressure that most often is not expressed and quite often is just "assumed" by the better players. They first assume the responsibility of being "counted on" to pull their team—and teammates—through. They then assume the pressure that is supposed to be a result of such responsibility.

It's a double-edged sword. The pressure we feel can be initiated by others or by our own imagination and/or assumptions. Enos Cabell's remark about stardom makes the assumption. Dan Schatzeder felt more than was being put on him by others. The minor league pitcher in the Cincinnati system expressed his own interpretation of the problem. In different ways, players feel this: "If I'm not 'coming through,' I'd better—or else. If I am 'coming through,' I'd better continue—or else."

Whether the expectations of others are real or imagined, the pressure becomes real. Either edge cuts. If the stress intensifies, the player becomes dysfunctional. Remember, a player not peforming up to a goal can change the goal. A player not performing up to an expectation must change his attitude. That's the distinction we wish to make: goals serve you, expectations serve others. Even teammates. It sounds noble to concern yourself with what you know or believe others need from you, but your concern must be on what you can do to enable yourself to perform to your capabilities.

Wally Joyner, in the 1987 season that followed his outstanding rookie year, was struggling in Anaheim. He started his sophomore season with 15 hits in his first 64 at-bats. He hadn't hit a homer since August 5, 1986. Said Gene Mauch, the Angels manager, "Wally's trying to please too many people: his family, the fans, his teammates, the media, Mickey Mouse, and all those other characters at Disneyland. What he should do is worry about pleasing himself."

Apparently, Joyner took Mauch's advice to heart. His 1987 stats showed a .285 batting average, with 34 homers and 117 RBIs.

It starts with Little Leaguers and continues on up through all levels. In the 1983 All-Star game, National League pitcher Atlee Hammaker of the San Francisco Giants gave up six hits, seven runs, and the first grand slam home run in the game's half-century history. His team's defeat broke an 11-game winning streak.

"I'm sorry I let the other guys down. I knew they wanted to win," said the dejected Hammaker, whose performance was also witnessed by some 60 million people watching on television and 43,801 others from the stands, including his wife and parents.

Hammaker's remarks came after the game; the pressure from his understanding came before. The result was not unusual. As we've said, it has happened to many players, before that particular event, and since.

When Andre Dawson, the 1987 National League MVP, was playing outfield for the Montreal Expos, he had a tendency to have hitting difficulties late in the season. His team had a history of not being where they were expected to be in the standings by the end of the season. And his teammates had a habit of looking to Dawson to shoulder the burden, which didn't help him—or them.

"There were times when I pushed myself too hard," Dawson admitted. "I tried to do too much too soon." It was one of the ballplayer's common explanations for a common predicament. It was a burden that should not have been bourne. It wasn't a responsibility Dawson should have shouldered, weakly or strongly.

But even the strong can weaken. During a frustrating 1984 season, Braves slugger Dale Murphy, the exemplary, authentic good guy of major league baseball, was put in the difficult position he had grown accustomed to: feeling the absence of power-hitting Bob Horner, who batted behind Murphy in the lineup. Horner's annual injuries, up to that time, had kept him out of the lineup for prolonged periods. Murphy was "expected" to compensate for the loss of Horner's productive bat. Whether or not the expectation was in others' minds, it definitely was in Murphy's. He was used to the idea by then, but he wasn't used to his flagging performance well into the '84 season. He suffered, and he took responsibility for his team's disappointing record.

One night in Los Angeles, Murphy came to bat late in the game with his team down one run to the Dodgers. The Braves had a runner on third, the tying run. The Dodgers brought a rookie relief pitcher into the game. Murphy struck out on three pitches. To say Murphy's next act was uncharacteristic of him is comparable to saying it's warmer at the equator than at the North Pole. Murphy went back to the dugout and beat up the water cooler.

"I am feeling the pressure," he said later. The confirmation was unnecessary. He was trying to do everything and be everything for the team, a behavior of which his manager at that time, Joe Torre, was well aware. Torre advised his centerfielder to play for himself, not for others. The advice was followed; the quality of the performance was very positively affected.

Flattery is all right, if you don't inhale. Whoever first spoke that clever truth would have been proud of Cincinnati outfielder Eric Davis, who heard excessive praise and high expectations for him coming from the likes of Willie Mays, Roger Craig, and others, before the 1986 season.

Davis' response was sensible. "I don't try to live up to anybody's expectations. You can't play that way. I've heard nice things about me before. It's tough when you're a young guy and everyone expects so much from you. All of us have to learn. Even when you're a success, everything is a learning process."

Parents and coaches often teach youngsters what is difficult to unlearn, making the process that much more difficult for the player. Girlfriends, brothers, sisters, local newspapermen, and fans — any person or medium may get into the process along the way, especially if they're inclined to set the expectations for the player. It's unfortunate for the player who doesn't realize what the effect on him will be. It's irresponsible of the player who is aware and allows himself to be governed in that manner. Any player old enough to read these words should be old enough to take the responsibility himself for setting his own goals and expectations.

At the other extreme, some people, coaches most often, expect too little from a player. That, too, is a problem, and the player is just as responsible for its solution. The low expectations of some may be just as unreasonable as the lofty ones of others. In this case, a player tends to give what is expected of him, no more. He lives up to the image of him created by other people. It's easy to; it can be accomplished without much effort. Then the "I told-you-so's" are heard.

Scouting reports are common carriers of this phrase. Many baseball scouts believe that what they expect of a player is all he'll ever give. They've seen it happen many times. Too many times it shouldn't have happened. The scout was wrong from the start; the player made him right in the end. Used to doing things the easy way, that player then tends to blame the scout.

All kinds of messages come to players through grapevines. The player hears that someone thinks he's "got no guts." Being young, impressionable — human — he accepts this view and behaves accordingly. Or, if he's the more determined type, he sets out to prove himself tough, concentrating his efforts on showing he does have guts. By doing this, he focuses his concentration on matters other than his game and his performance tasks. The right approach addresses performance tasks, not image.

He should apply the same proper strategy if he hears reports that rave about him. His strategy should have him being wise enough, organized enough, honest enough, and strong enough to set his own goals and know his own capabilities. This is playing from the inside out, not the reverse. It can be done. It is done by the most effective players.

The raves of others are usually the major problem, as Hartung, Gibson, Canseco, and a league of others can confirm. If a player doesn't live up to them, *he* is given the blame. Labels are securely attached to him: "Not hungry;" "Won't listen;" — or the all-inclusive, "Head case." The problems started when the player did not, for whatever reason, live up to the assessment of his ability, to the forecast for his future achievement.

We've noted that young players whose baseball experiences are launched under these conditions are not likely to go into orbit. Bobby Grich, a teammate of Doug DeCinces when the two infielders played in both Baltimore and California, saw DeCinces flounder during his early years with the Orioles. Grich respects what DeCinces went through and what he accomplished after the ordeal. "He (DeCinces) was able to survive when everybody was confronting him with high expectations." Of course, we also noted that DeCinces had very significant help finding the path after being so desperately lost.

Whatever can be known in advance can be helpful in avoiding that problem. That's why it's so important to distinguish between goals and expectations, as we have tried to do. The player who can understand the difference between where he is reasonably trying to go, as opposed to where others want him to end up, approaches his game from the right direction. He takes the initial responsibility of charting his own course. He then observes his movement and makes the appropriate adjustments, knowing where he is, knowing where he wants to be, knowing how to get there. One specific step at a time. He'll be a more relaxed, confident, and effective player as a result.

He will never *be* a failure. He will find out just how good he is and work at being that good consistently. In doing that, he'll become a better player — a happier one, as well, for he'll know he did his best. We think he'd call that personal success. We're tempted to expect that he would, but we'll resist the temptation.

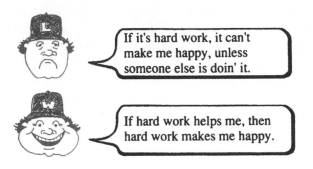

If it's hard work, it can't make me happy, unless someone else is doin' it.

If hard work helps me, then hard work makes me happy.

4
DEDICATION
Translating Desire into Action

Doing one's best is a popular *goal*. It's a rare achievement, however. In order to know his potential — and his limitations — a person must make the effort to go beyond what he is to become what he wishes to be. That effort is not made by the majority. The most successful people in their field are the exceptions, not the rule. Exceptional achievers are willing to push themselves further and higher. They have made a commitment to *themselves*. They've set goals for themselves and hold themselves responsible for attaining them. The next logical step, they know, is to work tirelessly to attain those ends — both the broad and long-term as well as the more specific and immediate. High achievers are willing to work hard. They *want* to work hard. Even those who don't enjoy some of the tasks still perform them vigorously, because they are committed to efforts that help them reach their goals.

Goals set without commitment are wasted. Successful people — successful players — know what they really want to accomplish and they construct their goals accordingly, fitting strategies to achieve them. They start with desire, build goals that spell out the desire and, further motivated by the goals, *they dedicate themselves to succeeding*. The more committed they are, the easier their efforts be-

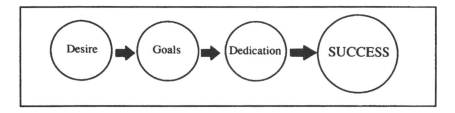

come. Mental and physical energies are devoted to what is defined as a challenge, not a burden or a threat. Their efforts do not drain them; the efforts vitalize them. For them, any effort is worth giving. Any problem is solvable. Any setback is temporary and instructive.

The player who commits himself in this way recognizes what must be done to improve himself and sees opportunities for doing so. The uncommitted player sees what cannot be accomplished and is discouraged. He is unwilling and/or unable to ake the great psychological investment required for the merging of attention, energy, and effort. Whatever his achievement, he does not consider himself a success. And should not.

The example of outfielder Darryl Strawberry provides a bridge over the gap between expectations and dedication. Again, a fine young ballplayer was highly acclaimed and loudly proclaimed to be a future Hall of Famer. He was called "a black Ted Williams" before he had played in his first major league game. Strawberry's first two years with the New York Mets, 1983 and 1984, illustrated to the young man—and to his observers—some of the problems that grow from premature and perhaps excessive expectations.

Strawberry's early performance with the Mets was weak. Everyone recognized the pressure put upon him. People were generally understanding and patient. After all, it was early. (There were no "Strawberry Fails" headlines.) With the help of a mentor, Jim Frey, then a Mets coach, Strawberry brought his talent above the surface of his tensions. He was named Rookie of the Year for 1983.

Strawberry's 1984 season began well enough. The performance of the young Mets team was surprisingly good. Well into the summer, Strawberry—and the team—slumped. The outfielder's problems at bat seemed to affect him in the field. Mets manager Davey Johnson benched him and spoke to him about his attitude and approach to the game, an approach some outspoken teammates openly criticized and resented. They felt he was sulking and not making an honest effort. The situation was ironic. In 1983, Strawberry had played under the strain of media build-up. The initial concern was that he wasn't as good as his press previews. In 1984, after the evident achievement at the end of the previous season, the suggestion was made that Strawberry now believed his press notices would speak for his performance.

The point to be made here is that *devotion to self-improvement is more apt to bring results than devotion to self-adulation.*

As is usually the case, much of the criticism leveled at Strawberry was made without regard for a true understanding of the individual and what he was going through. Strawberry publicly expressed a wish to have Jim Frey, "who understood," back with him. (Frey had become manager of the Chicago Cubs.) But every young player should understand for himself, whether he's struggling or not, the more he diminishes his physical commitment, the greater his problem will become before it is solved—if it is solved.

Strawberry's work ethic had never been highly acclaimed. His minor league managers and teammates, including a roommate and confidant, felt the young prospect's work habits "were not good."

The year before Strawberry's benching by Johnson, Frank Howard had sat the player down for the same reason. Howard, managing the Mets, had the support of his coach, Jim Frey.

"They felt I wasn't putting out enough, and they were right." Strawberry said shortly thereafter. "People let me know I had too much talent to be out there wasting it."

Frey understood what Strawberry would have to do in order to come close to his potential. "If he continues to try to improve and takes the game seriously, both offensively and defensively and as a baserunner, within three years Darryl Strawberry can be as valuable a ballplayer as anybody in the game," Frey told *Sports Illustrated* in 1984. "The whole question is his continued motivation and ambition and willingness to work." Strawberry's career, through 1993, has not been "understood" by those who have observed him over the years.

Ten years later, prior to 1994 spring training with the Los Angeles Dodgers, after years of injuries, insults, inconsistency, after reportedly clearing waivers and admittedly being the subject of trade talks, Darryl Strawberry said his troubles were behind him.

"I want to accomplish what Darryl Strawberry never accomplished," he said. "It basically boils down to, it's up to me this time." Actually, it's up to each of us ALL the time.

Strawberry skipped the Dodgers' final 1994 spring training game and was missing for nearly 24 hours. He was subsequently found and sought treatment under Major League Baseball's substance-abuse program. After months of rehabilitative treatment, he was signed to a contract with the San Francisco Giants in mid-1994. Before one knows what one has to do, one has to know who one wants to be. The presumption is that Strawberry has made that discovery.

Frey's formula also applies to players who won't be the "most valuable" in all of baseball. It applies to any player who wishes to get the most out of his abilities, whatever they are.

Charles Garfield, a clinical psychologist at the University of California School of Medicine, interviewed approximately 1,500 high-achievers as a project of the Peak Performance Center in Berkeley, which he heads. He drew the conclusion that "the single most powerful predictor of success in the long run (is) commitment"—not just a "willingness," but a *desire* to work hard toward achieving well-defined goals.

Success Magazine published an article in 1982 which made the point that some of our finest athletes are not "natural athletes" at all. Julius Erving, Bruce Jenner, and Tai Babilonia each gave more credit to attitude than to ability when discussing personal achievement.

"I played a lot of different sports in high school," said Jenner, the 1976 Olympic decathlete, "but I was never that good at anything. I certainly was no standout."

Jenner credited his dedication—decathelon training between 1972 and 1976, six to eight hours a day—for being a major factor in his gaining the gold medal he had coveted. "It was a lot of hard work. But it was fun. I had a ball."

Erving put in "an unbelievable amount of time" working on his basketball skills. Ice skater Tai Babilonia thinks her stardom came mostly as a result of "just hard work and knowing what you want out of your sport. I wanted it all."

There are many baseball players who could tell the same story, but probably the most representative and most articulate is pitcher Tom Seaver. Throughout his long career, Seaver spoke of his less-than-imposing physical stature as a high school player: 5'9" in height, 160 pounds in weight, and a body that tended (and still does) to fat.

"I was small and didn't throw very hard," Sever told *Sports Illustrated* in 1982. "In my senior year of high school I won six games and lost five. Even at USC (University of Southern California) I had to work hard just to be a starter. Pitching has always been hard work for me."

Toil, says the proverb, is the sire of fame. And joy, Seaver would say, is toil's perfect mate.

"Pitching is what makes me happy. I've devoted myself to it. I live my life around the four days between starts. It determines what I eat, when I go to bed, what I do when I'm awake. It determines how I spend my life when I'm not pitching. If it means I have to come to Florida and can't get tanned because I might get a burn that would keep me from throwing for a few days, then I never go shirtless in the sun. If it means when I get up in the morning I have to read the box scores to see who got two hits...instead of reading a novel, then I do it. If it means I have to remind myself to pet dogs with my left hand, then I do that, too. If it means in the winter I eat cottage cheese instead of chocolate chip cookies in order to keep my weight down, then I eat cottage cheese. I might want those cookies but I won't ever eat them. That might bother some people but it doesn't bother me. I enjoy the cottage cheese. I enjoy it more than I would those cookies because I know it will help me do what makes me happy.

"I've made up my mind what I want to do. I'm happy when I pitch well so I only do things that help me be happy. I wouldn't be able to dedicate myself like this for money or glory, although they are certainly consideratons. If I pitch well...I'll be able to give my family security. But that isn't what motivates me. What motivates some pitchers is to be known as the fastest who ever lived. Some want to have the greatest season ever. All I want is to do the best I possibly can day after day, year after year..."

Writer Pat Jordan, himself a former ballplayer, wrote that Seaver "is highly critical—one might almost say contemptuous—of less conscientious players." Said Jordan, "For Seaver, a man's talent is not just part of the man. It is the whole man, or at the very least a mirror of the whole man. Treating one's talent carelessly is indicative of a weakness in character."

Jordan reported that Seaver made the following comment about a pitcher who apparently had ruined a promising career through negligence: "What a fool he must be. To throw it all away like that. If you don't think baseball is a big deal, don't play it. But if you do, play it right."

How a man dedicates himself speaks for the man. What he achieves speaks for itself. So it is with Seaver and his achievements.

Of course, there are many "right" paths to achievement. As noted, Seaver's is representative. But Nolan Ryan's way led to where he wanted to be. His stay has been a long one. On a July morning in 1983—at 7:45 A.M., to be more precise—the then 36-year-old Houston Astros pitcher was found doing rigorous swimming exercises in a San Diego hotel pool, part of the extensive daily program Ryan follows. The previous night he had pitched his ninth one-hitter and 52nd career shutout, a 1-0 victory over the Padres. Ryan, a future Hall of Famer, retired in 1993 at age 46.

Pitcher Steve Carlton, elected to the Hall of Fame in 1994, had his own particular approach. His strength exercises and program of self-discipline influenced others and impressed many more. When Darrell Evans was playing for the San Francisco Giants, he said he "wouldn't be surprised if (Carlton) could pitch till he's 50. He's so strong."

Evans made his comment lightheartedly, with a laugh, but Carlton quite seriously, told friends he planned to pitch 10 more years. That was in 1983. Carlton's wife, Beverly, thought the goal not unrealistic. "As hard as he works, he just might," she said. He certainly tried.

There seems to be a distinct correlation between working and lasting.

Early in his career, Pete Rose wanted to become the first singles hitter to earn $100,000. He did. As his career progressed, Rose began to form long-range statistical goals. Now, his record-setting accomplishments are well known. But Rose was another player who considered his physical ability to be no better than ordinary. What is extraordinary, he said, was his attitude.

"Total dedication. I worked hard because I just can't go through the motions. The numbers motivated me, and I know what it takes to get those numbers. I dedicated myself. I worked my tail off. I took care of myself. I don't smoke or drink. I made sure I was ready to play every day, because to accomplish my goals, I had to play. You can't get 200 hits a year on the bench. Getting 4000 career hits excites me. There were a lot of days I didn't feel like doing the work I had to do, or I would've liked to do something else," Rose conceded. But he never yielded to the temptation to take it easy, if he ever really had one.

The temptation to take it easy can be strong. Many big leaguers have given in to it. Some perform halfheartedly. Others are malingerers. They have what is called "an attitude problem."

Some players are just not conscious of what it takes to be devoted to their profession. It isn't that they have bad work habits; they have no habits at all.

Pitcher Steve Trout altered his habits, with help from pitching coach Billy Connors, when the two were with the Cubs. Trout was 10-14 in 1983 for the Cubs, after having been traded across town from the White Sox. He had a reputation for enjoying himself rather than applying himself. Connors invited the pitcher to Florida in the winter of 1983 to work on Trout's mechanics—and his mind games.

Said Connors, "I had a lot of kids (who needed such work) in the minor leagues. But he's the biggest challenge I've had up here."

Both Connors and Trout responded to that challenge. Connors told his pitcher, "If you want to drink Don Perignon, you'd better bust yourself." The appeal was not exactly to the 26-year-old pitcher's professional pride, but it worked as an initial motivation. Connors kept after his pupil whenever Trout became lax, which wasn't often. Trout's 13-7, 1984 season was convincing enough to have Chicago re-sign him as a free agent. The pitcher's contract made Connors' forecast for "busting it" seem modest.

Trout called Connors his "avatar," a Hindu word meaning "a god's coming to earth in bodily form."

What Trout's avatar advocated was simply that earthlings in Cubs uniforms devote their bodies—and minds—to perfecting the skills of their trade and applying them. Apparently, the Cubs, National League Eastern Division Champions in '84, had quite a bit of success following that formula.

Many players work diligently with weights during the off-season so as to have greater strength during the playing season. Others dedicate themselves to specific programs which best serve their individual needs. Brian Downing and Lance Parrish of the Angels were two of the more conscientious players in the major leagues. "I've had my ups and downs in hitting," Parrish said while playing with the California Angels. "But...the improvement I've acquired took a lot of hard work. And it most certainly paid off."

There are many players, professional and amateur, who recognize the need for hard work, who have the opportunity, but who aren't motivated enough to put in the time and effort. We do not speak of those who are "burned out," but of those who lack the burning desire to improve themselves. They are not the dedicated practitioners of their game.

Practice alone does not "make perfect." The right kind of practice must accompany the right kind of dedication.

The Wrong Kind, An Example: An early selection of the Cleveland Indians in the 1983 draft was a catcher who came out of college with an extremely impressive batting record. His initial short season as a professional player was fair, but far from past performances and far from satisfying for the player, who admitted at the Indians' Instructional League camp in the fall of the year that he was "spoiled." Pro ball, he found, required more and gave less than that to which he had been accustomed.

The player had no idea of what batting practice should or could be. He went into the cage and swung away mindlessly. Purposelessly. Asked what he did when he saw he wasn't hitting the ball well, he responded, "I say, 'To hell with it,' and just turn around and bat lefty." (He was and is a right-handed batter, *not* a switchhitter.) When given an idea of what he could do to help himself in a more mature and professional manner, the player responded enthusiastically. The following day he dedicated hours of batting practice to the "right way." The way that led to better results. He has been working hard at all aspects of his game since and is a major leaguer now. His inclination had been sitting in a waiting room, waiting for the birth of an idea, a right idea.

Rusty Staub had the idea for many years. A major leaguer for 23 seasons, Staub set a number of pinch-hitting records in his last years with the New York Mets. His achievements had much to do with his method and manner of taking batting practice. His dedication to detail and serious work in the batting cage were particularly helpful to him when, used as a pinch hitter exclusively, he had one at-bat in a game without knowing when that game would come.

Staub did know that young, inexperienced players are not the only ones to be ineffective in the batting cage. He watched many major leaguers who unknowingly (or knowingly) took batting practice in a way that hurt their performance. Staub saw them every day of every season. They puzzled him. His own approach was no more than common sense to him. His persistence at it was no less than he demanded of himself.

"The most important thing I could ever offer a young person advice on is that he concentrate in his workouts—his batting practices and everything else he's doing—on something he wants to accomplish," said Staub. "When I take batting practice, I work on the bunt first. Then I work on hit-and-run, take the ball the other way. Then I put a man (imagined) on second base with nobody out, and I've gotta pull the ball to get the guy over from second with nobody out. And then, sometimes, I'll just work on hitting the ball a certain way. If I think a pitcher's gonna pitch me away, I tell the batting practice pitcher, 'I want you to work me away in b.p.' If I know I'm going to get a lot of breaking balls, I like to see some in batting practice.

"But the important thing that I try to do is keep my timing and thinking patterns going in the right way. It's like sharpening a tool. You don't ever go up there and just swing for the hell of it. If you're gonna use a knife, it should be sharp; if you're gonna use your bat, you should have honed those skills. That's a corny way of putting it, maybe, but it's the truth.

"I have certain situations I'll talk to people (players) about. I'll say, 'If you get down to the last couple of swings (in b.p.), then let's have two hit-and-runs. First pitch, you get the guy over; second pitch get the guy in.' Just trying to get everybody to think, around the batting cage, of circumstances they're gonna be in during the game.

"If you're mentally prepared ahead of time, if you've practiced these things, if you've *worked* at it—when you get in those situations, you're automatically going to do them, because you've worked on them every day. If you work on them on a routine, daily basis, instead of just goin' up there and trying to hit the ball out of the ball park every time, you're gonna be better prepared than the other guy."

By "other guy," Staub means the guy who hasn't committed himself to the appropriate physical and mental preparations—who hasn't learned to play winning mind games.

San Diego's Tony Gwynn signed a contract extension for $8.5 million through the 1997 season. A veteran of 11-plus seasons with the Padres, Gwynn hit .358 in 1993. Four National League batting crowns, 11 straight years over .300, a lifetime average of .329, eight All-Star Game appearances: it's more than skill according to Gwynn. To listen to Gwynn talk about dedicating himself to becoming a great hitter (he's used video more than any player in baseball) is to hear a contemporary Rusty Staub. But then, the music of excellence seems to be played in the same key.

Fielding is a neglected skill. The timeworn notion that good fielders are a dime-a-dozen has probably encouraged players at all levels to concentrate on hitting the ball more than catching it. Small wonder that it would be neglected. But it shouldn't be. Fielding is a very significant part of the game of baseball, and a player's dedication to fielding practice is as essential as his dedication to any other part of his game.

One particular minor league infielder who *used* to be with the Cincinnati organization was guilty of such neglect. He had hit well at the Triple-A level in 1983 (.322) but was regarded lightly because of his fielding weaknesses. The following year he was playing at the Double-A level, having been told his fielding kept him from being a prospect. He consented to the demotion, anxious to continue his professional career. He was hoping he could change some minds.

Hope was not enough. During the 1984 season the player admitted he "didn't spend very much time working on fielding." He said he "enjoyed hitting more." He hits well, he explained, and batting practice is more fun than fielding drills.

The tendency to enjoy most what we do best is normal behavior. Professional baseball players, however, are not the norm. And aspiring major leaguers can't afford to behave as if they are. Those who wish to advance to the top of their profession—or trade or class or whatever—*must work hard on their weaknesses*, in addition to working continually on their strengths, or they will never reach their goal—or even know if they were capable of reaching it.

Wade Boggs reached his in Fenway Park. His hitting skills were excellent enough to get him there. And, yes, he loves to take batting practice. His play at third base, however, did not impress many baseball observers, and it did not reach the standard that could satisfy Boggs. He has devoted considerable time during the season to his fielding, but he's dedicated entire winters to improving those defensive skills. The results of his work are very apparent.

Pre-game infield practice is a more-or-less daily procedure on any field where uniformed teams are preparing to play a game. The size of the people in the uniforms is of no matter: infield practice is a ritual for all. Unfortunately, the ceremony often is more form than function, to hear many professional players tell it. They put their bodies into it, but not necessarily their hearts—and rarely their minds.

That—the mind—is what needs the ritual most, according to frequent Gold Glove shortstop Ozzie Smith of the St. Louis Cardinals.

"Concentration is the key to fielding," Smith said. "You've got to be mentally prepared: knowing that you're playing the hitter properly; knowing his speed; knowing the speed of the ball—if you're on AstroTurf or high grass—the situation; knowing the rhythm of your pitcher and those things. You learn to concentrate well through practice."

Smith suggested that an infielder who just goes out and takes 100 ground balls off a fungo bat for, as Staub would say, "the hell of it" is accomplishing little. After all, a batter is called upon to concentrate on perhaps 25 pitches during the course of a game, whereas the fielder must sustain his concentration every defensive inning, for an average of 150 pitches per game.

Asked how many big leaguers use their infield work as such a mental regimen, Smith offered a sheepish grin under raised eyebrows. He gave a noncommittal shrug of the shoulders. "The ones that care a lot do," he said after a time.

Colorado shortstop Walt Weiss, the American League Rookie of the Year in 1988, is another example of "one who cares a lot."

During the 1983 National League Eastern Division's race for first place, Steve Rogers, pitching for the Montreal Expos, expressed his feeling that many teammates didn't care enough. The frustration he verbalized was a reaction to a game the Expos (and Rogers) lost at home in mid-July to the Reds. The game ended at 2:52 in the morning. The teams had to play later that afternoon.

Said Rogers, "The most frustrating thing is our players seem to think less of it as a race. That was an important game last night."

The game had been resumed after a two-hour, seven-minute rain delay with Cincinnati leading 1-0 in the top of the sixth.

"We go (back) out there into a game we're losing, and there was no perception of it being important. If we don't resume play, we lose it right there, but I didn't get the feeling (umpire) Lee Weyer's efforts and (Expos manager) Bill Virdon's efforts to get us back were fully appreciated (by many Expos players)," Rogers continued.

"It was more of a 'Why are we back here at 1:30?' and not a reprieve. The importance of each individual win is great, but it seems that unless a win is convenient, it doesn't matter. It's not easy to have that (dedicated) attitude. It was a tough-assed night. It's terribly difficult to keep your mental awareness. But if you're going to win, it's important...The problem is the intensity has been diminished..."

The early morning mind games that Steve Rogers was bothered by are in complete opposition to the dedicated attitude of a winner.

A Winner's Story: On April 19, 1982, the New York Mets were rained out of their game against the Expos in Montreal. Seaver was to have pitched for the Mets. His start was changed to the 21st against the Chicago Cubs. *Sports Illustrated* recorded the "event" which followed the rain-out:

> When the Mets returned to New York the night of the 19th, most of the players went directly home from La-Guardia Airport. Seaver, however, got a ride on the team bus to Shea Stadium, which was deserted and in darkness. He went directly to the locker room, put on his uniform, filled a bucket with baseballs and began the long walk across the diamond to the right-field bullpen. He moved with his graceless and plodding plowman's walk, his weight falling on his heels and his head listing to the right as if, with each ensuing step, it might collapse upon his shoulder. When Seaver reached the bullpen he stepped onto the warmup mound and began throwing baseball after baseball against the screen behind the plate. His throwing was illuminated only by the lights from the parking lot. He warmed up quickly but carefully in the mild night air. He was accompanied only by the sounds of his own exertion, and of baseballs plunking against the screen and dropping softly to the ground.

It was a typical behavior of a pitcher who always strives to get the best from himself. *Sports Illustrated* went on:

> . . . Seaver felt he had to labor that April night in the dark Mets bullpen. He threw until he reached the same level of effort and concentration he would have needed against the Expos in Montreal. He continued this pace for a while and then went home. . . . When asked why he put himself through such an inconvenience, he said, 'It was my day to throw. I always throw on my day to throw.'
> . . . Because of such dedication to detail, it would seem

Seaver: "... accompanied only by the sounds of his own exertion, and of the baseballs plunking against the screen and dropping softly to the ground."

the only thing that could keep Seaver from reaching the goal[s] he had determined for himself is an event beyond his control. . . .

The magazine article had exactly defined Seaver's intention — and the point of this chapter.

Seaver defeated the Cubs on April 21, 2–0. It was his second start of the season; it was his second shutout.

Roger Clemens is a more contemporary example of commitment and success. No sooner had he won his second consecutive Cy Young Award in 1987, than he began running and lifting weights to get his legs and shoulder in shape for the 1988 season. He reported to spring training in a condition less dedicated pitchers usually attain two months into the season.

"He's never satisfied," said Clemens' catcher, Rich Gedman. He credits Clemens' great success, talent notwithstanding, to hard work and preparation.

Don Mattingly is another fine example of a dedicated player. Listen to Chicago White Sox hitting coach Walt Hriniak telling *Sports Illustrated* writer Peter Gammons about Mattingly: "The guy's hitting .350, making a million-something dollars a year, his team is 10 games out, they got to their hotel at four in the morning, and he's underneath the stands in the cage at 3:30 in the afternoon. . . . Look at the way he plays the game. . . . He's the greatest I've ever seen, and he's everything this game *should* be."

Mattingly also spoke on the same topic — himself — to Gammons. ". . . I want to improve every day in every facet of the game," the Yankees first baseman said. "I hate to hear that a guy's not a good defensive player. There shouldn't be any bad defensive players, not if they work hard enough. It's as simple as that. There are tons of players who could be a lot better. I'd like to have some of the talent of those guys. Give me their talent and I'll do some *really* big things."

Ironically, former Yankee great Mickey Mantle was looking back on the ratio between his own talent and *dedication* during his playing days. He claimed to regret the years of hard drinking that he feels took years off his career and kept him from reaching some of his goals, as did his unwillingness to follow doctors' advice as to how he should have worked at rehabilitating his bad knees.

"Look at guys like Willie Mays and Hank Aaron and Pete Rose," Mantle told *USA Today* in May of 1987. "Those guys took care of their bodies and they played forever. I never thought it mattered, until now. It [ticks] me off when I see guys passing me on all-time home runs and I know I could have had a hell of a lot more."

Mantle added, "Kids should know they should take better care of themselves. I wish I had. Sometimes I think if I had the same body and the same natural ability and somebody else's brain, who knows how good a player I would have been?"

It's an apt question—one that can be asked by many who have played the game and who, retrospectively, realized that reaching goals has more to do with intensity than with intentions. With action, more than with words—or hopes.

Many other examples can be given of players who have been strongly committed to their goals. Dale Murphy, after having won the first of his two consecutive MVP Awards in 1982, sent himself to the Braves' Florida Instructional League camp at the regular season's end, so he could correct batting habits which displeased him. Mets pitcher Dwight Gooden was not satisfied with his pitching mechanics, despite the very fine statistics he compiled in winning the Rookie of the Year Award in 1984. Off he went to the Instructional League— and he won the Cy Young Award in 1985. Unhappy with batting average and his physical condition, George Brett undertook a dramatically rigorous winter conditioning program after the 1984 season. He was happy with both after the outstanding '85 season he had as a key member of Kansas City's World Championship team. Brett retired as a player after the 1993 season at age 40.

The great Roberto Clemente always worked vigorously and studiously in pre-game outfield practice, acclimating himself to the conditions he would play under on that particular day. He took batted balls off the grass, the better to judge the speed. He took balls off unusually contoured walls, so he could practice judging and handling the tricky caroms. He worked against the wind, the sun, the lights, as he would work in his mind against the opposing pitcher for the day.

In a biography of Clemente by Phil Musick (*Who Is Roberto?*), the author tells of a visit paid to the Clementes by a friend, attorney Elfren Bernier, during the 1971 season. On a rainy afternoon, in the middle of a downpour that threatened that night's ball game, Clemente suddenly informed his friend that they were leaving for the ball park immediately. It was two o'clock. "The field will be wet tonight," he told Bernier. "I want to try a couple of things."

Bernier described the "things." "He (Clemente) had someone roll the ball on the ground to make it wet and then threw it against the wall so that he could practice grabbing it barehanded. For a long time he did that and then ran back and forth, stopping and starting," reported Bernier about his hard-working and talented friend.

That's what the dedicated players do at every level of competition. The sooner the better.

Dedication and Success

We are very concerned with being clear about our definitions of "dedication" and "success."

In his book, *Winning*, Stuart Walker writes: "The mentally tough competitor recognizes that his [own] high expectations require — and justify — a high investment of self." We agree. *"Require and justify."*

In the preceding chapter, however, Walker had said: "The conscientious [athlete] expects that his high investment will result in a high reward . . . The unspoken corollary is, if you spend the amount of time, effort, and energy that I did, you are guaranteed success."

Here we cannot agree. Death and taxes and long-term contracts are the only guarantees about which we've heard ballplayers talk. The most inexperienced young player has played enough, we presume, to have tasted defeat, to have fallen short of his goals, to have learned that "success," as Walker seems to be defining it, is *never* "*guaranteed.*" The "success" of maximizing one's concern and effort is always possible, simply because that "success" is in the control of the individual himself.

Interestingly enough, Walker wrote elsewhere in his book, "Unrealistic expectations invite disappointment and discouragement."

A good example of an unrealistic expectation is the kind of "guaranteed success" suggested by Walker's words.

The idea seems to be more clearly and accurately stated by Michael

D. Scott and Louis Pelliccioni, Jr., in their *RQ* article, "Winners & Losers: Mastering the Mental Game." They warn that an athlete not try to be superhuman in his efforts: "We are not saying here an athlete should approach a competition with an attitude that it really doesn't matter. What we are saying is that the most successful athlete is one who stays loose. . . . Based on all of our research and the research of others, it is the *supercool effort* that enables an athlete to consistently come up on top."

Not always, but consistently. We agree—and having spoken to many ballplayers, we find that "supercool efforts"—the efforts of relaxed players—derive in large part from past success, confidence, concentration, and self-discipline. (These topics will be treated in later chapters of this book.) Much of which, say players, comes from dedication to *approach*—to technique—both mental and physical. "Success," say Scott and Pelliccioni later in the same article, "comes only when technique has become habit." Creating the good habit, we would say, is the first success.

The legendary Casey Stengel had his own way of expressing that same idea. Leonard Koppett's fine book, *A Thinking Man's Guide To Baseball,* includes some specific thoughts from the venerable "Perfesser" on dedication to task and technique.

> If a man has five good points, why wouldn't he work on the sixth point that can make him better? How many times have you seen a man practicing scoring from third on a fly? How often can you practice it in a game? You gotta hit a triple, right? But in batting practice, you can go down there every time after you hit.
>
> If a pitcher has trouble keeping a man close, why wouldn't he study and master it? If a man can't hit a curve, why wouldn't he get the batting practice pitcher to throw him curves instead of just seeing how far he can hit it at noon?
>
> Some of 'em complain they can't get the signs on this or that play, but why do you have to see the coach? Why don't you know yourself, while you're on deck, what I do if he doubles, what'll I do if he triples, this is probably what they'll want. Then you won't be shocked and taken by surprise when the sign is on.

Or running a base. Why do you have to look at the coach? Second base is right where it always was, they ain't moved it, have they? And there's no hills on the basepath or obstacle course, is there? So why not look at the ball in the outfield, and know what kind of arm the man has?

This is a form of the dedication we advocate, defined in the most profound Stengelese. We would also borrow the definition from *The American Heritage Dictionary of the English Language*: "The state of being bound emotionally or intellectually (or both!) to some course of action."

Course of *action*! Not the abstract idea of winning something. Not the fear of losing. Not the obsessive preoccupation that detaches a person from all else in his world. Not the drudgery of somber duty based on compulsiveness or guilt. None of that. Rusty Staub is a happy man, a gourmet chef, and entrepreneur, even as he was when he played big league baseball. Dale Murphy is a joyful family man, who works as diligently for his church as for his profession. Tom Seaver enjoyed golf and bird hunting and an occasional concert as he devoted himself to baseball.

These, and others like them, are real people. Multi-dimensional people. People in touch with themselves and the world around them; very dedicated people who believe they get out of something in direct proportion to what they put into it. And they are usually—not always, but usually—very successful at whatever they put themselves into. Baseball, for instance.

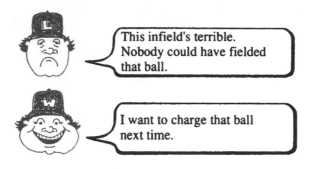

5
RESPONSIBILITY
The Player as Cause

When Great Britain's Prime Minister Winston Churchill said, "The price of greatness is responsibility," he didn't take the time to define the word so many people hear as scolding or blaming, as shaming, or even praising. It is none of these. At least, it shouldn't be. "Responsibility" is a term which defines the individual's (or group's) accountability for his (or its) own behavior and actions—performance, for a baseball player.

A player should not believe that he'll certainly be an outstanding performer on the baseball field just because he dedicates himself to that goal. We are not born with equal abilities. Whether we become ballplayers, auto mechanics, or writers, the hardest workers among us may never acquire and possess the abilities necessary to become exceptional in our field.

Fate hasn't treated us equally. Some of us were born into wealth, others into poverty. Some were born with what is considered to be a fine physical appearance; others are not particularly attractive in that way. And so it is, too, with our natural athletic abilities. None of this is within our control. Therefore, it is *not* our responsibility.

Our responsibility begins with a willingness to acknowledge who we are and what we are—and what we want to become.

Responsibility is the acceptance of our "selves" as the cause of our current situation, and it's the willingness to cope with that situation — to live vitally within it. Correct it; regulate it; *improve* it.

Whatever else responsibility might be, it is not actually something we *should* or *ought to* have. It's something that, as humans, we already have. We already are responsible for our thoughts and actions; for what we learn or don't learn; for what we like and dislike; for what we say and don't say. For the object and extent of our commitments. For our performance.

In *Release Your Brakes* Jim Newman writes of a "law of accountability," which proclaims, "People are responsible/accountable for everything they think and do, whether they like it, accept it, or even know it."

The best performers separate themselves from others by knowing it, accepting it, *and* liking it. In effect, they take an active responsibility for themselves.

The French author Saint-Exupery wrote, "To be a man is, precisely, to be responsible." We'll be less precise in the name of manhood and more so in the name of the "whole self": To be a self-actualized person is to be responsible.

Self-actualizing is the tendency human beings have toward fulfillment. It's based on the human need for positive regard — feeling good about ourselves. For cheers, applause. High-fives. Forearm bashes. Positive regard from others and from ourselves. Self-regard, in the latter case.

Responsibility is just one of the behaviors leading to self-actualization, like it or not, know it or not, as Newman says. Self-regard, then, is the barometer we watch — often unconsciously — to see what we think of ourselves.

The barometer is affected by many "conditions" of self: self-assertion, self-confidence, self-control, self-criticism, self-deception, self-denial, self-determination, self-doubt. There are many more, but we'll only add the following: self-importance, self-improvement, self-indulgence, self-pity, self-preservation, self-sacrifice, self-sufficiency.

Does all this have anything to do with playing baseball? Reread that list and decide for your*self.* Then add self-knowledge to the list.

If the list weren't in alphabetical order, self-knowledge would be at the top. Following that is accountability for our behavior and performance. Responsibility. Do we "own up" to what we've done or caused to happen? Or to what we haven't done? Or prevented from happening? All very much related to what pitcher Frank Viola meant when he finally took responsibility for his failures on the mound and said, "I'm a new man." It comes easier on the tongue than, "I'm getting closer to being a self-actualized person." Easier to the ear, also.

Many players don't behave as if they're responsible for what they do or cause to happen. They try to give the responsibility away, or take only a share of it, at most. By not "owning up" they forfeit control of their actions. They can't be "in charge." Improvement for them comes at an extremely slow rate, if it comes at all, and the player's "potential" is neither reached nor approached. *The degree to which each player holds himself accountable and responsible for his actions will be a major factor in determining the degree of his learning, improving, and succeeding.*

Relief pitcher Bill Caudill was with the Seattle Mariners in 1983 when, on June 25, manager Rene Lachemann was fired. "You can't point the finger at one individual, but if you do, you have to point it in my direction," said Caudill, nearly two months later. "I think I let Lach down. I didn't do it on purpose, but if I realized what I know now, I think he would still have his job."

The self Caudill became aware of apparently did not make him proud. He had made a habit of arriving at the ball park at his own convenience and preparing himself in a less-than-dedicated — all right, irresponsible — manner. Caudill didn't help *himself* reach the goals he wanted on the field. And he didn't help Lachemann reach some of the goals the manager had set for the team.

"My shoes aren't so big that I can go out and, just because of who I am, get people out," Caudill added. "I've got to have that killer instinct every time I take the field. This has made me grow up a little. The last two months (remaining in the '83 season) I have to see if I've become a smart pitcher. I hope so. I've been successful, but not the type of success I want to be. I want to be a relief pitcher that people will remember."

The following year, pitching for the Oakland A's, Caudill had a 9-7 record — with 36 saves and an ERA of 2.71.

ACCEPTING RESPONSIBILITY

1. Player is in control of his own fate.
2. Player recognizes choices.
3. Player learns from mistakes.
4. Player feels in charge.
5. Player feels enthusiastic, aware of personal power.
6. Player "wants to, is free to, loves to" approach activity.
7. Player feels he has caused his own success, which reinforces confidence in future successes.

REJECTING RESPONSIBILITY

1. Player controlled by luck, fate or the breaks.
2. Player doesn't recognize available choices.
3. Player doesn't learn from mistakes.
4. Player feels threatened.
5. Player feels pressure, frustration, resentment.
6. Player feels, "I have to; I should; I must" get things done; or, "Why bother?"
7. Player uses excuses as a defense against failure.

Look again at the lists above. You might wonder why a player would want to give away responsibility or you might already know. But it's likely that both those who wonder and those who know have, at some time and/or another, found a necessary reason for relinquishing responsibility.

SOME COMMON REASONS
FOR REJECTING RESPONSIBILITY

1. To immediately reduce or avoid the pain after a mistake or poor performance.
2. To protect self-image.
3. To protect reputation.
4. To get sympathy and/or attention ("Poor guy; it wasn't all his fault").
5. To maintain a sense of superiority ("I'm too good to make a mistake like that").

6. To avoid or eliminate the fear of being criticized (felt by those players with a particularly strong need for approval).

There are a number of reasons for avoiding responsibility. All of them are used to protect our pride. The need for approval—our own and others'—is very strong. We resort to equally strong measures to satisfy the need—and to keep it satisfied. Because we're all imperfect, we've got to learn to live with our failures; to accept the fact that some of the attempts we make at success will be failures; to recognize that we, ourselves,—the persons—are not failures. This understanding makes it much easier to learn how to take responsibility—and use it to help the self that seeks approval and awareness.

Probably the most common device used by a ballplayer attempting to avoid responsibility is the excuse. Through its use, the player eases the disappointment—the pain—of a failure to reach a specific goal. He also gives himself a satisfactory explanation for his performance. What he's produced may be an "acceptable" reason, but it is not an "accurate" one. Primarily, the player is trying to fool others. He may end up fooling himself, which is more likely—and more harmful.

Whether done consciously or unconsciously, excuse-making is an attempt to say that any other player would have performed in the exact way, under the exact conditions.

An occasional excuse can be an effective coping mechanism—a necessary one sometimes. *Sometimes.* But frequent use of that technique indicates a greater failure than the one the player is trying to cover up: the failure to be honest with himself.

Being a compulsive excuse-maker can also indicate that the player believes he must take responsibility for everything—for everyone. He rightly feels this to be more than he can handle. *It is more than anyone should ever attempt to handle.* It can't be handled, and it shouldn't be handled.

This subject will be expanded and clarified shortly. First, let's identify a few excuses players use in shifting responsibility for poor performance by blaming other people, circumstances, conditions, or unknown forces:

Reprinted by permission of United Feature Syndicate, Inc.

1. The *wind* was playing tricks with the ball.
2. The *umpire* blew the first pitch, and then I couldn't concentrate.
3. What kind of attitude do you expect me to have, the way *they* treat me?
4. I didn't *try* to do that; something just happened. (blaming an unknown force)
5. The catcher insisted I throw the curve instead of the fastball.
6. I can't pitch in *cold weather.*
7. That's what happens when *they make me* play *hurt.*
8. *He* doesn't use me in my right *position.*
9. I gotta *play every day* to be effective.
10. They only caught me because the *ump* blew a balk call.
    And so on . . .

At the Cleveland Indians Instructional League camp in 1983, a young minor league outfielder emphatically stated, "I can't play in the morning," having discovered the next day's game was to begin at 10 A.M. Asked how this "fact" had been revealed to him, the player explained that he had played badly, in the field and at bat, in the two previous morning games in Florida. He was excusing, in advance, the third such poor performance. This attitude, of course, was doubly dangerous because of its potential to convince the player — before the "fact" — that his next game would be another bad one. A self-fulfilling prophecy lurked in the shadow of a shifting responsibility.

All this was brought to the player's attention. He agreed to try to adjust his approach. While his performance that morning was not Hall of Fame calibre, it was respectable enough to support his belief in the approach. In addition, he gave assurances that, even if he had had a bad game, *he* would have "shouldered the blame."

"Taken the responsibility" would have been a more desirable phrase. A good player doesn't point the finger away from himself; he points it at himself. *But he doesn't wag it!* Self-blame diminishes a player; responsibility makes him grow. Too many conscientious players confuse the two. Accepting responsibility is just recognizing the facts, stating them clearly, learning from them, and applying what has been learned in the future. Blame, shame, and self-degradation are wastes of time and energy. They sap a player's power.

The young outfielder in the Cleveland organization went from one poor extreme to another before he moderated his mental approach to a particular problem. Infielder Ron Washington solved the same type of problem more directly — but he wasn't a "young" infielder when he addressed it.

Ron Washington had trials with the Kansas City Royals and the Los Angeles Dodgers before making it with the Minnesota Twins as a 30-year-old in 1982. Washington had been capable of playing in the big leagues for a long time, but no one was willing to tolerate the high number of mistakes he made — and the explanations that went with them. After Washington had "screwed up," he would always have an explanation, such as, "I know I goofed. I'm not making excuses, but I want to tell you why I did it that way. (In his mind, he was *not* making excuses.) I know I did the wrong things, but I have a good reason."

Washington would not completely concede he'd made mistakes. Consequently, he kept making the same ones again and again. By the middle of the season, the total of his errors in judgment was almost as great as the total of all the other Twins together. Even before a play began, Washington was preparing to defend himself against criticism. He didn't realize what he was doing, focusing defensively on his "self," instead of his task. All of his thinking — his "concentration" — was destructive, not constructive.

By June, a great transformation was evident in his attitude. Washington began to take responsibility for all his errors and mistakes. He began to learn from them. During the second half of the season, he made very few — and never repeated one he had made before.

People also give away responsibility by saying, "I have to," or "I must." Usually, the words are spoken without any thought. Those words can cause problems. They suggest that the speaker doesn't have any choice in his actions. No alternatives. Since he's "forced" to act in a particular way, he isn't responsible for that action, he reasons. *But he has a choice.*

For example, "I *have* to be on time."

No one *has* to be on time. People *choose* to be on time: so that they aren't fired from their jobs; so that they make good impressions on others; because they don't like to be kept waiting, so they don't wish to make others wait; because they like order and organization.

A player says, "I *have* to play for the Moscow Mavericks," but he is really *choosing* to, rather than be fined, suspended, or released.

Another player says, "I *have* to do what my coach told me to do."

Not so, but most players *choose* to do so — in order to take advantage of the coach's experience; out of respect; in order to keep from antagonizing the coach and suffering the consequences.

Someone saying, "I have to," is saying, "I have no control over what I'm doing." These "have-to's" create pressure, tension, resentment. We don't generally like to do things we "have to," even if the requirement is self-imposed. "Have-to's" are pushy. We resent and resist being pushed and, therefore, we'll seldom do anything as well as we are capable, when we "have to" do it.

Catcher Tim Laudner, early in his career with the Minnesota Twins, claimed he would hit better if the hitting coach, Jim Lemon, would let him hit his "own way."

The player was asked, "Why don't you hit your own way, if you know you can hit better?"

He answered, "I *have to* hit the way he told me to hit."

Then the player was asked, "Is he (Lemon) holding a gun to your head? How is he forcing you to hit his way? What will happen if you hit the way you want to?"

After a moment of thought, the player responded, "He'll get mad at me."

Perhaps Lemon would have. Most likely not. With still more thought, the player began to recognize the fact that he had a choice in the matter. He could hit the way Lemon had suggested, or he could hit his "own way," and put up with Lemon's anger, should that have been the result. When he consciously made his choice,

"Hit my way—or else!"

the player took responsibility for *his decision* to bat a particular way. He stopped resisting; he started hitting more effectively. (He took Lemon's approach, not his own, incidentally.)

To whom are we responsible/obligated? — and for what are we responsible/accountable? We can be responsible/obligated to others, but we cannot be accountable *for* what others think or do, because we can't control their thoughts or deeds. Players have responsibility *to* their families, friends, and teammates. This is just an extension, really, of the responsibility they have to themselves. But players who start to feel responsible *for* others — for everyone and everything, as we mentioned earlier in the chapter — create pressure for themselves. This pressure is more than a player should have to cope with. It can be avoided.

Occasionally, a fine player will mistakenly begin to feel responsible *for* the performance of his team. Andre Dawson and Dale Murphy were mentioned earlier as two who have felt that "responsibility." A player who feels that way usually finds, as did Dawson and Murphy, that his performance suffers. Former big league catcher Butch Wynegar went through a more prolonged experience than did the two National League sluggers.

In 1976, Wynegar was a 20-year-old rookie with Minnesota. Selected to be a participant in the All-Star Game that year, he became the youngest catcher ever to play in the game. He was an All-Star again the following year. From that time on, however, his production slipped. By the time he was traded to the Yankees in '82, he was a disappointment to the Twins and to himself. A short time after having joined the Yankees, his play improved. The base hits came consistently for the first time in years.

In June of that '82 season, the *New York Times* quoted Wynegar as saying, "I am more comfortable with the Yankees than I was with the Twins."

The writer asked him, "How can you possibly be more comfortable in this zoo, with the pressure from the press and management, than you were in Minnesota?"

Wynegar responded, "In Minnesota I was expected(!) to be the leader, to drive in the runs. I knew I had to do well or the team would not win. That put a lot of pressure on me. I felt responsible for(!) the Twins' winning or losing. With the Yankees, they have guys like Piniella, Winfield, Nettles, and Gamble, who are paid a lot of money to drive in runs. Anything I contribute is gravy."

Wynegar hadn't felt responsible for making the Yankees win, only for his own performance. That relieved great pressure, freeing him to play the way Butch Wynegar was capable of playing.

A minor league pitcher in the Cincinnati system was trying to explain why negativism seemed to creep into his thinking while he was pitching. He was questioned about past difficulties and current fears, but, to his own surprise, he "discovered" that his baseball career had been rather successful—and that he hadn't really ever been a fearful person.

He was told that, whatever the case may be, *he* was responsible for his thoughts. His "discovery" would make it that much easier for him to grasp responsibility.

"How can I be responsible for thoughts that just suddenly come into my head from nowhere?" he asked.

A search was conducted for "Nowhere"; it was located. The travel route of his thoughts was mapped out clearly. Seemingly automatic thoughts from nowhere were thoughts the player had had before. Some were learned responses and reactions. In order to control his thoughts, he first had to become aware of what he was thinking. He would think about what he was thinking, so to speak. When his thoughts were identified as useless, inappropriate, or counter-productive, and he wished to get them out of his mind, he'd begin to guide and direct his thinking by substituting other thoughts. *Useful—appropriate—productive thoughts.*

Remember the reference to Steve Sax's problem at second base? "I am not going to throw the ball away" was a thought recommended by some would-be problem-solvers. That thought focused the player's mind on committing a throwing error, thereby directing his body to do just that.

"I'm going to hit the first baseman chest high—nice and easy" would have been a better suggestion. It focuses on relaxed function, positive function, target.

The Cincinnati farmhand began to successfully apply his understanding to his own particular thought pattern and positive commands. His greatest enthusiasm was inspired by the recognition of the power he held in his own mind.

He learned that he was, indeed, responsible for his own thoughts, because he could choose what he thought about. He didn't have to think about matters he didn't want to think about.

He learned he should control his thoughts, or his thoughts would control him.

Steve Carlton's training and self-discipline were exceptional. Asked how he handled a situation in which a negative thought popped into his head, the pitcher said, "I don't allow that to happen."

Very effective, but very exceptional. Yet it's possible, with effort, for anyone to achieve. That effort should be made by each of us inclined to believe that our life is what our thoughts make it.

During the 1993 World Series, Philadelphia pitcher Danny Jackson struggled with the opposing Toronto hitters, with the weather, and the field conditions. Seemingly uncomfortable on a mound made wet during a rain delay, he never found a pitching rhythm. He gave up four runs and six hits in five innings. After the game, Jackson replied to reporters focusing on the conditions, "You guys make a big thing out of a rain delay. I don't want to hear excuses about the delay. The delay had nothing to do with it."

Players have a tendency to think of their behavior—their performance—as being either within their control or outside it. Those who believe they are in control are convinced their performance is determined by their own efforts: dedication, preparation, persistence, all the physical and mental approaches they use. *They take responsiblity for whatever they do.*

The players who think matters are outside their control are the ones who speak of (give responsibility to) "luck, fate, and the breaks." Even when things are going well, they "thank…lucky stars," or say, "I just got the breaks today." By not taking credit, they won't have to take blame. The attitude is neither a winning one nor a responsible one.

Of course, it isn't possible for a player to completely control the *results* of his performance or the *outcome* of a game. But he *can control* and is responsible for knowing what it takes to win: to have a "good at-bat"; to pitch as well as he is capable; to field and run bases as well as he can; to execute the proper play in a given situation.

We mentioned outfielder Gary Ward and his turnaround during the 1982 season with the Twins. Ward saved his career, as well as his season, by defining and taking responsibility for those things he could control in his game. He had labored in the minor leagues for seven years before becoming a full-time major leaguer in 1981. He hit three homers and drove in 29 runs for Minnesota in 85 games that year. Near the middle of June the following season, 1982, the Twins were trying to "unload" Ward (who was hitting .220 with 19 RBIs in the throes of his struggles). No one was interested in him.

Ward thought only about getting some hits and "hanging on in the Show." But he had no control over that, though it worried him very much. He could hit four balls "right on the button" and still not get a hit. He could come to bat frequently with no baserunners for him to drive in. And management alone would make the decisions about his future with the Twins.

Ward came to realize he couldn't control those matters, and he decided to eliminate them from his thoughts and focus his attention on what he could control. He listed them:

1. Having a disciplined batting practice.
2. Controlling emotions and tension level.
3. Knowing the pitcher and the situation.
4. Not being intimidated by the pitcher's reputation, the situation, or the ball. (This item was stated in negative terms and is an example of an improper mental suggestion, though the basic intention is good.)
5. Being aggressive; making every single swing a good swing.
6. Being ready mentally and physically for every pitch.
7. Seeing the release and the spin on every pitch.
8. Tracking the ball all the way.

Just past the middle of June, Ward was holding himself responsible for the behaviors on the list. He put himself in control. He also judged himself severely, but only in relation to those controllable behaviors. With that approach, Gary Ward had an outstanding second half of the season. He hit .355, drove in 74 runs, and hit 22 homers during that period.

Certainly, the acceptance of responsiblity is a key to controlling our lives and careers. The player who takes that responsibility will be in control of the situation on the field more often and more effectively. He'll also be in control of himself.

A SUMMARY AND REMINDER FOR PLAYERS

1. Think about what is being thought and imagined. It's what you say to yourself and what you visualize in your mind that count— that will determine your behavior and performance.

2. Change "I have to" and "I must" to "I have decided to"— "I choose to"—"I want to," etc.

3. When involved in something that doesn't seem to be working to your satisfaction ask, "What can I learn from this?"

4. Become aware of when and how excuses are being made. Ask yourself why you need to use them. Start to catch the justifications, explanations, and blame before they are expressed to others. Then work at eliminating the thoughts, so you don't even express them to yourself.

5. Practice taking risks and accepting the consequences. Observe and compare how the good players and the poor players deal with personal responsibility.

6. Define what can and cannot be controlled in your life and on the field.

7. Examine and judge yourself honestly. (Tom Seaver said, "I am like a kangaroo court. I am my own judge and jury.")

8. Remember this: one of the strongest principles of behavior lies in human choice. If you do not take responsibility, you have *still made a choice*. A wrong one.

Another o-fer-four. And tomorrow I'll have to face a lefty. I never get a break.

I'm seeing the ball good. I'm swinging good. I'll get my share of hits.

6
ATTITUDES
Great Means to Greater Ends

A True Story: A little boy is being accompanied by his father. They're walking toward a school bus stop, where the boy, a five-year-old, will board the bus on this, his first day of school.

"Kindergarten is sure going to be fun!" exclaims the father, glancing out of the corner of his eye at his hand-grasping son. Then, trying to suggest a positive attitude to the youngster, the adult adds: "You're excited, I'll bet."

"*You're* excited," responds the boy. "*I'm* scared!"

True also is the fact that the two walkers had distinctly different thoughts about the event to follow — different attitudes, therefore. The reason, in this case, may be obvious. So much about the two were different, including age, experience, and involvement in the upcoming activity.

Yet, a pair of "identical" twins about to perform the same task will differ to some extent — perhaps to a great extent — in the attitude each brings to the task. Each twin is unique in certain ways and, more to the point, the entire world is populated by people different from every other person. Because of the differences, each person's "world" is not the same as anyone else's. The differences stem from biology (inherited) and experience (acquired). They keep us from having the exact perceptions as anyone else involved in the same activity at the same time. Whether they are relatives, friends — teammates.

In addition to our being distinctive in biological make-up and past experiences, we differ also in our purposes, that is to say, in our *specific* purposes. We do share some *basic* purposes. They're generally referred to as *basic needs*:

> *the need to survive:* having food, clothing, shelter, family — and protection against the danger of harm or loss.

> *the need to be wanted:* having the appreciation, approval, and love of others.

> *the need to thrive:* having a feeling of growth and satisfaction as one lives his life.

We do have common purposes, but the *intensity* with which they're felt varies with the individual. Also, plenty of "sub-purposes" exist: the specific and personally unique purposes we have within the framework of our daily routine, for example. Each of our lives is a sequence of actions meant to achieve our purposes. And before we can understand ourselves, we have to understand the purposes that move us into action, that motivate us, for better or for worse, that express our dominant needs.

An invented true story: Three major league baseball players walk onto the field together before a game. Their similar, immediate purpose is to play the game, but each has his own larger purpose. In this group of three, even the basic needs aren't the shared needs.

Player A's major purpose for playing that game is simply to abide by the terms of his contractual agreement. He plays and he gets paid. His salary provides food, clothing, and shelter for his family and for himself.

Player B plays for approval. He wants to be appreciated. Few people ever get to be big leaguers, he knows, and he enjoys being in that inner circle, admired by others. Envied. He's going to make the fans love him today. A couple of hits, a dinger, maybe — and he did sign a whole bunch of autographs earlier.

Player C flat out loves the ole game of hardball. He has a great time "being a man, getting paid to play a boy's game," as he says. He's very content with his place on the team, at home—in the world.

These three players with different purposes may have the same goals—result goals—*but their governing purposes (needs) will have much to do with whether or not the goals will be attained.*

Let's get more specific. Player A we will call the "survival" player. Let's say he's primarily interested in how his performance will affect his next contract. Even the type of contract he now has can affect the way he plays that day he walks onto the field with his two teammates. The more secure he feels financially, the less devoted his mind has to be to "survival," to doing what's necessary in order to "stay in the Show," as Gary Ward put it. Former Baltimore Orioles pitching star Jim Palmer, having had a long-term contract himself, said in a *New York Times* interview: ". . . Up until 1975, my next year's salary always depended on every pitch I threw . . . I never took anything for granted. It would seem hard for some players to have that kind of intensity after signing a multi-year contract."

His reference, it seems, is to some players whose purpose is based on "survival." Recent findings and psychologists' statistical evidence (*Psychology Today,* March 1982) indicate that long-term contracts *do* have a negative effect on the performance of professional baseball players. Not all players are affected this way. Player A types are most susceptible.

When Gary Carter played for Montreal, he had a tendency to try to please fans and media-folk. He irritated some of the other Expos as a result. Though he admired Carter's ability and style of play, Pete Rose, having left the Expos to return to Cincinnati, criticized his former teammate for what he considered to be Carter's "immature" attitude. Simply, Carter's need for approval and love were considerably greater than Rose's—and many other players. Carter could qualify as our hypothetical Player B.

Hall of Famer Willie Stargell, the former Pittsburgh Pirates slugger, would be a good candidate for Player C. Tom Seaver also qualifies, though his subpurpose was different. Stargell claimed that baseball itself was a joy, not a job. "Umpires shout, 'Play Ball!' not 'Work Ball!'" Stargell said, explaining his viewpoint. The pleasure and satisfaction he gained from his playing career was evident to all around him. And contagious. The Pirates brought him back as a first base coach in 1985, hoping he would be a visible and vocal role model.

Seaver, on the other hand, took a quiet joy from the game. A joy of competition against his own potential, a joy of learning, growing— and observing the changes in self. Working at being the best (as did Stargell). Thriving through striving. Also a Player C.

So there they are: Players A, B, and C. Different genes; different experience—culturally, economically, religiously, politically, racially. Therefore—different attitudes.

Attitude: Our state of mind as we approach and experience our lives. Each year; each season. Each day; each game. Each situation; each pitch. Always us; not always the same attitude. *But always within our capability to control it*; within our responsibility, as we've said.

We're more likely to take that responsibility if we understand the *extent* to which attitudes influence us. They influence our appearance to others, the words we speak, the actions we take. Attitudes influence the way we feel, both physically and mentally. They influence the degree to which we're successful in *achieving our purposes*.

So many times baseball people have identified gifted players whose poor attitudes (lazy? uncooperative? selfish? disruptive?) stood in the way of the player's development and success. Players around him identified him quickly.

But the "identifiers" themselves, baseball "experts" included, are not free from judgment. They have their own attitudes, and the evaluations they make of others may be distorted by their own bad attitude (jealousy? resentment? intimidation? prejudice?). Everyone has an attitude: those who evaluate, those who are evaluated. Coaches and bat boys. Club owners. And they all—we all—have reasons. Purposes.

As basketball coach Pat Riley so emphatically states in his fine book, *The Winner Within*, "It's strictly attitude that lets you learn— and learning leads to change."

WHAT DOES IT TAKE TO CHANGE A POOR ATTITUDE TO A GOOD ONE?

1. Becoming aware of your existing attitudes (an honest evaluation).

2. Trying to understand why those attitudes were developed (an aid to self-awareness).

"Yeah, yeah, right ... Like I didn't know that."

3. Recognizing the importance of learning (no one knows everything, ourselves included).

4. Dedicating yourself to your work (sound familiar?).

5. Being enthusiastic about your daily activities (and life in general).

6. Welcoming the prospect of change (being open to new methods and ideas, instead of believing one way is the only way — and that happens to be your way; not taking criticism personally).

7. Expressing a sense of humor (not taking yourself so seriously; having fun at what you're doing, which helps you to relax).

8. Having an interest in others (in *their* needs and difficulties).

9. Trying to understand the point of view of others (their thoughts, feelings — reasons).

10. Being a good listener (trying to learn from others).

11. Working/Playing effectively as part of a group/team (to attain common goals).

12. Keeping yourself from criticizing others (first judge yourself: when perfect, move on to others).

Easy? Not a bit. But, again, worth the effort, you'll find. *Just the desire to improve an attitude is a sign that positive results will follow.* And once we see results, we want more. It takes time, but time well spent for a good cause: self-improvement.

And should you find some spare time, check back to see how many of the 12 suggestions can apply to players and situations already mentioned in previous pages of this book. Yes, baseball players are very human. From that truth comes the "rhyme and reason" in the list above. Recommended even for umpires.

It's important to understand that an attitude is not really an emotion. There are similarities, but attitudes are built primarily by thoughts, whereas emotions are built by feelings. (Many of these feelings never get to be identified.) Thoughts give direction and control; emotions, most often, provide arousal and energy.

Another important understanding to have is that there are wide varieties of "bad attitudes." An attitude doesn't have to be antisocial to qualify as "bad." A lazy worker has one kind of bad attitude; a dedicated perfectionist may have another—if he's never satisfied with what he does. In the case of a ballplayer, *any attitude leading to actions that keep the player from achieving a peak performance is a bad one*—bad for the player, in that it keeps him from playing as well as he's physically capable of playing.

You can see how very important a player's thoughts are. What he thinks about, especially as he performs, makes all the difference in the world in what he'll do—and how he'll do it.

Here are three major leaguers: each has an attitude toward "o-fers"—games in which he, the batter, goes hitless. 0-fer-three; o-fer-four; o-fer-more.

Gary Carter, you remember, would put tremendous pressure on himself during his final at-bat on a prospective o-fer-day. His intense desire to have a hit to "show-fer-the-day" tightened him up, especially after he heard his do-or-die command (thought), "I gotta get a hit!" His body worked against that purpose. He wasn't relaxed; he wasn't confident; he wasn't properly focused. He was losing his mind games.

Carter's thoughts, through his experience, had built a generally poor attitude toward o-fers. It was specifically brought into game situations which had him at bat for the last time on days when he hadn't yet gotten a hit. That last at-bat became a give-away most often.

Rusty Staub, a scientific and pragmatic hitter, nevertheless admitted that he too "was intense" when he was younger and working on an o-fer.

"I don't like o-fers. Who does? If I could hit the ball really well a couple of times, psychologically it could get to you a little bit, because you're hitting the ball good and you've got no hits. But you've gotta know *you're swinging the bat well.* If you're not swinging the bat well, and you go o-fer-four, that's when you should think about going out and taking some extra b.p." Staub said.

"The most important thing is knowing why you made an out. If you know the pitcher got you out, you gotta clap your hands and say, 'Great for the pitcher.' If you got yourself out—by moving too quick, by trying to pull the ball, by coming out of your crouch, pulling your head off the ball—you should know that each time."

And when it's the last time at bat on a potential o-fer-day, those behaviors are most likely to happen to those who most dread o-fers. Essentially, Staub was advising hitters to look at today's at-bats in the name of function, rather than looking at tomorrow's box score in the name of embarrassment. The former is a winning attitude; the latter is a losing one.

When Ray Knight was playing third base in Houston as an every-day player for the Astros, he spoke about his attitude toward o-fers. Said Knight, "I never go up to that last at-bat saying 'I gotta get a hit.' All it does is put more pressure on me."

Knight then changed the subject a bit, but stuck to the theme. He told of a game earlier that season ('83). "I was 4-for-4 in Chicago, and I went up in my last at-bat and said, 'I've got to get that fifth hit.' I popped up. I didn't *have* to get that first or second, third, fourth one. But when I *had* to get the fifth one, I swung too hard and popped it up."

Back on the main track, Knight explained that he didn't even recognize the existence of o-fers any longer. He said, "I know I'll have four at-bats today and four tomorrow and the day after, and so on for the whole season. So I'm never thinking o-fer-four—or even four-fer-four—anymore. I'm whatever I am for 600 or so at-bats over a whole season. My at-bats stop at the end of one game only until the next day, and then they continue. I know over the course of the season, I'll get the hits I want. I always have, so why worry on a particular bad day? There are plenty of tomorrows."

(And, we'd reiterate, swinging well and hitting the ball hard four times is not a "*bad day*," even if there are no hits to show for it. The batter had done as much as is within his control. *That's the attitude he should have*.)

Circumstances change, feelings change. These new circumstances and feelings can lead to new thoughts.

Ray Knight was a part-time player with the Mets in 1985, after being injured much of 1984. From 1979 to 1983 he had been a regular. Playing irregularly, sometimes as a pinch hitter, Knight struggled. The New York fans chose him as the target of their abuse. He was booed. Being sensitive, he, like the Carters and Schmidts, was affected.

Knight told *New York Times* writer George Vecsey, "In Cincinnati, in Houston, I was always a favorite player . . . One year I batted .385 with men in scoring position. I was a clutch hitter. At least, that's what I think I am."

He had had a chance in the clutch two days earlier. "I thought I had a great at-bat," Knight said. "Four or five fouls, seeing the ball real well, straightening them out, and then I hit into a double play. I like to died . . .

"I've always played every day. I never thought about the next game. I'd go through my regular routine. Now I think about it. I don't play for three games and then I feel uncomfortable if I go 0-for-4. I was never o-fer-four in my mind before this. I was always 200-for-600," said Knight.

In 1986, Knight regained his status as a regular with the Mets, and he regained his former good *attitude*. He also gained recognition as the Comeback Player of the Year in the National League — and was the MVP in the '86 World Series.

An attitude can change — or be changed. We are never stuck for life with an attitude we don't want. But we — not the situation, not other people — must control the change, so that it's a change for the better. And if we have a good attitude in a good situation, we must know in advance that our attitude will have to battle whatever bad situations we meet — or we and our attitude will be taken prisoner.

The three examples above illustrated differences in an attitude related to one common situation — o-fers. The three examples to follow identify a very common influence in the lives of most young ballplayers. These three ballplayers became major leaguers.

The influence: a boy's father. The players: George Brett, Ray Knight, and infielder Roy Smalley.

Jack Brett was extremely critical of his youngest son, George. A poor performance by the boy in a Little League game would greatly disturb the father, who would become angry and voice the anger strongly.

John Garrity, in his book *The George Brett Story*, noted that the father would compare George, unfavorably, to the older brothers. Garrity quotes the adult George Brett: "I hated my dad...I was intimidated. I was scared to death of him."

Garrity reports a frequently told story about young George striking out twice in a game and riding home in a silent car with his father. Then, George recalled, "I remember I got out of the car in my uniform, my head hanging, and the next thing I felt was a foot coming right up my ass! For embarrassing the family. That's probably where I got my hemorrhoids."

Ray Knight's father was demanding, but instructive. He made his son labor hard at the sport. Knight did suggest that his attitude toward working hard at the game—and playing hard—was shaped by his "daddy." (The Mets infielder said he believes his father to be most responsible for his son's attitude toward pain—to be discussed in a later chapter.)

It may be surprising to some that Roy Smalley's father, a major league shortstop himself in the '40s and '50s, projected a much more relaxed attitude toward the ballplaying of his little boy. No pressure; no work program; no prescribed footsteps in which to follow. (Young Roy's uncle, Gene Mauch, was also a big league player and manager.)

Rod Dedeaux, the younger Smalley's baseball coach at the University of Southern California, felt, "Roy (the elder) has done everything possible a father can do the right way. His approach (to the son's interest and involvement in baseball) has been sensible and sound."

How and how much each father (and mother and high school coach) affected the attitudes of these players isn't to be considered here. Only the players fully know, and *this* point is what is served by their example: the influences are varied and real, and so are the attitudes that result. Some of us have better talents than others; some of us have better influences. *But, as we become adults, we all have the same responsibility for our attitudes and actions.* We should each know as much about them as possible—as ballplayers seeking to improve our performance; as people seeking to improve our lives.

You're familiar, perhaps, with the illustration of the standing glass containing water that reaches mid-point from top to bottom. If so, you're also familiar with the two people asked to describe the glass and its contents.

"Half empty," says one, and his attitude has come to represent the pessimist's.

"Half full," says the other, optimistically.

That's the way we see our world—our situation. If we see the glass as half full, we think of what we can do with what we have. If we see it as half empty, we think of what we've lost and the prospects of losing what's left.

The optimist will, as the old song lyric told us, build castles in the air. The pessimist, wrote columnist Walter Winchell, will build dungeons.

Baseball players don't express their attitudes by describing water glasses. They reveal themselves by the way they approach and play the game. They reveal themselves, as we do, through what they *do,* though what they *say* can give a hint of what will be done—and how it will be done.

Out of Left Field. That's the title of Bob Adelman's and Susan Hall's account of Willie Stargell's 1973 season with the Pirates. In it, Stargell expressed himself candidly on many subjects, including our current subject.

"You could tell the guys' attitude from the clubhouse. All the guys are complaining. Early in the season, people criticized (catcher) Milt May, saying he wasn't able to handle pitchers. Pitchers complain about the rotation, saying they're not being given a chance to pitch. Clines wants to play every game. Hebner doesn't like being platooned. Zisk doesn't say anything . . . We got a lot of unhappy guys on this ballclub . . . Pittsburgh is a disturbed place, and the results show it . . ."

That was obvious negativism. But at the other extreme is a not-very-obvious optimism which can bring just as poor results. An apparently carefree person projects this attitude, with no good sense to back it up. The attitude is not the positive one it may first appear to be.

A *sensible* optimist is inspired by an authentic positive attitude, which gives him vitality and hope, where others lose their spirit and quit. He holds his head high as he moves into the future. The *fool-*

Reprinted by permission of United Feature Syndicate, Inc.

ish optimist cheerfully ignores a bad situation, pretending it isn't bad at all, or tolerating it. Foolish — and weak. An attitude, nevertheless.

An example is a player who prepares himself to lose with "style and grace." He's more conscious of the attitude he shows after losing than the one he shows during the game — the one that influences his performance. He wants to be a good loser or "laid back" or "cool." He says, "I'll do the best I can and if it isn't enough, so what? I'm not a loser because I've tried." The problem with this "positive" attitude is that it accepts defeat. It becomes an easy habit, a habit of the mind. A loser's attitude.

Accepting the possibility of defeat is realistic, and it can be beneficial. (No guaranteed success, remember.) Accepting the possibility does not mean being *willing* to be defeated. It does not mean accepting defeat before it results, opening the door to welcome it in.

This is most often expressed in the name of good sportsmanship. Even professional players, playing in a big game, can "give in" to it — in a World Series, in a Super Bowl. Most players aren't aware of doing so.

The Super Bowl of 1978 matched the Dallas Cowboys and the Denver Broncos. Denver quarterback Craig Morton said before the game, "I anticipate playing a good Super Bowl, but it won't burden us if we lose." In other words, "Look how well we've done up to this point. We don't have anything to prove. If we lose today, it really doesn't matter."

Denver lost. It did "matter," though not in ways Morton was aware of when he expressed his thoughts — and attitude.

A situation: A pitcher starts a baseball game optimistically, anticipating he'll pitch well. (This isn't always true in reality, of course.)

Things begin to look bleak. The game is going badly; the pitcher starts to think of his excellent chance of losing—and looking bad in the process. He says to himself, "I just want to get out of this game. Just get it over with." He becomes preoccupied with the image others must be forming of him out there on the mound. "What must they be thinking?"

What is the pitcher thinking? Of preserving his image to others and to himself. Not of winning the game. Not of pitching effectively. Not of the next pitch he's to throw. He's thinking of "getting it over with." He's giving himself relief from tension and frustration. He is "helping" himself—to lose his competitive spirit, his positive attitude. He's giving in. The process speeds up; it becomes "caving in."

The original "positive attitude" was only a shell. No inner substance. When the going got tough, the attitude got going—in the opposite direction. We'll speak further of this pitcher when discussing "mental discipline."

There are many ways to skin a cat—or salve a psyche. Such as the "There's-nothing-I-can-do-about-what's-happening" application. The helpless attitude is frequently expressed by pitchers who are having "all the breaks go against them" in a particular game or streak. A few breaks can go against every pitcher (or hitter). Many breaks, perhaps. *But the way he pitches after he's lost a positive attitude will create "all the breaks" needed for him to lose control of himself.*

The way he might otherwise keep his positive attitude and control, despite breaks—or adversity of any kind—working against him, will keep him playing aggressively, like a winner, regardless of the result of the game.

Sometimes the result will also reward the effort. Pete Rose told "a true story" to his Cincinnati players at the beginning of his first spring training as their manager. The topic related to "being aggressive; not quitting"—Rose's kind of attitude.

"Let me tell you about running out everything," he began. "...Back in the '60s, Ray Washburn of the Cardinals was beating us, 7-0, late in the game. With two outs, I hit a one-hopper right back to him. I kept running and he threw high to first base, and by the time Bill White came down with the ball, I was safe. By the end of that inning, we had an 8-7 lead."

Former tennis great Virginia Wade summed up what every great athlete comes around to as a prevailing and governing attitude. "...I spend each minute out there doing everything I can to win, then I've gone the limit," Wade said. "If I can do that, I win. If I don't, then I come off the court and say, 'I didn't do everything I could.' Period."

Rooted in that attitude are goals, dedication, responsibility, and, yes, aggressiveness.

Aggressiveness is missing from the approach of many players who need to be liked by their opponents. Pete Rose, for one, never had that problem. Yet, even at the major league level, players *can* be found who *are* concerned with being "Mr. Nice Guy" on the field of play. Their opponents most often do like them, but rarely respect them. A pitcher who is this type may think, "I'm trying to get you out, but I'm a good guy, and I'll be nice to you." He'll "give in" because of the threat of conflict—or of any indication he might be threatening his opponent.

Toronto pitcher Pat Hentgen used his aggressive attitude to win 19 games in his 1993 rookie year. "Being competitive is one of my assets," said Hentgen, in looking back on the season. His high school coach, Mario Borrocci, an obvious admirer of his former player's rookie achievements, nevertheless felt it essential to note: "The first thing about Pat is that he is a much better person than he is a pitcher." It can be done.

Attitudes, all. Real ones. Real players, for sure. Real people, like us.

So many of us love the game of baseball. We've enjoyed the experience of playing and have been rewarded in some way—or ways—by our involvement. Needs have been served. We were motivated to want to do the best we could, even if we didn't always know how to go about it.

But what of the "unmotivated" player? The one who doesn't hustle; who doesn't seem to enjoy himself; who isn't a willing listener or learner; who appears to be negative about the game itself. He's the player labeled as being a "bad actor." Assuming the label is correct, why does he act the way he does?

Simply, his needs aren't being satisfied. In many cases, the player has brought his attitude to the game from elsewhere. In any case, he doesn't seem to get what he needs from the sport, and this is usually because he doesn't know what he wants from the sport. His goals are either scattered or non-existent.

He can choose to change that situation, and if he knows he has a *choice*, he should know he has a chance—to be more effective as a player and as a person, if he makes that choice; to have a winning attitude rather than a losing one.

Many winning attitudes will reveal themselves within the chapters that follow. [A list of "Winner's Choices" will be found in Chapter 14.]

All winning attitudes lead to that most important one: self-confidence. It isn't inherited, it's acquired. Every outstanding baseball player has had it. It deserves a separate chapter, because, though *confidence is a state of mind*, many players consider it to be an emotion—a "feeling" they either have or do not have.

One young minor league pitcher listened to Don Sutton talk about aggressiveness on the mound during a spring training session. "That's easy for Sutton to say," said the minor leaguer. "He was born with confidence."

Not so. Please read on.

7
CONFIDENCE
A Very Top Priority

Whether for individual purposes of material gain, for recognition or personal satisfaction, the young person driven to be a baseball player has as his most powerful purpose the desire to be an outstanding performer — a great player.

He sets *goals;* he dedicates himself to working hard to attain them. He drives forward, taking the responsibility for developing his skills and attitudes.

Behind that drive lies the attitude players say will most influence their success: *confidence.* The lack of it, they say, most influences their failures.

No one sets failure as a goal, but failure is a statistical *probability* in the game of baseball and a player needs to face the *possibility,* at least. He can't be afraid to fail. Confidence isn't gained by the timid and fearful. As anxious about his tasks as he may be, a player must find the courage to face them and perform them with strength and aggressiveness, despite that ever-present possibility of failure.

The development of confidence requires risk-taking. It comes through gradual (step-by-step) success. Each success encourages us to persevere as we struggle with the next step. That's why the specific goals a player focuses on each day are so important. They are achievable; they are easy to evaluate. And as we attain each goal, we then give ourselves credit for the attainment. Our confidence will grow with these daily, identifiable successes. Our total performance will improve.

It's a simple formula, but one that isn't commonly used, because people tend to jump to ends while disregarding the means to those ends. Performance, after all, is an end. It isn't the only basis for true confidence. The start of confidence-building has nothing to do with whether we're right or wrong; whether we win or lose; whether we get a hit or strike out. *Most important is what we think about ourselves.* What we are to ourselves matters more than what others see us as or what they see us doing. So that's where confidence is found. Inside. *Inside each of us.*

We may express it—show it—or not on the outside, depending on the situation we face. Some situations we handle easily; we're confident in our skill to do so. Other situations are very difficult for us to deal with; we aren't as confident in our ability to manage them as we face them.

This is the point at which we can take the big step forward. We may not be confident in our ability in this particular situation—in our skill—*but we can always be confident in ourselves as people.* In that confidence is the freedom to do what we wish and to see how capable we are; to make the attempt; to attack any situation—even a situation in which, up until now, we've lacked confidence in our skill.

We'll focus more effectively on what we have to do. Center on the object that requires our attention—the ball; the catcher's target. Breathe deeply and slowly. Relax and enjoy the challenge. After all, what's at stake? Don't we understand that just functioning the way we want to makes us successful? Makes us *winners* as competitors?

Yes, we know it rationally, but our emotions interfere with that understanding when we're faced by a challenge we don't think we're up to. So we have to recognize the emotions that are inhibiting our bodies' easy movement, and control them with winning mind games—strong, positive thoughts focused on function. And we evaluate our behavior—our performance. We make a few adjustments. And we try again. And again. We make some progress. And *feel* better. And find that it helps us play better.

Confidence is near; down the road—straight ahead.

The greatest obstacle on the road to confidence is fear. Fear of embarrassment from o-fers and errors; fear of humiliation from booing fans and lost games; fear of a father's wrath or a manager's displeasure. Fear of not making the team—or the big leagues. Basically, fear of failure.

George Brett's hitting mentor, and the guru of many major league players, was the late Charley Lau. The players Lau worked with claimed that he was as much a psychologist as he was a hitting coach. Lau recognized that fear prevents a hitter from keeping his mind free from distraction as he hits, as he prepares to hit. (Willie Wilson, as a rookie with Kansas City, was a fearful hitter. According to Lau, Wilson was intimidated by the big league atmosphere, primarily the big crowds.) Lau would first have his students admit to their fears, instead of denying and suppressing them. The fears ranged from being hit in the head by a pitched ball to the very typical one that troubled Wilson. Admit and conquer, Lau told the players.

Fears come from uncertainty, and the uncertainty indicates a lack of confidence. What's most unfortunate is that the confidence is so often missing in the player's view of himself. He believes his self-worth is at stake. Surely no situation can provoke the kind of fear he feels if he recognizes his own real value, if his world is in perspective. A strike-out, he should know, can't make his world collapse. If he labels himself a failure, his biggest failure is in having a distorted sense of reality.

No one can make us feel as if we're failures without our own consent. Confident people never consent. They approach risky and challenging situations without the possibility of *being* a failure. They relish the challenge, all the while knowing they may fail at their task, but that is all. They remember that they've succeeded in the past and will again in the future. "Next time, in fact," they say to themselves, should they not succeed this time.

Fear is a motivator. It can work *for* a player, as well as against him. That's up to the player. Everyone experiences fear. Athletes, singers, corporate executives, mountain climbers. The successful performers don't prevent fear. They can't do that, but they can and do learn to cope with it successfully. The great ones learn to *control it*, rather than be controlled by it—*to use the energy fear creates in a positive way.* Dennis Eckersley, winner of both the Cy Young Award and MVP Award in the American League in 1992, is a profound example.

Reprinted by permission of United Feature Syndicate, Inc.

The late Cus D'Amato was the renowned fight manager of former heavyweight champion Floyd Patterson, former light heavyweight champion Jose Torres, and, most recently, for Mike Tyson. D'Amato had exceedingly strong convictions that he passed on to his fighters, most of them stemming from his own belief that, above all, "mind triumphs over matter . . ."

D'Amato had this to say about fear: "Fear is your best friend or your worst enemy. It's like fire. If you can control it, it can cook for you; it can heat your house. If you can't control it, it will burn everything around you and destroy you. If you can control fear, it makes you more alert . . ."

California Angels pitcher Mark Langston told Franz Lidz of *Sports Illustrated* that he has a tendency toward fright—and that he can now enjoy it. (Langston was afraid of the dark until he reached junior high school age.) The most frightened he had ever been on a ball field was prior to his major league debut on April 7, 1984, against Milwaukee.

"Loosening up was so nerve-racking I thought I'd go crazy," he told *SI*. "It was the same kind of scared I felt in (the movie, watching) *Halloween II*. But it wasn't a *scared* scared. It was more like unsure scared."

But Langston kept his fear and himself in control. He struck out lead-off hitter Paul Molitor. His fright left.

It leaves the baseball players who throw up before games, break into cold sweat or just have a universal collection of "butterflies," until the action starts "between the white lines." The players who are ready to win—to succeed—cut loose and go after the challenge between those lines. The players who are afraid to lose—to fail—bring with them as they cross the lines a tentative approach, often covered by a false front. They try to *look* courageous, instead of playing that way. Some can't even do that. The fear can be seen in their eyes — and in their play. They're distracted by fear. They're slowed by it, stifled by it, not propelled by it, not stimulated in a positive way.

Examining Fear

Before looking fear in the face, let's look at its whole form. What exactly is fear that it keeps a player from being confident and from achieving maximum performance?

First, fear is a monstrous liar. It tells us that situations are more threatening and harder to handle than they truly are, and it tells us we aren't capable of dealing successfully with these situations. It suggests to us that there are terrible, unnamed consequences for failing to handle these situations. The Monster, fear, breaks down our confidence, brainwashes us, makes us play losing mental games.

And we built the Monster! Out of our own imagination. We feed him, so he grows larger and stronger. Paul Molitor was much more threatening before Langston struck him out. The other team's great won-lost record is much more significant until we beat that team and prove to ourselves they aren't invincible. Has any opposing pitcher *ever* had the "unhittable slider" the Monster tells us about before we go to bat?

"The young fighter always perceives his first-time opponent as bigger, stronger, and faster than he is," said Cus D'Amato. Boxers have Monsters also. They all have the same form.

Children, Mark Langston included, are afraid of the dark because they fear the unknown. But after years of walking into their dark rooms and turning on the lights, they learn the truth — from experience: nothing in there will harm them. That fear is weakened and eventually dies.

We starve our Monster when we disregard our fears and *act*. In spite of being fearful we walked into those dark rooms. We faced the *now* and eliminated the *future* that threatened us and distracted us. That's the way it should be when we perform — play ball. *There can be no future for the performer; there can only be the present.*

If there's no future, there's no distraction. No Monster.

Knowing When Fear is Here

In July 1983, when pitcher Bruce Hurst was with the Boston Red Sox, he talked about his manager, who "hates walks." Said Hurst, "Especially in this ball park (Fenway Park), he hates walks. He's afraid of walking anyone here. So one of the priorities in my mind before I go out there is, 'Don't walk a lot of guys.' "

His manager's fear became Hurst's fear. The reader has heard the negative language before: "*Don't* walk a lot of guys." That language, that self-talk is one of the first signs a player has that fear is near— or here.

"I gotta get a hit"; "I can't let him hit this"; "I gotta win this game"; "What's going to happen if I don't drive these runners in?" Such is the stuff of which fears are made—self-talk that indicates and accentuates the player's lack of confidence.

His body will also give him clues. Breathing particularly is affected by fear. Tightness in muscles and chest, heart pounding, sweaty hands, and a cottony mouth are some other signs that fear has set in.

Fearing to make mistakes will lead to mistake-making. Fearing to lose will make a loser. What can be done about it?

Working Against Fear

Self-awareness comes first, of course. If we've paid attention to the signals, we're aware of what's happening to us. We don't like what's happening. The thing to do is *stop* what we've been doing. Stop and look fear in the face.

Get ourselves out of the batter's box when we hear our "Gotta get a hit"; when we feel our hands squeezing the bat and our stomach tightening. Take a long deep breath. Let the air out slowly. Same procedure twice again. Change our self-talk, so that it focuses on what we *want to do* in this situation. "Hit the ball hard up the middle." Get back into the box. Another deep breath and slow exhale, while giving the command in a relaxed tone: "Just see the ball." Then we center our eyes on the ball as it's released.

The routine is similar for a pitcher. He hears and/or feels what he doesn't like and gets himself off the mound. He, like a batter, separates his environment. He doesn't allow himself to be controlled by fear or uncertainty in his place of function—the pitcher's mound (or batter's box). He moves away from that environment and gets himself in order. The breathing, the changed self-talk. "All right, I'm gonna throw a fastball in." He visualizes exactly where he wants to throw the pitch. Up on top of the mound, he inhales again; exhales slowly; takes his sign and centers on the catcher's target. No thoughts now; just that singular focus. He winds; he pitches. *He functions.* Fear, as Jimmy Pearsall would say, strikes out.

Nervous fear is very often the fear of discomfort—the discomfort of embarrassment and humiliation and all else we've mentioned before.

Cardinals first baseman—and 1993 All-Star—Gregg Jefferies was a temperamental and unhappy player with the New York Mets and the Kansas City Royals. In 1992, Jefferies' 46 errors were the most by an American League third baseman. Said a happier first baseman now: "One of my problems was throwing the ball from third base. A lot of time I had mental strain. If I threw the ball away, I'd think about if for a long time. I didn't have confidence in myself. I was very uncomfortable over there."

Those who have "the will to bear discomfort" can be functional and successful in their performance. That's what the players illustrated in the examples above. They acted in spite of bad feelings. They achieved. That's what the goal is: to conquer, not just to cope. To master each situation in competition not only with skill, but with will. The will to face fear, discomfort, or the guy who has the wicked side-armed delivery with the same self-control—always. Before and after, yes, but especially *during*, while the *doing* is being done.

Check Reality and Chuck Fears

Each time we confront fear we gain courage. We become more confident that reality is not as bad as the threat. A friend of ours has great confidence in "reality checks" as a means of becoming more confident in an uncomfortable or threatening situation. A "reality check" is what the character Fagan is going through as he sings in the film *Oliver Twist*, "I'm Reviewing the Situation." Exactly. We're checking our reality when we review our situation—examine it in a clear and thoughtful way. When we're uptight, our emotional self has made an initial evaluation and has given a hasty, first opinion. We need a second opinion. We take the responsibility away from our emotions and give it to our rational self, which looks at our situation in a more sensible way. Inevitably, whatever difficulty exists in the situation is reduced to its actual size. The situation doesn't disappear, but fear does. Now we're left to confront the situation with all our resources working for us—our natural and acquired resources. We can play the game the way we know how— with our talent, our determination, and our understanding of what needs to be done and how to get it done.

And we gain confidence by knowing just that.

Three "Games" in the Reality-Check League

Watching an opposing pitcher warm up in the bullpen before an Instructional League game in Arizona, an Oakland minor leaguer is extremely impressed by the pitcher's speed and seemingly deceptive body movement. He points out these qualities animatedly— nervously—to his teammates.

The game starts. The impressed player says to each batter who returns to the dugout, "This guy's throwin' serious cheese, huh?" It's a rhetorical question. He doesn't even listen to the hitter's assessment.

Three consecutive A's batters hit the ball hard. A double; a line drive caught by an outfielder on the run; a triple.

"Can't be *that* serious," says the original "scout," as he gives a "five" to the teammate who scores from second on the triple. And he steps up to bat with an *attitude*—a confidence level—quite different from what it had been *before* he saw the opposing pitcher get hit. Those hard-hit balls helped him check his reality. But what if the pitcher hadn't been hit hard? Could the reality have been checked in advance? It could have, but it probably wouldn't have, in this case. The fellow's first at-bat could have helped—even had the pitcher thrown "serious cheese." But why give away that first at-bat? The quickest reality checks can be as simple as these: "No one is unhittable. This guy's a minor leaguer too. It's easier for the guy to throw that loose in the pen than in the game. Hey, here's a good guy to go to right field against; I've been working on that."

Any or all of those—or other *positive self-talk* which puts the situation in proper perspective—will do.

How did the player do? He swung wildly at the first pitch, a curveball in the dirt. He stepped out and "gathered himself"—thinking about being patient and waiting on the fastball, taking a deep, slow breath to relax himself. The next two pitches were outside, not close. The batter then hit a belt-high fastball, on the outside part of the plate, hard on the ground to the right side. The second baseman went into the hole and threw him out. The runner scored from third. No further talk was heard about the pitcher's ability, though he settled down and pitched four innings very effectively after the two-run first.

A young pitcher in Cincinnati's farm system was changed from a starter to a reliever. He had been an effective starting pitcher and, therefore, wasn't enthusiastic about the change. A typical situation; a typical reaction. He showed some signs of anxiety, but he went ahead in his new role and soon after turned in a string of outstanding relief appearances. He developed great confidence in his ability to save and finish games.

The team's pitching rotation became disrupted. There weren't enough starters. The newly-developed reliever was tapped for return to the rotation. He was distraught. He'd become so confident as a reliever, he hated the change back. He felt great anxiety. He panicked. He felt his career was in jeopardy; he'd never be effective as a starter.

The player had completely dismissed from his reality the fact that he had already been an effective starting pitcher. His confidence as a relief pitcher had improved dramatically, but his performance as a pitcher had not significantly improved. He'd done some maturing by coming into difficult situations created by other pitchers. He felt much less pressure as a reliever. *He* hadn't put those guys on base. They weren't *his* responsibility, he felt. Now he was going to be the one to need relief.

His talk and tone anticipated catastrophe. He was reminded that he had developed a part of himself, including a confident attitude, that hadn't existed when he had been a starting pitcher. He had grown as a person *and* as a pitcher. He'd learned more about himself and his game. He was told to remember that *the successes we achieved in our past are more real than the failures we fear in our future.*

Those successes should be brought forward—into the present. The fear of failure shouldn't be dragged backward.

The young pitcher said he'd never thought about that. The fact was, he hadn't *thought* about anything; he had only *felt*. Thinking—checking reality—put him firmly into the starting rotation. Firmly and successfully.

This was a player who had "anticipated catastrophe," who expected the worst to happen. Fear has a fine way of getting us to do that. How can we resist?

It's clear that recalling success from the past is helpful. That's a convenient and easy solution for some, but it actually doesn't address the real question: What really *is* the worst thing that can happen? The process is called "catastrophizing": thinking of what consequences can actually come to be. We usually find a few things out quickly when we do that.

First, by examining the fear, rather than pretending it doesn't exist, we gain courage and reduce the threat immediately.

Second, through self-talk that starts in our minds, we hear true possibilities, rather than imagined ones. Sense instead of nonsense.

Third, we look carefully at this truly possible future and the "terrible" consequence and we discover it is *not* catastrophic. It won't destroy us. It may be unpleasant. Maybe. Uncomfortable? Maybe. Manageable? Probably. Survivable? Definitely. Likely to happen at all? We'll see what we can do to prevent it.

And that's the last step. We are able to see what's within our control and what isn't. "What can I do about this situation?" is a very reasonable question to ask *after* we've examined what the situation actually is. Being kept on the bench, being sent to a lower classification, being traded, failing in a crucial game situation do not bring on catastrophe. Only the player brings it on when his imagination is in control.

When his reality is checked, his good sense regains control. His mind games can be won. He continues to work diligently. That, he can control. He rises after a failure to perform the way he wished, breathes deeply and slowly a few times, gives himself functional, positive commands, and performs. He continues his effort to reach the limits of his ability. He knows the body ususally follows the will's command. Fearful? Why should he be?

But What About Doubtful?

"The fearful Unbelief," Thomas Carlyle wrote, "is Unbelief in yourself." To nit-pick over the difference between fear and self-doubt is not our purpose, but many of us who deny being fearful will admit to being doubtful—doubtful of our ability to succeed. We lack confidence within the framework of a goal, a requirement, or a situation. Self-doubt translates itself into negativism. The self-fulfilling prophecy waits for the command—positive or negative.

Bruce Berenyi, when he was with the New York Mets, pitched a four-hit shutout against Los Angeles on a warm August night in 1984. "Tonight," said the very pleased pitcher, "I had a positive attitude...I've had negative thoughts my whole career. I've thought the worst and the worst would always happen."

The difference between fear and self-doubt may be considerable. Either one stands between a player and confidence. "Think positively" is an empty command. And just changing "I can't" to "I can" will

"Be the hunter, not the prey."

not break down any barriers. *The player must believe in the self-talk he articulates and act upon it aggressively*, or doubt will remain—and weak performances continue. So we get back to the strategies we have for approaching our lack of confidence, whatever the cause.

A REVIEW

Examine the situation.

Assess its true degree of difficulty.

Identify the worst possible consequence of failure.

Recall the successes we had in similar past situations.

Bring successful past strategies forward.

Recognize what else the current situation may require.

Focus positively on those required and desirable actions.

Face the challenge with confidence in our preparation.

Documenting the Case for Confidence

Finally, it seems appropriate to support the view that gaining confidence is a player's priority. It doesn't take much effort to find that support. The daily sports pages offer it, as do magazines, books, television and radio interviews. Any informal or formal discussion with a player about the quality of his play will come around to the subject of confidence.

A keen observer can watch the body language of players to get evidence of its existence—or non-existence. Walking with head down, kicking dirt, shaking head sideways, slumping the body, making tentative movements—these are non-verbal displays of the lack of confidence.

Most ballplayers are verbal about periods during which their confidence sags. But only a few bring some very hard truths to their lips. Milwaukee great Robin Yount, the 1989 American League MVP, was an 18-year-old rookie shortstop for the Brewers. "Those stories about me quitting baseball to play professional golf were told because I was having a terrible time up here. I doubted my ability. I had no confidence at all. I wanted to run away," Yount said.

George Brett and former outfielder Bill Almon both had spells—as major leaguers—when they hoped (prayed) the batter wouldn't hit the ball to them. It happens at *all* levels, though the higher the level, the less likely the admission is to be made. Brett recalled struggling through a batting slump, being in the on-deck circle, seeing a lefthander warming up in the opposing team's bullpen—and hoping his teammate at bat would make the third out, so the lefty wouldn't be called in to face Brett.

Just by telling that story, Brett made it easier for any player to face his own lack of confidence. It's not inherited, we remind you. And it's acquired, without a lifetime guarantee. We've earned it when we get it.

And when we have it, we're glad to tell about it! "It's the most wonderful thing in the world..." said Gary Carter. "When I've got my confidence, I feel as if I can go up there and stand on my head and still get a hit—or hit the ball hard."

When former major league outfielder Paul Householder was with the Reds as a youngster, he had some very trying times. But after a winter of physical and mental rehabilitation, he came back a more confident player. He remembers going up to the plate on one particular occasion. "I was certain I would get a hit. I just felt it. I felt great. I was tickled (to feel that way). In fact, I felt so good I stepped out of the box to enjoy it."

He said he did get a hit, but that isn't the point. He—and Carter—were having the "flow experience" about which athletes talk. They "have it together," they say. They know it and feel it. Their concentration is keen because of it, because of confidence. As a result, "the ball looks like a grapefruit instead of a pea," as Carter said. They can't wait to get up there for their next at-bat.

And pitchers throw effortlessly. "All I can see is the catcher's glove when I'm going good," said Dan Schatzeder, who also knew how it felt when going poorly. "I never hear or see the crowd when I'm going good. It's like I'm in a dream. Everything is so easy."

When everything isn't very easy, and confidence erodes, "the field shrinks," said Householder. "My concentration lags. I look for the ball too late. I try too hard. I overreact. It hurts more than it helps."

Sparky Anderson wasn't happy to lose Roger Craig when the Detroit pitching coach "retired." Said Anderson, "He's a fine psychologist...a positive thinker who doesn't permit pitchers to wallow in problems or slumps."

When Craig became the San Francisco manager in 1986, one of his first transactions was to get pitcher Juan Berenguer from the Tigers. There seemed to be a correlation between Craig's presence and Berenguer's confidence. The pitcher's performances were enough evidence for Craig to bring him to San Francisco.

Tom Hume went to Tom Seaver when the two pitchers were teammates in Cincinnati. Tom Hume went to Tom Seaver for a prescription to cure lack of confidence. Giants outfielder Brett Butler said he went to religion, while playing for Atlanta. Pitcher Ken Dayley went to St. Louis after having played, without confidence, in Atlanta. Dayley said his confidence got the "boost" it needed with the Cardinals.

Players, managers, coaches, and *confidence* come and go.

Frank Viola knows from where his lack of confidence came. "I know my insecurity stemmed from not really thinking of myself as a pitcher," he told the *New York Times* in 1984. "Until now, as I'm throwing one pitch, I'm doubting it. When you doubt your pitch selection, you don't have anything. You end up throwing the 'other' pitch, and you don't give your all because you're not really committed to it. I feel now I have a commitment to every pitch I throw."

Bruce Hurst remembers doubting pitches as he was in the midst of his wind-up. (Many pitchers have the same memory, some from very recent games.) "I should be throwing the slider," Hurst has said to himself. Naturally, that doubt was distracting and if affected his concentration. A pitcher isn't in control of the pitch—or himself—at such times.

Phillies pitcher Tommy Greene had an impressive 16-4 1993 season. Prior to that season, observers seemed to be more impressed with Greene's ability than Greene himself. "He finally believes he can get hitters out," said teammate John Kruk. "Before, I think he was in that doubting period where he wasn't sure. Now, he works quick. He works ahead in the count."

A frequently asked question is: Which comes first, confidence or success? We've often heard the term "beginner's luck" applied to those who immediately succeed at a "new" task. If it is truly "luck," the success will be short-lived. Whatever confidence might have developed from that initial success disappears with the "luck."

We suggest that confidence actually preceeds true success, whether the activity be familiar or unfamiliar. As we stated, the confidence comes from the manner in which the participant has prepared for the activity. This confidence is built one step at a time, coming in steps as each task-specific goal is achieved.

The baseball player must first identify the fundamentals of the activity (hitting, pitching, fielding, etc.) or skill he's working at mastering. Next, he converts these fundamentals into functional goals (see Appendix). Then, he works—and works—on one goal at a time until he is very confident of his ability to execute/achieve *each one*. These achievements are the "building blocks" for confidence.

The "building blocks" are:

Self-evaluation (What fundamentals do I have to learn, develop, or improve?)
Goals (Fundamentals converted to functional goals.)
Preparation (Conscientious, positive, effective work at the task/activity.)
Persistence (The continued commitment to achieving— until confidence results.)

Greg Maddux, Tony Gwynn, Pat Hentgen, Greg Jefferies, Ryne Sandberg, Tommy Greene—all the players already mentioned in these pages, and any other player who speaks, has spoken about the influence confidence has had on their play. It's the most sought-after commodity in baseball—in any sport, for that matter. Larry Bird could certainly confirm this view. (We'll hear from the Celtics' basketball star in the next chapter.)

Paul Lindblad said that pitching great Catfish Hunter was so confident, he passed it on to his teammates. Gene Conley said that Ted Williams was so confident, he took it away from his opponents.

Pitcher Sid Fernandez, now a Baltimore Oriole, is another formidable talent who has struggled with that self-recognition. With the Mets in 1988, he stated: "My confidence this year has been much better, especially in the second half of the season. I go into a game now and I don't care *who* I face." He credited his improvement to mental work he had done on fixing "negative and (recognizing) things I can't control." He was still working on it in 1992, when he won 14 games. Many people voiced opinions on the growth Fernandez displayed. His catcher, Charlie O'Brien, was the most succinct—and probably the most accurate: "Self-confidence."

Pitcher Ron Darling summed it up nicely in Marc Gunther's *Basepaths*: "You can't last in any sport without being confident. Even if you're not the best, you've got to be confident that you're better than the other guy...Ninety percent (of pitching) is mental. There's enough guys who can throw breaking pitches over and have the physical ability, but when you believe that you're better than that hitter, I think that's the most important thing.

"This game is a game played with confidence because this game is played with your head. Most people have physical ability to play this game. To excel in it, I think it's in your head," Darling concluded.

What should be in our heads is a positive outlook and a good feeling for the competition ahead of us. Any expressions we make to that effect will help us, but perhaps more important is the attitude expressed by Virginia Wade earlier and by Wade Boggs here: "If I'm prepared, I'm confident. I can control that, so I do everything possible to be prepared. That's as much as I can do."

And, we believe, that's as much as any player *should do* if he's in pursuit of confidence and excellence on the baseball field.

8
LEARNING
Preparation's Start

The working definition we have of "confidence" is simple as we apply it to a baseball player: the attitude, the feeling, a player has that he will perform well. Successfully. Not that he—or his team—will win, though that may happen, of course, but rather that he will go into the competition with a sense of positive anticipation and well-being. The player doesn't consider the competition's *outcome* as the focal point of his good feeling. He does consider that he, himself, is physically and mentally prepared to take on the opposition successfully. He's prepared to do what needs to be done, using all his knowledge, understanding, and practice experience. He knows he has prepared well, so he is confident he will play well.

It may sound too simple to be true. Nevertheless, it *is* true. There's a catch, however. The typical athlete goes all-out during competition. That's easy. The exceptional athlete also goes all-out to prepare for competition. That's difficult. Demanding.

It may seem clear to all of us that preparation is essential. But the catch's question is this: How many athletes act out what they know? Those who care enough, according to Ozzie Smith.

Former NFL receiver and head coach Raymond Berry sums up our point nicely. "The most prepared are the most dedicated." he said. Every reference to a successful — yes, confident — player in the earlier chapter on "Dedication" addresses and supports Berry's view.

> For all your days prepare,
> And meet them all alike:
> When you are the anvil, bear —
> When you are the hammer, strike.

Prepare; be consistent; know yourself and understand your situation; act appropriately. That's the message in Edwin Markham's poetic and brief statement. Our message is essentially the same, though we need two chapters to make it.

To be a dedicated baseball player is, we believe, to learn as much about the game as he possibly can and to work at that game as energetically and regularly as possible. Players don't set limits; they set goals. And they prepare themselves to reach the goals through diligence and devotion to learning and practice.

Joe DiMaggio cast an enormous shadow when he played center field in Yankee Stadium. But Yankee rightfielder Tommy Henrich didn't play in that shadow. He established a reputation apart from that of the "Yankee Clipper." Henrich always seemed to do exactly what needed to be done. Talent had nothing to do with it. Henrich knew he couldn't match DiMaggio's great skill, but he also knew he could match anyone's knowledge of the game.

"Catching a fly ball is a pleasure," Henrich said when he played. "But knowing what to do with it after you catch it is a business." Henrich had learned his business. Players and fans paid recognition and paid tribute to his approach — his learning and preparation — which carried over to his performance. He became known as the Yankees' "Old Reliable."

Learning: Growth Through Change

First, a confession: we don't know everything, not even all those things about which we're supposed to be expert. Ourselves, for example. Furthermore, we haven't ever met anyone who does know everything. We *have* met quite a number of people who *acted* as if they did. We weren't impressed. In fact, we don't think they themselves really believed it. Still, it's a bad act. It's an act that stunts growth.

"How do *you* make that kind of adjustment?"

You've heard of growing pains? Well, it's often painful for people to find out that an idea they've cherished—an idea a parent or close friend or trusted coach cherished—is useless or wrong. In that sense, learning can be painful. It's more often just uncomfortable. A character in a George Bernard Shaw play (*Major Barbara*) says, "You have learnt something. That always feels at first as if you've lost something." It may be a long-held idea or a habit of which we've rid ourselves—a change in outlook or a change in behavior. But such learning is a change for the better, we think, though the discomfort is very apparent to us. We've "lost" something to which we'd grown accustomed.

We change reluctantly. Unless we have—or develop—an attitude which is compatible with our desire to be as effective as we can be. Then, learning is a joy.

During Wally Joyner's 1986 impressive rookie season with the Angels, Reggie Jackson seemed most impressed with the young first baseman's relentless desire for knowledge. Said Jackson of his teammate, Joyner, "He asks about everything. He wants to learn."

During that same season, Houston Astros rookie lefthander Jim Deshaies had been unrelenting in his desire to avoid change. Late in July, he changed his delivery and had, to that point, his "best outing" as a major leaguer.

"I've been stubborn," Deshaies admitted after the game. "But I made an adjustment in my delivery tonight, and I couldn't believe how it worked." In 1994, after having experienced a number of changes in his approach, he's still working as a big league pitcher—with the Minnesota Twins.

"You've gotta believe," as Tug McGraw used to say so often. We gotta *want* to believe—and know.

INTENTIONAL LEARNING: WHAT TO WANT

We want to look for better ways of doing "our thing" and have an open mind.

We want to experiment with these new approaches. We never want to be satisfied with our knowledge or our skill.

We want to recognize that new ways are not immediately comfortable.

We want to give these new approaches a fair test of time—and effort.

We want to think and talk about the solution, not the problem.

We want to use our minds and control our emotions.

We want to keep what works and discard what doesn't.

We want to be persistent.

We want to remember that mistakes are first steps to learning and should not be labeled as "failures."

We want to remember that many people avoid learning new ways of doing things because, in addition to not wanting to feel uncomfortable, they "don't want to look bad."

We want to remember that good learners "risk" doing things badly, in order to find out how to do things well.

We want to remember that had we waited until we could have walked perfectly before we made our attempts, we never would have attempted.

We want to recognize there is always a need to learn.

The ability to learn and make the necessary adjustments is highly valued by the outstanding ballplayers. Small wonder. They know value because they were willing to pay the price. They learned on and off the playing field. And they realized great profits.

Everyone learns, even without trying. *Intentional learning,* however, is what separates the mediocre players from the stars.

Hall of Famer Carl Yastrzemski, at age 43, could be seen experimenting during spring training and, from time to time, during the season. We might think that after 20-plus years in the major leagues, Yaz would have found one style and stuck to it. But we should know better by now.

The year before his illustrious career ended, Yaz, speaking about his approach to hitting, said, "I am always looking for a better way. I am never satisfied. You have to be honest with yourself. Sometimes you get yourself out, but sometimes the opposition beats you. When that happens, you have to adjust. You can't be afraid to change."

A major reason for Yastrzemski's productivity over those many years was his *learning attitude.* Many players never develop one— and thereby fail to develop their talents, to say almost nothing of their "selves."

A good start at developing a learning attitude is to *want* the "wants" listed previously. Those players who can put them all into action—remembering what needs to be remembered and doing what needs to be done—have already made the Learner's All-Star team. Hitting over .500 on that list puts him on the road to the Learner's Hall of Fame.

Let's pick a few items from the list—big league requirements. We'll scramble the order and be a bit more expansive about these strategies for intentional learning.

1. *Never be satisfied with your knowledge, performance, or skill.*

Socrates was credited with being the wisest man in Athens about 2500 years ago. When asked what made him so smart, the Greek teacher/philosopher responded, "My wisdom lay in this: unlike other men, I know how ignorant I am."

In other words, if we know we don't know everything, we're smarter than the guy who thinks he does, and we strive to learn more. Getting less ignorant all the time, Socrates would say. Getting smarter, we'd say.

Mike Schmidt was named the Most Valuable Player in the National League in 1986. (The third player in National League history to win three MVP Awards.) When asked about his feelings after winning the award, the former Phillies third baseman/first baseman responded, "I'm already thinking of ways to improve."

In other words, if we don't set limits on our abilities and performance, we will continue to seek perfection, Schmidt would say. And surely get closer to it, we'll say.

In still another way, Yastrzemski's earlier words speak to the same point.

A specific example: Al Williams broke into the major leagues with the Minnesota Twins in 1980. As a starting pitcher he won six and lost two with a 3.51 ERA. In 1981, his record was 6–10; his ERA 4.08. By July 1982, it had become obvious that his performance was on a steady downward slide.

In mid-July, Williams was sent to Toledo for some work on fundamentals. When he returned, he was a much-improved pitcher. He had learned more in five weeks than he had learned in his three years in the big leagues. He fielded his position much better; the opposition could no longer run on him at will. He changed speeds more effectively. He appeared to be a "new" Al Williams. He won six in a row to finish that season.

Williams was asked, "What happened? Why the sudden improvement?"

He explained that when he had gotten to Toledo, he had a meeting with himself. He said he realized he had become satisfied with being a starting pitcher in the big leagues, and with the money he was making.

"When I screwed up in the field or someone stole a base, I used to just tell myself to get the next guy out. I didn't worry about it. I didn't recognize the need to be better fundamentally, even though the coaches were telling me. At Toledo, I took a look at myself and how I had been losing games. Then I started working on those things."

The need to learn and improve is always present, but players who become comfortable and satisfied will seldom recognize the many ways and opportunities to do so. Obviously, those who are immediately aware of that need are far ahead of those who take years to make the discovery—or who never make it at all.

2. *Think and talk the solution, not the problem.*

When a person justifies, explains, or blames, he's making it difficult for himself to be an effective learner. He is dwelling on the problem, not the possible solution.

It's easy to understand why we all have a tendency to behave this way. As children, we were taught to dwell on negative behavior or the problem, rather than the possible solution to it.

First, we were told what *not* to do: "Don't step on the cat"; "Don't drop the dish"; "Don't spill the milk"; "Don't slam the door."

Then, we were asked to defend our behavior: "Why did you do that?"; "What *were* you thinking of?"; "What went wrong?"; "What made you do that?"

The next step was for us—the children—to ask ourselves those questions before someone else did. We wanted to be prepared with an acceptable answer. Whether we were answering to ourselves or to others, that kind of talk led us into a habit which prevented us from thinking about how to correct the mistake or solve the problem. That is one of the primary reasons people make the same mistakes over and over.

Of course, we must recognize our mistakes and learn from them. But too many people dwell on them, get bogged down in them—and find themselves overcome by them. They never do get their heads turned in the right direction, where the correction can be found.

Twins centerfielder Bobby Mitchell chased down a drive by Ricky Henderson in the left-center gap. Mitchell got to the ball quickly and came up firing, but he missed the cut-off man, and Henderson cruised into third base.

When Mitchell came off the field, a teammate asked him, "What happened? How come you didn't hit the cut-off man?"

Mitchell answered, "I know that Henderson can fly and that I didn't have much time. So I made the play as fast as I could. When I turned around, I didn't see the cut-off man where I thought he would be."

Mitchell said later that even after he had stopped talking about the play, he was still thinking about it. Thoughts such as: "My foot slipped some on the warning track; I hope it didn't sound like I was blaming the shortstop."

All that Mitchell had said and thought focused on the problem. Had he simply asked himself, "Next time, on a similar play, what will I do differently?" he would probably have led himself to an appropriate answer. "I'm going to take more time when I get to the wall and make sure I see the cut-off man before I throw."

After he figured out what he wanted to do next time and mentally rehearsed it, he could have started getting ready for the next play. This approach saves a lot of time and eliminates a lot of mental energy. Negative energy, that is.

We usually know what mistakes we've made and what the problem is without spending much time thinking about it. The more time we spend with it, the more likely we are to repeat it.

The two steps involved in learning from mistakes are:

Ask yourself, "What will I have to do differently next time?" (or words to that effect)

Visualize yourself doing it correctly.

Willie Stargell explained it as well as anyone. While playing with the Pirates, he said, "I think about what I didn't like and I fix it in my mind. I don't analyze it. I see, feel and hear myself getting the results I want."

Numerous stories have been told about American POWs in Vietnam who, during their imprisonment, "learned, practiced, and played" golf every day — for years — in their heads. Dog legs left and right, water holes, sand traps. Their mental simulations helped them survive — and did wonders for their "real" golf game when they returned home.

3. *Keep the emotions under control.*

The first and most typical reaction of a ballplayer who fails to perform up to his expectations is one of frustration and/or anger — "I should have killed that pitch"; "I never should have walked that hitter"; "Why didn't I catch that ball? I should have"; "I shouldn't even be in this situation."

The player must give the emotions time to quiet down. (Stepping out of the batter's box; getting off the pitcher's mound.) Then, his brain back in control, he substitutes positive, functional thoughts that help him learn and adjust. (He can use the rapid two-step process above.)

When emotions are strong, it's difficult to understand, learn, and retain. After mistakes or errors, emotions *add pressure,* rather than reduce it. And people have a tendency to revert to their "old ways" (the ways that lead to mistakes) when under pressure. They usually don't intend to do so — or realize they are doing so.

Let the intellectual system, not the emotional one, correct mistakes and solve problems.

4. *Have an open mind*

A closed mind is a door closed on the opportunity for improvement. While people recognize this truth, they often do not clearly see another truth: that they themselves have shut the door — and locked it behind them.

Why do people close their minds? There are a number of reasons:

Self-satisfaction.

The "sophomore jinx" is a phrase used to describe the phenomenon that occurs when a second year major leaguer, after having had a good first ("freshman") year, falls flat on his face in his second ("sophomore") year. When that has happened, "sophomores" have been heard to make such statements as: "I know what it takes and what I have to do; nobody has to tell me. This approach worked last year. That's what got me here. It will work again, I just have to stay with it. I don't need anyone telling me what to do."

What happens in most cases is that the league adjusted to the "sophomore," but because his mind was closed, the player didn't see what had happened and failed to make his own adjustments.

Minor leaguers who were very successful in college have suffered from the same affliction, as have college players who were outstanding in high school; high school players who were . . . The point is clear.

Prejudgments.

When we prejudge a person or situation, our thoughts may be: "He doesn't know enough to be telling me how to do this; my coach last year knew more than this jerk." Or, "This is boring." Or, "I'm wasting my time." Or, "I can't learn anything from all this, it's too complicated."

People who think they know more than everyone else certainly won't be able to learn from others. But not for the reason they have in their heads.

Remember the following: *Who learns more in a conversation between a "wise" man and a "fool"?*

Consider: The wise man has more to offer, no doubt, but the fool is a fool because he doesn't learn from others—or from his own experience. The wise man is wise because he seeks to learn from everyone and everything he confronts. Our wise man will learn something from the fool; our fool will get nothing from his contact with the wise man.

We all have the choice in every conversation we have. *Will we choose to be wise — or foolish?*

Distracting thoughts.

Instructions come in three forms: a) *Direct* ("Try this; Take the ball out of your glove this way."); b) *Questions;* c) *Criticism* (usually meant to tell someone he may be able to find a better way).

Instruction in any form is meant to help people reach their potential, but it isn't always seen that way by the person being instructed. It isn't unusual for a player, let's say, to feel, "The instructor is telling me, 'You're no good; you don't measure up.'"

When that happens, the player has distracting thoughts, such as, "Why is he on me? I did my best." "It's not my fault. I was told to do it this way last year." "I'm doing as well as everybody else. Why should I change?" "I wasn't *trying* to do it that way." And so on.

When we become defensive — take instruction as a personal attack — we close ourselves off or "lash back." Either of those behaviors prevents us from learning and improving. We want to remember that, no matter what kind of tonality or language the instructor is using, *our aim is not to be distracted* by his behavior or attitude, but to *listen* to his *words* and *evaluate them, rather than him.* That will keep our focus on what might be able to teach us something. And the more we pay attention to what we *want* to learn, the better we will learn it, because *attention itself is a learning reinforcement.*

If we are feeling extremely defensive — threatened perhaps — while being instructed, we may resort to the distraction of verbalized justification or explanation. We may feel the need to tell, "This is why I'm doing it this way." Remember, internally or externally expressed, those explanations are dwelling on the past. They distract from what we want to do. Our desire is to improve in the future. We can best do this by focusing on the present, on how we *now* want to act or perform. The more we use our thoughts to find a better way, even a completely different way, the more choices we'll have, and the better prepared we'll be.

The best way to have an *open* mind is to *be curious*—have a questioning attitude, as Socrates had. He was always asking, "Why?"— so he always received information. Other questions can help us improve our preparation, our game, and ourselves. Try these: "What is he trying to tell me?" "How can this apply to me?" "Where and how can I use this?" "Why does he see this as important?" "How can I take advantage of his experience?"

5. *Use failures to learn*

The great players experiment and change. They know that all improvement comes from change. They are willing to risk and tolerate temporary failure to gain long-term success. They find better ways and continue to stretch toward their limits.

A person can learn from every failure if he takes the attitude that it's an opportunity to learn. St. Louis Cardinal quarterback Neil Lomax was benched in November 1986, after 52 straight games as the team's starter. The Cardinals made it known they were trying to trade him. It was a curious decline since 1984, when Lomax had seven 300-yard passing games.

Lomax made the best possible public statement: "I'm going to take this as a positive thing, a chance to sit back, reflect and look at things and ask what I can learn from this situation. I need to improve. I know that."

He was reinstated after a week. His performances did show a marked improvement. They were a result of "reflection"—his learning.

Trial and error is one of the most common ways to learn. Trial and error is, essentially, trial and failure. Failure tells us that we have to do something different or differently. John Wooden, the legendary teacher and basketball coach at UCLA, said, "Failure is not failure, unless it's failure to change."

Change for change's sake is not the answer. It's important to know when to change, to be sensibly discriminating—not changing constantly. That was the message "Dr. J"—Hall of Famer Julius Erving—gave when he was playing basketball for the Philadelphia '76ers. "I stay with the things that work well for me, but the fun comes from exploring, trying to discover new moves."

Erving didn't *employ* the new moves until they *proved to be effective.* Even the moves that eventually became very effective didn't click immediately. Some never panned out. If Erving treated his day-to-day results as a measure of his worth, he would have used all the wrong instruments to measure. Those of us who do that — and Erving obviously did not — are not likely to take the risks so necessary to reaching our potential.

But if we treat our successes and failures the same — as equal opportunities to *learn* and *grow* and *improve* — then we discover the rewards that come from the process.

After all, we should realize that how *others* view our errors and mistakes must be *their* problem, *not ours.* We must develop our own goals, irrespective of what others expect of us. And we must also develop our own philosophy of learning. We won't be effective learners if we concern ourselves with what others think we're doing, instead of what we know we're doing.

6. *Be persistent.*

Even the most conscientious learners are usually impatient with the time it takes to learn. Baseball players seem to be particularly impatient. They think they should "be getting it faster." Their intention to be good learners can be cancelled out by this attitude. When they don't learn something quickly and easily, they have a tendency to move on to something else. The best players are persistent. After others have quit, the "winners" will still be working, looking for another approach (mental and/or physical), trying to find another, better way.

Pete Rose is a great example. We first saw Pete in 1961, in a Cincinnati Reds minor league camp at the old Fair Grounds in Tampa, Florida. He had mediocre physical ability. Nothing was easy for him. He fought ground balls; he was tight throwing; he wasn't impressive at the plate. There were many players in that camp with more physical ability.

What Rose did have was a *mental toughness* in its earliest stages: *desire* and *persistence.* He was the first one on the field in the morning and the last one off at night. If he were trying to learn something, he wore everyone out until he got it the way he wanted it.

Desire and persistence were Rose's trademarks throughout his career. He became the only man in the history of baseball to be an All-Star at four different positions. He could not have accomplished that without his persistence. Rose was a model player. His attitude toward learning contributed to that model.

For all he knew, Ted Williams also wanted to know more. ". . . I want to know the answers," he wrote (*My Turn at Bat*). "I want to know why. I think 'why' is a wonderful word."

In *The Quality of Courage,* Mickey Mantle wrote: "It's unbelievable how much you don't know about the game you've been playing all your life."

What are your limits to learning? It's generally agreed upon that typical humans utilize 15 to 20% of their brain capacity. How much are *you* using? And how effective are you being?

Brain work uses energy, needs effort, requires some imagination. The dedicated player gives it, along with his physical energy. That's paying the *whole* price. And we get what we pay for.

Those who may argue that their improvement "didn't result from change, but from being more consistent" have failed to learn that the improvement in their consistency came about through a change in attitude or mental process. They learned something despite themselves.

Surely, we *consciously* change through *learning.*

Much of what you read in this book you will already have known. Even so, you can learn, because:

1. The reinforcement of what you know and agree with will give you more confidence.
2. You may find that some of what you know is more important than you previously thought.
3. Your reading may lead you to tie pieces of information together, making your knowledge more unified and complete.
4. You may discover that the information you have can be applied and utilized in a variety of situations and circumstances.

Of course, we hope to provide some information and insights that are new for you, some *new* learning. And that can come about in a number of ways. We've found that in baseball, and, generally speaking, in life itself, we are hindered not so much by what we don't know, but by what we believe to be true that actually is not true. So original ideas are sometimes less important than the re-examination of long-held ideas.

Therefore, it's very important to continually reevaluate what we believe to be "the best way" of doing things. Don't believe that "nothing changes." What was true yesterday may no longer be true today. What worked yesterday may no longer work today.

With that in mind, the challenge is to examine and experiment with every thought and suggestion in this book, especially those with which you are not comfortable. Then reevaluate and decide for yourself. Using that process, all of us cannot fail to learn.

When we fail to learn, we've learned to fail.

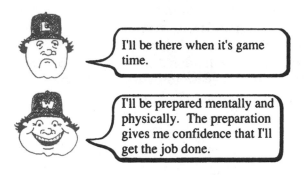

I'll be there when it's game time.

I'll be prepared mentally and physically. The preparation gives me confidence that I'll get the job done.

9
PREPARATION
The Action and Reinforcement of Learning

If a player has made himself aware of the fact that there is something to be learned in everything he hears and sees, he's one step away from being a model athlete. It's a giant step, however, taken only by the few, not the many. Many players are aware of what needs to be done next, but few are able to put the awareness into action — which is the final step in learning and preparation. The best players all have a program which they follow in a regular, routine, regimented, repetitious way. We call this *consistent* behavior. And we say that consistency is the key to confidence and maximum performance. The best players put their learning into form through diligent, conscientious, and effective practice routines. They learn further through these routines and they continue to make the necessary adjustments and applications.

The driving force is a mental one; one of desire and discipline. The desire to learn (intellectual) joins with the discipline to work effectively (psychological). The body then makes it a threesome.

We used to be told: "Practice makes perfect." Now we hear, more appropriately: "Perfect practice makes perfect." Simply, that means that we best prepare ourselves for the attempt at perfection in competition by making the same attempt during practice.

120

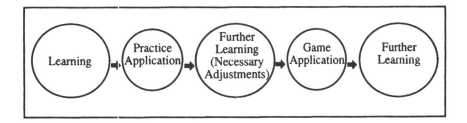

And so on — until we know it all.

Why do so few make the commitment to prepare in this manner? The answer is an easy one for any reader who's ever made the attempt. The process is extremely difficult. It is a demanding one: time-consuming and arduous. Physically and mentally. "Boring" is the description we hear most often. We consider the source and agree. It is boring to those who don't actually want to become as good as they can be. And we understand them completely. They admit they "don't want it bad enough." But what about those who say they do want it, yet won't make that commitment because "it's boring"? We won't claim to understand them — though we have some very strong suspicions. Everyone makes a choice, remember.

Effective preparation incorporates and brings forward a number of mental elements we've already discussed: dedication, goal-setting, responsibility, to name a few. It should become clear, as this book progresses, that all the chapters are related, interdependent, in fact. Rusty Staub's dedication in batting practice was evident, but Staub had a specific, functional goal he was trying to achieve with every swing he took. He took the responsibility of being prepared.

As did Tom Seaver. Whether he was eating cottage cheese or taking late-night, solitary pitching practice, his acts reflected his dedication and preparation. He didn't allow internal temptations or outside forces to interfere with his pattern of preparation. He took complete responsibility for his behavior.

Ozzie Smith's approach to his infield practice is a reflection of his attitude toward his profession. The same is true of the behavior of the others we've mentioned and will mention. But Smith attributes his approach to his learning that preparation "makes it happen." The fans see his acrobatic skills in the field, yes. That's the "easy part" of his game, he'd say. He knows how much time and attention he dedicates before it's time for competition and how intensely he concentrates. And that, as he said earlier, is what he thinks anyone should do. Anyone "who cares enough."

Ozzie Smith is thought by some to be the best fielding shortstop in baseball history. His numerous Gold Gloves, his soaring, spinning, whirling, diving plays have certainly impressed all who have watched him. Second baseman Tommy Herr was most impressed by Smith's consistency.

"What is overlooked about Ozzie," Herr said before the 1985 World Series, "is that he always makes the routine plays. Most guys can make a lot of good plays, and a lot of guys can sometimes make a great play, but they'll blow the easy ones, and that hurts a team. But Ozzie has tremendous powers of concentration. He won't take the easy ones for granted."

Smith responded to Herr's assessment: "Because I wasn't born with a lot of size, I've had to maybe work harder than some others. Or concentrate harder. You play the way you practice, and so I just don't go out in infield practice for the sake of taking some ground balls. I have a purpose in what I'm doing out there—testing the infield bounces, working on my moves."

Smith gives complete attention to every ground ball hit to him in practice. There are many infielders not "born with a lot of size," who don't practice the way Smith does. And some are born with a lot of size. Physical size isn't the issue. Smith and others like him are giants. They're the "big men" in the league of the mental game.

"My mother told me that if you don't put anything into something, you won't get anything out," Smith explained. "I want to look back and say, 'I got everything out of all I had.'"

No one can have a higher goal. It's difficult to know if we ever attain it. But we are successful if we can honestly say, "I did everything I could to get there . . ." We then have no regrets, and we don't have to mouth the familiar phrase of failure, "If only I would have . . ."

So, we get to this: "If you know it, show it." Convert learning into quality practice. Use mental practice, as well as physical. That is a prerequisite for effective preparation. By being disciplined enough

"Hit me a couple dozen more; I wanna work on comin' in on this high grass."

to concentrate on all 100 ground balls hit at him during a practice session, an infielder is approaching practice in the same manner he'd approach a game. He positions himself properly on every ball; he sets up properly on every ball; he moves properly on every ball; his eyes follow every ball properly off the bat and into his glove. Every ball. Over and over—and over again.

This infielder is doing more than improving his ability to field ground balls. He is developing his *mental stamina.* Through the discipline he applies—even as he gets "tired"—he creates good mental habits in practice, thereby preparing himself for the game. That is the most he can do. And he becomes confident in the knowing and in the doing.

The pitcher in the bullpen: thinking selection, location; simulating situations; knowing that every practice or warmup pitch has a purpose; throwing the pitch with that purpose clearly in mind. That is the structure of preparation.

Hitters should reread Staub's approach during batting practice. That approach, as well as the infielder's (Smith's) and pitcher's (Seaver's), simulates game conditions in practice and leads to developing an effective game attitude. It keeps the player's mind on his business: the function of the moment.

Through repetition and simulation in practice, a player can quickly get to the point at which the playing of the game is, in a relative sense, "easy."

In his *Coaches Training Manual to Psyching for Sport,* Terry Orlick writes of Chinese table tennis players, who, in practice, "serve thousands of balls . . . Chinese gymnasts do routine after routine, divers do dive after dive, often for an entire training session." Orlick notes how hard they work, but adds that just as important "is the quality of effort and concentration that an athlete carries to the task."

Dr. Keith Bell in his book, *Winning Isn't Normal,* writes about what it takes for an athlete to be "a winner." We have expressed the idea before, but Dr. Bell's words are particularly to the point of this chapter. He states that the athlete most likely to succeed is the one willing "to stand out and act differently." The exceptional athlete "can't train like everyone else. (He has) to train more and train better."

We'd like to refer to three exceptional athletes whose great success in their sport has been attributed, by themselves and others, to their mental preparation.

Joanne Carner became the first woman golfer to reach $2 million in career earnings. She claims that striving for perfection is the only way to be the best.

"You have to want to win," said Carner, who has won the Vare Trophy for the lowest stroke average five times. "And if you want to win, you stay in there and practice totally different. What I try to do is chip every ball in the hole. You're not going to do it every time, but that's the attitude you have to have.

"I won't let myself out of the bunker until I hole one out," she said of her practice routine. "I do that with everything I do, and a lot of times I have to stand out there longer than I want. But I stay sharp and consistent."

Larry Bird explains his basketball greatness simply: "I work hard all the time. I've always been one willing to learn and get better."

Bird gets better through relentless practice, during and between seasons. The Milwaukee Bucks beat Bird's Celtics four straight during the 1982–83 Eastern Conference finals. Afterward, Bird said, "I'm gonna go back home this summer and work harder on basketball than I ever did before."

He did. "I went back to French Lick, worked my tail off . . . We won the title and I had my best year ever." NBA fans will find that Bird has continued to improve.

Bird's physical assets have often been questioned. He waddles when he walks and runs flat-footed. He is strong in body at 220 pounds, but the NBA has many stronger, faster, higher-jumping forwards. Why, then, has he been considered "the best"?

"Practice and hard work," said former Celtics coach K.C. Jones. "I have been around basketball for a long time . . . but I have yet to find anyone who has Larry's determination . . . He is a student of the game and a perfectionist."

Bird claims his "habit-forming days" began in fourth grade. As a high schooler, Bird would go to the gym to practice at 7 o'clock in the morning.

"Larry might not have appreciated getting up early in the morning then," Jones said. "But he is benefiting from those work habits now."

Before Celtics practices, and after everyone had left, Bird would remain to work alone. He had a consistent pattern: one day he focused on foul shots and shots from the left side of the court; on another he'd concentrate on off-balance fall-away jumpers and three-point shots. Over and over—with consistent intensity.

Bird made mental records of opponents' moves, the better to defend against them. "You can get a lot of steals that way," he explained. Of course, Bird's passing and rebounding simulations have also helped him develop what Dave DeBusschere, a former New York Knicks player and executive, considers to be "a most rarely wrapped package."

Raymond Berry had limited physical talents, most experts agreed. Nevertheless, the former Baltimore Colts (1955-1967) receiver rose from being a 20th-round draft choice of the Baltimore Colts to becoming a member of the Pro Football Hall of Fame. Berry has credited teammate Johnny Unitas' arm and his own mental preparation.

Steve Sabol, who produces NFL Films, revealed some of the lesser-known habits Berry formed. "About the final half-dozen years he played for the Colts, Berry would spend two or three days and nights at a studio in Philadelphia going over every play he participated in during the season," recalled Sabol.

"He told us he was trying to measure how precisely he had run each route, how he placed his hands to catch the ball, his reaction to being tackled, a lot of things. He actually would log the quality of the spiral of the passes, and check them against weather conditions."

Sabol and Berry would identify the films he wanted put together for further examination during the winter. "We'd do it for him," Sabol said. "After all, he was the best receiver in the NFL, and no one else asked us anyway. For that matter, no one has asked us...since then."

Berry had studied and prepared himself for years prior to those extensive film-viewings. He'd concluded that there were 88 ways of avoiding a defender to catch a pass. He had practiced them all. He improved his greatest physical asset, his hands, through the strengthening exercise of squeezing Silly Putty. He's practiced catching off-target passes. He's practiced falling on fumbles. He's laundered his own uniform pants to be certain they fit properly. He's used different contact lenses for different conditions, and he used shaded goggles to cope with the troublesome sun on the West Coast. He did whatever he could to make himself a better performer.

The three athletes above are exceptional in their preparation, not in their natural physical attributes. What our genes do for us is one matter. What our actions do for us is another. Once again, any athlete has the choice to be exceptional — or ordinary — in his actions.

The number of games played during a baseball season — particularly at the professional level — makes it easier for a player to develop a consistent approach. The nature of the game makes it more necessary than in other sports.

Every effective athlete prepares for his performance with consistency, because he seeks consistency in the performance itself. When a new element presents itself, the effective athlete factors it into his routine. For example, recall Roberto Clemente's outfield preparation prior to a game on a wet field. The thickness of the grass, the changing directions of the wind, the contour of the outfield wall were always factored into his preparation through action, not just awareness. He noticed, then he practiced.

Clemente was both an exemplar and a teacher.

Willie Stargell told us in the spring of 1981 that Clemente had taught him to prepare for games and at-bats. Stargell's process:

> **Review**: "After the game I think of what I did that I liked: the balls I hit hard and the good plays I made.
>
> "Next, I go over swings I didn't like: bad pitches I might have chased, any fielding plays or baserunning that I wasn't satisfied with. I relive them in my mind and get them right."
>
> **Preview**: "Now, I want to know who is pitching the next day: the starter and all possible relievers. I usually pick up a bat, go through my routine of getting ready and then visualize how they pitched to me last time and any

changes they might make. I picture the pitches coming in, I hit them on the sweet spot, and see them go to all parts of the field. I even see myself staying off of bad pitches. When I leave that out, I'll chase those pitches just like I did when I was a rookie.

"The next day, I watch every pitch the pitcher throws. I want to know if he is throwing anything differently, or new."

Self-Coaching: "In the on-deck circle, I remind myself to keep my shoulder in. I check to make sure my bat, hands, stance, and stride feel good. Then I tell myself, 'Yeah, feels good.'

"Before I step into the batter's box again, I visualize the pitches and how I'm going to hit them."

The At-Bat: "Once I get into the batter's box, I don't talk to myself at all. I don't think about anything but picking up the ball and seeing the spin on it. If anything else comes into my mind, I get out of there and start all over. After every pitch, I look down and take a picture of where my foot landed. I have a tendency to open up. If I do, I step out of the box, and in my mind I fix it. If I don't see the ball the way I want to, or swing and miss, I do the same thing. I'm not in any hurry.

"The first at-bat, I want to make the pitcher throw as many pitches as I can. I want to see everything he has. My picture, then, is so strong, if he makes any kind of mistake, I don't miss it."

If the batter's box is a hitter's "place of business," a pitcher's "office" is the mound. Many of the pitcher's behavior patterns around and on the mound are similar to those of a hitter outside and in the box, though the focus and function are different. A pitcher's daily and pre-game routine will vary, depending on whether he's a starter or reliever. (See "Pitching" chapter.)

One important aspect of preparation for any pitcher is learning the strengths and weaknesses of opposing hitting. Just as Stargell and others study the tendencies of pitchers, so do conscientious pitchers learn and retain as much as possible about the guy facing him in the batter's box.

Tom Seaver started "doing his homework" early in his career. On days after starts, he jotted down, pitch by pitch, what he had thrown to each hitter and what the hitter had done, or not done, to each pitch.

Seaver told John Devaney:

> I will never forget the crucial pitches, the ones that brought a key strike or led to a double play. I jot down in the book as a performance record of what I have done to every hitter and what every hitter has done to me.
>
> I get in a situation where I have to apply all I know, mentally and physically, on just one pitch . . . I have to think what I should do, and then make my body do it. A light goes on in your head, and you realize that everything you've done in your life has been for this moment . . . Suddenly, you're the most confident person in the world.

Wade Boggs is perhaps the major league player most confident in his preparation, in its order and structure, in its completeness. Few could duplicate it. Fewer would want to try.

Growing up in a military household is conducive to order and structure. "Some kids wouldn't have liked (it)," Boggs told *Sports Illustrated* writer, Peter Gammons, in 1986.

> . . . It was the greatest thing that happened to me. Dinner was always at 5:30, and if you weren't home at 5:30, you didn't eat. So you learned to always know where the clocks were in your friends' houses, and to this day I always notice clocks. I woke up at precisely the same time every day for 18 years. If I woke up, say, 30 minutes late, I was out of sync all day.
>
> (On game days, Boggs leaves his apartment at 3:00, punctually.) That way it's always between 3:10 and 3:15 when I walk in the door of the clubhouse.
>
> (His dressing and bat-checking rituals take him to 4:15 or 4:20, at which time he goes to third base for 20–25

minutes of ground balls. After a drink of water, he trots to center field for some mental preparation.) I like to focus in on who's pitching, what he, the catcher, the manager and the defense are likely to try to do with me, who's available in the bullpen—everything I'm going to face. It's nothing more than preparation. Then, I'm ready to take batting practice. (Of course, Boggs has a batting practice routine—and another one prior to his game at-bats. When he gets to the on-deck circle, he arranges the pine tar, the doughnut, the resin and uses them in that order. He studies the pitcher and keeps his head clear. In the batter's box, he draws a symbol: the Hebrew letter Chai. He is now prepared.) Almost every hitter has a routine when he gets into the box. Pete Rose. George Foster. Carlton Fisk. Yaz. Mine has evolved from Little League through the minors, part by design, part born of superstition, but mine's the same as theirs—only it takes a little more than 5½ hours.

Boggs is considered to be everything between unusual and eccentric. He eats chicken every day; he does his running at 7:17 before every night game. He strictly adheres to the program he's developed. An excessive one? Tedious? Who is qualified to make that judgment? It's easy to question the actions of others. In this case, we would better use our energy searching for our own pattern of control.

Boggs' verdict: "Baseball is fun. I love it." Other judges may wish to refer to his achievements. Case closed.

Off-Season Preparation

Baseball players have sometimes been considered to be the worst conditioned of professional athletes. Dr. Frank Jobe, cofounder of the National Athletic Health Institute and medical adviser to the Los Angeles Dodgers, disputes that view: "Maybe that was true back in the days of the Babe (Ruth) and perhaps up to 15 years ago, when players drank too much, ate too much and lay around in the winter getting fat, then spent spring training trying to get into shape."

Jobe is certain that is no longer the way things are.

Players' routines have changed dramatically since "the days they rolled off the train and into spring training," according to Kansas City Royals trainer Mickey Cobb. "That won't work anymore."

Said former Toronto outfielder Mookie Wilson, "My idea is to play the best I can for as long as I can, and now that means not letting yourself go between seasons."

In 1993, Phillies outfielder Lenny Dykstra had his best season, an MVP-type performance. "I worked hard all winter and it's showed. I'm as strong as I was at the start of the season."

"Conditioning is in the head and heart, not just the legs," said former NFL coach Bum Phillips. Any off-season program—particularly working with weights and running—means that the player continues to work within the framework of his plan for successful performance. His mental self is as much the beneficiary as his physical self.

In 1986, Andy Allenson, catching for the Cleveland Indians, was named to the Topps Rookie Team. Allenson himself was very unhappy with his season's performance, at bat and behind the plate. His manager expressed the view that Allenson's errors and low batting average were results of "lack of confidence." The catcher spent the last month of the season on the bench, his confidence sinking to new depths each day.

During the winter that followed, Allenson formed a program of study and conditioning. "I never really lifted before," he said in late November. "I knew it would make me (physically) stronger, but I already feel more confident. I feel like I have a sense of purpose—something that gives me control."

In college, especially, and in the minor leagues, baseball had come easy to Andy Allenson. Like so many others, he was not prepared for the challenge waiting at the next level. Unlike so many others, he learned that an immediate adjustment was necessary. And he made it.

Preparation is always in season.

Superstitions

It's fitting that Wade Boggs attributed part of his preparation to superstition. The thread of superstition can be found woven through the fabric of most people's everyday lives—for sensible and non-sensible reasons. It can be based on fearful thinking or wishful thinking. Occasionally, we all seem to find some element of luck,

Reprinted by permission of United Feature Syndicate, Inc.

good or bad, in our daily lives. When that happens, we ignore facts or logic and our thoughts and actions can be strongly influenced by superstition.

The structure and pace of baseball, the repetitive actions of the players and their desire for good results have all allowed superstition easy access to the game. Superstition, in fact, has become part of baseball lore.

Listen to Houston Astros pitching coach Mel Stottlemeyer, who was pitching for the New York Yankees when these words were spoken:

> I will never step on a foul line. We (the Yankees) were playing the Twins a few years ago, and I was headed for the bullpen to warm up before the start of the game. I avoided the foul line and Jim Hegan (Yankee coach) said I shouldn't be superstitious, and that I should step on the line. I did.
>
> The first batter I faced was Ted Uhlander, and he hit a line drive off my left shin. It went for a hit. Carew, Oliva, and Killebrew followed with extra base hits. The fifth man hit a single and scored, and I was charged with five runs. I haven't stepped on a foul line since.

If avoiding foul lines, wearing "lucky" sanitary socks, using a "hot" bat, carrying a rabbit's foot, or eating chicken every day can give a player confidence, then he should, by all means, help himself to have that feeling. It may be an important part of his preparation.

We believe in the feeling, not in the charm's powers. We believe in the power of belief. We know that many people who have good, strong faith can make what they believe become a reality. That's why we frequently say that, if there are a dozen traits in every outstanding baseball player, 12 of them are confidence.

The only problem we have with superstitions is that they may offer an immature person an excuse — an opportunity to blame some power beyond himself for his bad fortune or bad performance. We believe in a player's individual responsibility for that performance, in the player's own ability to affect outcomes. We have never heard of anyone inducted into the Baseball Hall of Fame because he was lucky.

Superstitions aside, consistent and repeated thoughts and behaviors are the elements of effective mental preparation. Learning and saying and doing the right things again and again will lead to the confidence that will bring the desired performance in competition.

Bill Curry, head football coach at Kentucky, identifies mental preparation as "repetition, faith, and expectancy."

Says University of Indiana basketball coach Bobby Knight, "Don't go out there thinking you're ready to play. Go out there *knowing* you're ready."

Knowing You're Ready

The most compelling part of Wade Boggs' extensive preparation relates to timing. We've noted his regularity, how he felt "out of sync" if he woke up late. The same was true if he went to sleep at irregular times. Flying from coast to coast can put us "out of sync." Most of us have had the feeling. Our "internal clock" was affected. People who work night shifts have had their internal clocks adjust to their routine. A "clock" that works regularly makes life easier for all of us. It allows an athlete, particularly, to ready himself for competition in a consistent way, as individual as that way may be.

Actual clocks and internal clocks count outstanding athletes down to competition time. Everything Boggs does, from the time he goes to sleep until the time he puts his cap back on after the national anthem, has become part of his focus on performance. His behaviors lead, step-by-consistent-step, to his at-bats and his positioning himself at third base. It eliminates the psychological gear-stripping experienced by so many players who, at game time, have to kick their energy into high from a dead-stop. For most players, this kind of readying process is unnatural and ineffective. The body needs a regular warm-up to ready itself. So does the mind. Its warm-up must start well before the body's.

The control people seek in their lives comes from the internal world. In a player's case, if his existence is helter-skelter and his preparation haphazard, he allows the external environment to control him. He does things as he's bombarded with the desire, need, or obligation to do them. Preparation in athletics is the *act of control* —controlling behavior and environment, in order to be ready to attain a goal.

The specific readying process includes a number of considerations:

> *Time*: The internal clocks of starting pitchers, relievers, and position players move at different rates of speed. But no one makes a real clock move faster or slower. So every player creates his own schedule: between starts, between appearances, between games, whatever. Everyone knows how much time remains before the game will be played. Each player fills that time differently. Filling it with comfortable, consistent, purposeful behaviors is the key to readying through time. All of the activities that follow fill time.

> *Sleeping*: The time a player wakes up is as important as the time he goes to sleep, perhaps more important. The conscious countdown to competition begins when a player awakens. Therefore, any consistent program of preparation should include a reliable schedule. In other words, a player who wakes up at different times each day will, by necessity, alter his activities and therefore be inconsistent.

> *Eating*: Eating or snacking before competition is unwise, regardless of the fact that many do just that. The "many" do not justify the behavior. They don't change physiological truths, either. It's best to complete a meal the same number of hours before a game—daily. Regularly.

> *Traveling*: Whether he rides a school bus or a chartered

plane, the player doesn't control the schedule for games played away from the home field. He does control his promptness and what he chooses to do en route. Length of trips vary; the player's activity during the trip doesn't have to.

Arrival time for home games is controllable by the players. Late arrivals mean rushed routines. Effective readying doesn't include a pressured approach.

Dressing: For baseball players, dressing has become a ritual, whether it's conscious or unconscious. By high school a player has dressed so many times during school season and summer leagues, he has probably created his own way of putting on the uniform, ordered and comfortable for him. It should be a very important part of his preparation. Everyone has to do it. So it should be used by the player as a means of creating a consistent, relaxed internal atmosphere.

Readying Place: Usually a player's place in front of his locker is the most convenient and sensible place for getting emotionally and mentally ready for the game. Some players like to move around—to use "nervous energy." Others like to still themselves. Whatever the preference, a player should find the place that suits him best and use it in his program.

Socializing/Isolating: Each player comes to know if he prefers solitude or society when readying himself for a game. Perhaps, he enjoys or needs the company of others until a specific time, at which time he draws inward. Again, it's a matter of individual preference, but it's an important preference to establish. Certainly, at some time, the player has to direct his mental focus to the upcoming event, which means he has to detach himself from the company of others at that time. Many players find it easier just to have an extended time alone. A consistent schedule is once again essential. (Yaz even isolated himself for a period after each game. He sat, staring into his locker, thinking his thoughts. No one interrupted those thoughts.)

The higher the level, the greater the distractions. Visitors, media, and fans can become intrusive. It's up to a player to establish the ground rules for these people. The player who allows someone to interfere with his readying process loses control of the process and himself. It comes back to whether the player is working to meet his own goals or the expectations of others.

Warming Up, Physically and Mentally: Warmups should also be regulated. There is a time to prepare the body and a time to prepare the mind. Both need stretching. The readying place is usually a good one for going over mental strategies and getting emotions to their familiar arousal level. Boggs prefers the outfield; Clemente came to the park very early and stretched out on the trainer's table. (He did *not* sleep.) Consistent behavior at a regular time is the key.

This type of preparation helps the player to develop a program of consistent behavior, in which he can have a feeling of confidence and, as Andy Allenson put it, "a sense of purpose." Behavior becomes automatic. This is just how the player wants to approach his at-bats or pitching: with a muscle-memory that allows performance to happen without the interferences of confused, irrational, self-conscious, or fearful thinking. The player has prepared so well, so intensely, that, ideally, he responds to each situation in competition in the same manner he approached it in practice.

San Diego Padres outfielder Tony Gwynn said of his preparation, "I've been doing it so long, I *can't* stop . . ." That is a man with an ingrained habit speaking. In his case, a good habit. Isn't that what every player should want to develop?

"Big Games"

Every player feels the difference in stimulation before a "big game," but every effective player has prepared for it as he had for every other game. In other words, he continues to exert *self-discipline*, thereby maintaining *consistency*, thereby building *self-confidence*.

Every game is played the same way, so every game should be approached the same way. *Preparation should not vary greatly.* If field conditions change, that change is integrated into the preparation. Great players make necessary adjustments, not drastic changes. Change is made because of physical, environmental, or situational conditions. Emotional changes should not trigger a change in approach. The sameness of preparation will help to control and stabilize the nervousness and "butterflies" that precede a particularly important game or series.

Excitement or nervousness levels do normally increase before "big games." That's the excitement of competition. That's what all the preparation is for. That's the challenge—the opportunity to feel the joy of playing a great game against worthy opponents. The opportunity to be the "gamer,"—the "winner." All those feelings should be enjoyed. But the greatest joy for an athlete is the joy of competition itself.

The best know they are always ready. Regardless of the significance of the game, they are prepared to perform in the same manner they've prepared themselves: with *dedication, purpose, consistency,* and *confidence.* They've been doing it so long, they won't be able to stop.

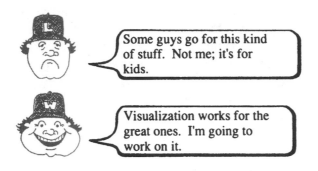

Some guys go for this kind of stuff. Not me; it's for kids.

Visualization works for the great ones. I'm going to work on it.

10
VISUALIZATION
Practice and Play on the Mind's Field

The reference may be to "visualization," or "mental rehearsal," or "imagery," or "mental practice," depending upon who is discussing it. The process, as we discuss it, refers to the ability to recall information in physical forms and images, instead of words. And the process begins in the imagination, which Barbara Brown, author of the book *Supermind,* considers to be "the ultimate energy." We enthusiastically agree.

One of the most effective ways for a player to prepare is to realize and activate his imagination, so he can develop effective visualization techniques. Most athletes vividly imagined when they were children. Baseball is, essentially, "a kid's game," but somewhere during the years of growing up many players lost their imagination. Many still think that imagining is for kids.

National League MVP (1988) Kirk Gibson doesn't. He employed mental rehearsal techniques before his now historic game-winning home run in the first game of the '88 World Series. We already spoke of Willie Stargell's technique. Such behaviors are part of an on-going preparation.

For example, after a poor at-bat, the player reviews what he did and what he wants to do next time he comes to the plate. The player then "sees" himself making that adjustment in his mind's eye. He's *visualizing;* he's preparing for his next at-bat.

A great advantage of visualization is that it can be used away from the baseball field. In a way, your mind becomes the practice field. That field is always accessible. Someone can always be there to throw b.p., or catch, or hit the ball to you on defense.

Actually, researchers have found that in many instances mental practice is more useful than physical practice. Our recommendation is that both are required at the ball park and that mental practice, exclusively, should take place wherever and whenever it's appropriate for the player. (New York Yankees first baseman Don Mattingly uses visualization techniques while he shaves.) But it should take place!

During the 1986 season, relief pitcher Doug Corbett made four consecutive appearances for the California Angels, in which he earned four saves and held the opposition scoreless in his 12⅔ innings. He gave credit to sports psychologist Ken Ravizza, who had been working with the Angels pitching staff.

Corbett, who spent time on the disabled list during each of the previous three seasons, said, "In the past I pitched five minutes on the side every day to stay sharp. Now I can do that pitching in my mind and save the wear and tear . . ."

Many players in the past incorporated visualization techniques into their preparation. Whether through instinct or trial-and-error, they had developed the skill to the point that it became a big factor in their successes.

Listen to these "old timers," whose pre-game and game plans called for visualization long before the advent of sports psychologists.

Carl Yastrzemski:

"The night before a game, I visualize the pitcher and the pitches I'm going to see the next day. I hit the ball right on the button and know what it's going to feel like. I hit the pitches where I want to. I keep some bats at home. If I want a stronger picture, I pick one up and do some hitting in the living room.

"If there is anything I want to work on mechanically, I go to the park at about 2:30 and take some extra hitting. Once the regular hitting starts, I never think about anything but seeing the ball.

"When the game starts, I see every pitch, from the release point to the catcher's glove. I want to see the movement and speed. I don't like surprises. I never think about mechanics, only seeing the ball.

"I anticipate by seeing [visualizing] what I want to see."

Duke Snider:

"I did my preparation in the afternoon. I liked to lay down for an hour before I went to the park. That's when I went over the pitchers in my mind. We didn't call it visualizing then, but I sure used my imagination."

Reggie Jackson:

"When I want to turn it on, I have a routine I go through. I get away from the plate. I stretch, control my breathing, and slow up my heart rate. I slow up.

"I start toward the plate, and I imagine myself putting the 'sweet spot' in the hitting area just as the ball is getting there. I see a line drive going to center field. It's important to me to see myself putting that bat there and not swinging it. When I visualize, I feel my approach and the contact.

"I remind myself to see the release and the spin on the ball. Then, I 'see it' the way I'm going to see it.

"I don't want to try too hard or tense up. As I step into the batter's box, I mumble [talks under his breath], 'All right, Reggie, just let it happen, just let it flow...Now, let it happen.'

"Then, I am quiet."

George Brett:

"When I'm going good, in the on-deck circle I can see myself hitting line drives all over the ball park. The ball looks like a volleyball."

It's interesting that Brett qualified the successful use of his visualization technique with, "when I'm going good." The question of cause and effect arises. Must a player be playing well *before* the visualization becomes effective? Or does his performance improve, in part, as a result of visualization?

We believe in the latter. We believe that visualization should always be a part of preparation. When things are going bad, some players' routines break down. In a sense, that is giving in, losing confidence. It is allowing an important ingredient for confidence to slip away. Just "seeing" oneself being successful can and does help.

One of the reasons players forget to visualize or don't do so at all (assuming they're familiar with the technique) is that they think they are no good at it. Most people are much better at visualization than they believe themselves to be. We've heard many players say they "just can't seem to do it," without actually having tried. Some, very obviously, didn't know the first thing about how to go about visualizing. They said they couldn't close their eyes and see themselves performing clearly, so they knew they were "brutal" when it came to visualizing. They wanted to; they "just couldn't."

These players seemed to think that they should "hallucinate" visual pictures. Few of us do that. Most of us first recall the pictures in a general shape, passing through the mind quickly. We do not necessarily see the ball in every detail. We do perceive it vividly enough to allow us to see ourselves doing what we want to do in a successful way. Through that image, we've told our bodies what we wanted it to do, how we wanted it to respond. We have prepared it, minimally. Programmed it, maximally.

Visualization programs the nervous system, muscles, and fibers of the body. The clearer the image—the more detail—the greater the effect on the body. Imagination can trigger nerve and muscle response. Do you recall your heart beating in joyous anticipation of an event such as Christmas or a birthday, when you were a child? Did you ever have "the dreads"—accompanied by sweaty palms or whatever? Your heart, breath, nerves, and muscles all got the message from the internal picture you had drawn and sent to your nervous system. You had visualized, without even trying.

Any time we get together with old friends, we draw forth, in a random, free-wheeling way, experiences we shared long ago. We clearly bring out the rather detailed images of those times and activities. We visualize without even trying, often without even being aware.

The most effective visualization will result for those who do try to create specific and detailed images. The baseball player surely has enough specific experience to do just that. He knows what he wants his body to do.

He should understand by now that his mind can give guidance to his muscles. For an athlete, appropriate guidance greatly increases the chances for successful performance.

Have you ever imagined something so vividly you thought it really happened? Well, the more real the experience—the mental practice—the more effective the performance will be. To have it be that real, a player has to visualize as a participant, not as a spectator.

When visualizing this way (subjective visualization), you are performing. Your emotions are included in the experience. Visualize performing in some pressure situations. Feel the approach and contact the tension level. Hear any sounds associated with the performance. (Not crowd noise.) See things from the eyes as they will be seen during the actual performance. Don't rush it; make the timing true to life.

Direct the intentions (with self-talk). For example:

Hitter:
"I am going to hit the ball on the ground between the first and second baseman."

Pitcher:
"I am going to throw this fastball low and away."

Outfielder:
"I am going to hit the cutoff man when the ball comes to me."

Infielder:
"I am going to see the ball all the way into my glove."

Baserunner:
"I am going to watch the pitcher's shoulder and go when it turns in."

Early in the 1983 season, the Oakland Athletics were visiting Fenway Park in Boston. In the second game of the series, before his last at-bat of the game, Boston's Wade Boggs saw A's centerfielder

Dwayne Murphy playing particularly shallow. Boggs stepped out of the batter's box and visualized himself hitting the ball over Murphy's head. Two pitches later, Boggs hit his first home run of the season, a line drive into the bleachers in left center, over Murphy. Boggs told about the experience the next day, prior to game time.

"What," he was asked, "will you do if you see Murphy in the same place before your first at-bat today?"

"I'll do the same thing," Boggs responded. "I'll see myself hitting a line drive over his head. And I'll wait for a pitch I can do it on."

Murphy was still shallow. Boggs swung at the third pitch thrown to him. The result: a line drive over the centerfielder's head for a double. Murphy played deeper during Boggs' subsequent at-bats.

Whether used before, during, or after competition, visualization is a formidable tool for a player. Athletes in all fields of sport have discovered its great value: Chris Evert, Dwight Stones, Olympic steeplechaser John Gregoreck, half of the world-class gymnasts—and the number is growing. Robert Nideffer, in his book *The Inner Athlete,* notes that the late Pete Maravich would replay the entire basketball game in which he had participated. Nicklaus plays every shot in advance of his real swing. Tennis players, wrestlers, runners, every athlete who trains to win, wins first in his "mind's eye."

Amad Rashad, many times an NFL All-Pro pass catcher while playing for the Minnesota Vikings, said, "My imagination was the key to my success. I got ready for a game by imagining every possible move a defender might use to try and stop me. I even gave them moves they didn't have. My imagination is stronger now than when I was growing up. I developed it. It was a tool."

Charles Garfield's article, "Peak Performers," appeared in the February 1986 issue of *Success.* In the article, Garfield wrote:

> An experience that happened to me several years ago illustrates the powerful potential of mental rehearsal. I met a group of scientists from East Germany, Bulgaria, and the Soviet Union who had been studying optimal achievement for more than 30 years. To test their theory that performance can be improved—deliberately, systematically, predictably—I agreed to lift some weights.
>
> In times past I had developed my strength to world-

class levels, once bench-pressing 435 pounds, but it had been more than seven years since my last serious training. (In bench-pressing, you lie on your back and lift the weights straight up.) At the time of the experiment I seldom lifted more than 280 pounds. "How long," they asked, "should it take you to get into shape to lift 365 pounds?" I told them it would take nine to 12 months of serious training. When they asked what the absolute maximum weight was that I would be willing to try, I said 300, although I felt sure I could not lift it. The scientists hooked me up to various measuring devices—EEG, ECG, and EMG— and asked me to begin. To my surprise, I did, after several warm-ups, lift the 300 pounds.

Then we went on to the next step. They added 65 pounds to the 300 I had barely pushed off my chest earlier. Any weight-lifter knows that you increase the weight in small increments, not 21 percent at once. But these scientists wanted me to try. They guided me into a deep state of relaxation. Then they talked me through a series of mental preparations. In my mind's eye, I saw myself approaching the bench. I visualized myself lying down. I visualized myself, with total confidence, lifting the 365 pounds. I imagined the metal bar as I wrapped my hands around it. I felt a surge of strength filling my body . . .

Suddenly, I became apprehensive, but the scientists talked me through more relaxation, more visualization. All the while they checked the monitors. At length, everything began to come together for me, just as it does an instant before you know you are going to succeed in some task for which you have been preparing. In my mind, I became convinced I could do it. The world around me seemed to fade. I lifted the weight!

This most impressive experience is meant to convince those who are uncertain about the potential of visualization. But what of those who only doubt themselves and their own visualization skill? Or those who have never known how to make a first attempt? Our aim is to convince everyone that the skill can be learned and developed.

Mental rehearsal initiates concentration, which is what every player values in competition. But the many players we referred to in the preceding chapter—the ones who "just go through the physical motions" when they practice—are not concentrating. Theirs is hardly "perfect practice." Rather, their approach to practice increases the likelihood that they'll repeat any mistake their body makes. The wrong movement, unattended to and therefore uncorrected, is left in the body's program. The error is likely to be habituated. Errors cannot be corrected on the playing field or in the mind unless a player is willing to exert the mental energy essential for concentration.

Visualization requires concentration. We *cannot* just go through the motions. If we do, we lose whatever image we've created. Sustaining concentration is difficult. That is why so many people say they can't visualize. In reality they won't—or don't know how to—expend the effort necessary to make visualization work. Remember, Garfield, a highly respected sports psychologist well versed in visualization techniques, still had to be guided through it by the scientists. It is not easy, but the player whose goal is to reach his physical potential doesn't look for the easy way, physically or mentally. He does look for the most effective way.

Let's look for that way through visualization. Let's imagine three baseballs are resting on a table before us. From left to right, the balls are colored Dodger blue, Cardinal red, Oakland green. Blue, red, green. Left to right: blue, red, green.

Now with our right hand, we pick up the Dodger blue ball that is on the left and place it back on the table so that it's now at the right. We visualize the new order: red, green, blue. There they are in our mind's eye now: red, green, blue. We've watched our hand move that Dodger blue ball. If it wasn't clear to us, we'll do it again. There—done. One more time. See the balls in their original order, from left to right: blue, red, green. We see our hand pick up the blue baseball. We see it place that ball to the right of the others. We see the new right-to-left order: red, green, blue.

We have visualized.

We used a number of memory senses. We "saw" the baseballs on the table; we "sensed" their colors, (some of us saw color more vividly than others, but all of us "sensed" color); we "verbalized" (self-talked) the colors as we "saw" them, thereby identifying them—even associating them with the team uniforms, if we're familiar with them; we used "muscle memory" to pick up the baseball, feel its cover, the seams. And then we "know the movement" of our hand as it goes toward the right and places the ball back on the table.

Visualization, then, is more than just the use of mental pictures. We suggested earlier that the player feel and hear as he mentally rehearses. In doing so, he uses a variety of thought forms which merge and then provide an internal simulation of the performance.

Karl Albrecht, in his book, *Brain Power,* discusses visualization as it includes, "All non-verbal thought forms that (the) brain organizes into a spatial pattern, not just a mental picture." What follows is the enabling process:

> . . . As you perceive some physical situation for the first time, your eyes feed their retinal images to your brain, with their aspects of shape, brightness, color, motion, and so on. Your ears feed in whatever they receive at the moment, your nose provides olfactory inputs, your skin and other tactile sensors send their data, and even the taste information from your mouth goes to the brain. In addition to these well-known sense inputs, your whole-body kinesthetic sensation — your "feelings" if you like to simplify the term — goes to your brain. The current status of your feeling response as well as the details of the sensory data form a complete "package" of data, which your brain receives and puts together in a whole pattern. *If the scene you are perceiving has a high level of personal meaning for you, then you will tend to imprint it more intensively and later you will be able to recall many of the features of the situation . . .*

We italicized the preceding sentence to emphasize the fact that highly motivated baseball players: A) are not "perceiving the scene for the first time," and B) certainly do give their performance "a high level of personal meaning." Both of the above factors lead us to believe that these players are therefore capable of developing strong visualization skills.

Research shows that anyone can improve these skills by being more conscious of them and more attentive to them, and by employing them in one's daily routines, whatever they may be.

A baseball player should set aside the time and include that time in his regular preparation schedule. A minimum of 10 to 15 minutes a day of mental baseball practice should be a requirement for those who visualize effectively. The beginner should probably spend a bit more time.

A number of simple practice techniques can be employed by those who wish to improve their skill. The first is the most obvious: become a more careful observer. (We have, in the past, recommended this to players to improve their concentration, as well. Many of these recommendations will serve both visualization and concentration.) Do more than notice the elements of your environment. Look and then *see*.

> *Observe* everything in and of your bedroom. See it the way an architect would; see it the way a detective would; a foreign visitor. Away from your room, days later, re-create it. *See* the spatial relationships of the furniture, the windows, the door; *see* the colors and designs on the bedcover; *feel* its texture; *smell* the fragrances—wood, a kitchen smell wafting by, a plant. Study and visualize any room or place you choose.

> *Practice* the exercise mentioned with the colored base-balls. Change their order: take the red one from the middle; move the green one from the right to take its place; put the red one in that spot. The next day, add a fourth ball. A white one. *See* the name of the company that manufactured it before you put it in place. *See* the order of the colors. Put them in a new order every day, placing them on the table one at a time, when you begin the practice, rather than having them already appearing on the table.

> *Invent* a vacation spot: a beach, a ranch; a ski mountain. *Feel* the sun and *hear* the tide come and go; *feel* and *smell* the horse under you; *see,* through your goggles, the snow flying past you. *Hear* the cold wind and *feel* it sting your face. Be as inventive as you can.

> *Imagine* a paper bag with some "unknown" in it. Pull it out. Perhaps it will be a peach, or an eraser, or a piece

of velvet. "Discover" it. *Feel* and *taste* the peach. *Feel* the texture and shape of the eraser. The velvet *feels* smooth, right? Does it *smell* of perfume? That's up to your mind's nose. Draw out a number of such objects. Focus on as many senses as possible.

Those exercises are good starters. Whether visualization has always come easy to you, or whether you are now developing and improving your skill, you're ready to work with visualizing baseball.

Improve an aspect of your game. Get your baseball self onto that field. Start working on the part of your game that least satisfies you. (Frustrates you?) That's the skill you're going to work on today — now.

Put yourself in the batter's box, or in the field, or on the mound. Get out there aggressively, confidently. Start the practice session. *See* and *feel* yourself performing just the way you wish to. Do it again — and again. Keep your attention directed to this practice as you would want to keep your attention during the real practice.

You're improving. You're getting it right. It wasn't quite right? Fix it. Focus on the part that wasn't executed the way you'd like it to be. Just do that. Hit to the opposite field. Stay on the balls of your feet at second base. React and dive more effectively at third. Get better jumps in the outfield. Keep the breaking ball down. Do it again — and again. Run that play over. Get it just right. See it. Feel the ground on the proper dive to the left. Jump right up; set your feet; make that throw — He's out!

The sooner you can get to the real field now, the better. Visualize before you take your position. Then go to it. You may still have trouble getting it the way you want it. Patience. More mental rehearsal. More physical practice. More visualization.

You're preparing for success: dedication, determination — imagination.

View yourself "doing your thing" — the physical part of the game that is your strength. Be a scout, a coach,

Mental replays of effective performance.

a manager watching your every move at bat, in the field, on the mound or base paths. See exactly how you take that smooth swing—how you push off the mound with force—how you explode toward second base. *Feel* the rhythm and force. That guy is awesome! Watch him do it again. He gets better every time. He's worth seeing often. Go see him. In this exercise, you're a spectator. This is called *objective visualization.*

To be fond of practice is to be near success. It's easy to be fond of this type of practice because it's as relaxing as it is rewarding. At least it should be. And, as we've said, there is no physical restriction. A player can visualize whenever he wishes. Nevertheless, a regular time should be set for visualization within the player's preparation schedule.

Finally, it's important for the player to establish and set the proper conditions for visualization:

> Find a spot that is private and quiet. One in which you won't be disturbed by others and in which you are not likely to distract yourself.

> Be certain you bring yourself to this setting in a relaxed condition: your mind, body, and spirit. If you're not just that when you arrive there, spend some time calming yourself before attempting to begin your visualization.

> Whenever conflicting or intrusive thoughts interfere with the activity, stop visualizing. Deal with the interfering thoughts, rather than trying to block them out. Having done so successfully, begin again the visualization process. If the interference continues after a number of restarts, end the session, and try to resolve the matter of those thoughts by the next scheduled time for visualization.

Mental involvement is essential as the player practices and performs physically. Visualization allows the player to devote his mental powers entirely, without the demands or distractions of the playing or practice environment. He creates his own ideal environment.

The player can also ready himself for every possible circumstance he'll meet on the field. He can think, see, and feel his way through these circumstances so that if and when he meets them in competition, he'll know he has already confronted them — experienced them — handled them.

The player may very well feel the real experience as a *déjà vu*. He'll know what must be done; he'll have the confidence to do it. After all, he's done it before. Over and over. Successfully.

His preparation has been complete.

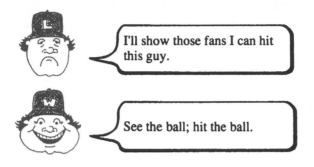

I'll show those fans I can hit this guy.

See the ball; hit the ball.

11
CONCENTRATION
The Control of Attention

According to Ralph Waldo Emerson, concentration "is the secret to success in politics, in war, in trade; in short, in all the management of human affairs."

According to our view, concentration is firmly linked to everything we've already said about the very human affair of playing baseball. It is the largest connecting link in the chain of behaviors that attaches the ballplayer to his performance. *Outstanding performance requires outstanding concentration.*

According to most sports psychology sources, concentration is defined as the skill of focusing one's attention on the function or task at hand. In baseball, the focus is a target: a ball, a spot to throw to, a movement, a key.

To fully concentrate is to truly concentrate. Anything less than complete concentration indicates a disturbance or distraction. An interference, whether it originates externally or internally, is irrelevant to what the player is trying to do on the field, and thus it keeps him from playing as well as he can. It's common for a player, while preparing to perform or actually performing (during a wind-up, while a pitch is being thrown, a ball batted, etc.), to have several thoughts fighting for center stage, in the spotlight of the mind. The conflict creates divided attention.

According to Cal Ripken, Jr., of the Baltimore Orioles, "The most difficult aspect of baseball is concentration. Being able to put everything out of your mind while standing at the plate is not easy."

According to the many major league and minor league players who have spoken with us over the years, concentration is easiest when confidence is greatest. (Of course, we believe that confidence is greatest when preparation is most complete. And so on down the links — back through the chapters of this book.) Both directly and indirectly, the players indicated that when things are going well for them, they concentrate well.

Our great concern with this truth is that many players we spoke with also indicated that they either try to force things to happen or they wait and/or hope for things to go well. In one case, they lose their sense of focus. In the other, they lose their sense of control. In either, they lose their concentration. We'll deal with these problems and their solutions later in the chapter.

First, a few words from players:

George Brett:
"When I'm going good, I'm simply unconscious."

Gary Carter:
"When I'm on a streak, I'm confident and seeing the ball like it's a grapefruit, I could stand on my head and hit. When a player's going bad, he thinks too much and gets himself out."

Bruce Hurst:
"When I'm pitching well, my concentration gets better. I remember a game I pitched earlier in the season (1983) against Britt Burns and the White Sox. I knew I'd have to bear down, because he'd be tough. I hadn't given up a run after four innings, and I told myself they weren't going to get another hit off me. My concentration got even better in the seventh, eighth, and ninth," (Hurst gained a shutout victory.)

Robin Yount (He was playing shortstop for the Milwaukee Brewers at the time):

"There's no doubt that if I make a couple of errors, I lose some of my confidence. And when that happens, I don't concentrate as well — until I get control of myself again."

Dale Murphy:

"When you're hitting well, you're not really thinking too much. With any athlete, you can't force things and can't calculate things . . . When you don't hit good, it's usually because you're thinking too much about everything else except that ball. And when you're hitting good, you're not really thinking about anything. You're able to concentrate — I don't know — you don't even have to concentrate. You're not trying to concentrate. You don't have to work at it. It's kind of weird."

The "weirdness" Murphy senses is based on the simple, paradoxical truth that players can't be effective when they concentrate on concentrating. *The complete focus of attention should be effortless.* It should flow like a graceful physical movement, like a gliding bird. Concentration isn't thought about; it's just there.

The players quoted above give evidence to the fact that "going good" produces that effortlessness. When a player is not "going good," he starts to press, to analyze his mechanics. It's said that "analysis leads to paralysis." Confidence slips away; the player's attention to the ball or to the catcher's target is interfered with by his feelings of uncertainty, by sounds of booing, and so on. His sight is then affected. His focus is diffused. Too many conflicting senses are vying for his attention. His senses are in control of him.

The player tells himself to concentrate — or is commanded to do so by a coach or manager. He doesn't get any positive result. In fact, the harder he tries, the poorer he plays. His preoccupation with the demand/command has intensified the distraction.

What the player must do is focus, not force, his attention on his immediate function, exclusively, to the very moment — the very target. Last inning's error or the last bad at-bat increases the likelihood of the next error or the next poor at-bat, if it's dragged from the past into the present. The player who's "going good" has a clear mind, a loose body, and a positive anticipation of performance. As Reggie said, he "just let it flow." A player who's going bad is worried and tight—and tries to force everything to happen. In these cases, "going bad" becomes "going worse." —

That is why concentration seems just to be there when all is well, and can't seem to be found during bad times. Concentration can be found hiding behind control: controlled thoughts; controlled focus; controlled self.

Concentration is a skill and can therefore be learned. It may be true that some players naturally seem more able to concentrate more effectively than others. But any player can train himself, through practice, to enhance his ability to control himself, to gently keep himself from being distracted by irrelevant thoughts and signals; to attend to the task at hand.

Note that we stress the task, the performance, not the person or the personal. *The ego must get out of the body's way.* The ego, we've found, is the number one nemesis of the player's mind and body. It is a formidable adversary.

In the introduction to his book *Zen in the Art of Archery,* D.T. Suzuki writes of the archer who "ceases to be conscious of himself as the one who is engaged in hitting the bull's-eye which confronts him."

A player who allows his ego to swing the bat or throw the ball is surely a distracted player. Most often he's also a tentative player or an angry one. The resultant frustration or anxiety—or both— have stripped him of his confidence. As sports psychologist Bruce Ogilvie determined years ago, self-doubt is "the main interference in performance."

A player may know all the right approaches to performance, yet too often he lets himself be controlled by what he feels—a Little League parent; a high school coach; a girlfriend at an American Legion game; a scout; a minor leaguer's own deep desire to become a major leaguer; the disappointed, booing fans at major league stadiums. All of these can dramatically affect the ego, can cause self-doubt in the player and prevent or ruin his concentration. While Gary Carter was hearing the crowd chanting his .195 batting average in 1983, his play suffered—as he did. The fan—and teammate— support in New York helped Carter bring a different "person" to the plate, or one with a different level of concentration, at least.

We made an early reference to Mike Schmidt's sensitivity to the booing he received in Philadelphia. When Schmidt reached the age of 37, after he had led the National League in home runs eight times, in runs-batted-in five times, and had won the MVP three times, the booing diminished greatly. Not entirely. But Schmidt's acknowledged strong will — his *mental discipline* — had helped him overcome the interferences caused by his feelings of reaction toward the fans' view of him.

Darryl Strawberry is a classic and more recent example of what we consider to be this most important interference to a player's concentration.

An earlier chapter forecast the problem Strawberry would have because of fan expectation. Late in August 1986 (his fourth year in New York), Strawberry's problem became most apparent. Wrote George Vecsey in the September 1 edition of *The New York Times*: "There have always been a few fans eager to let Strawberry have it when he watched a called third strike, but the boos on Saturday were surprising . . .

"The boos began Saturday when Strawberry struck out with a runner on base in the third inning and intensified when he flied out with the bases loaded in the fourth. They got worse in the sixth when he was called out on strikes but they reached their peak when Bill Matlock's hard single bounced right past him, in the late afternoon glare."

Did the glare interfere with Strawberry's concentration on a bouncing ball as much as the events of the day — and the feelings they triggered in the player? We ask that question rhetorically.

Said Strawberry after the game, "Maybe it's time to be somewhere else, if I'm not wanted . . ."

The Mets had a 19-game lead at the time. A few weeks later, Strawberry's feelings were bruised again when a Mets rookie, making his first appearance in the big leagues, was grandly applauded and cheered as he came to bat for the first time. Strawberry remarked bitterly that he had worked hard for four years in New York and was booed, and this "unknown guy" was given enthusiastic support. It isn't hard to guess the depths of this young man's hurt.

To what extent is a player's concentration affected when he plays regularly in front of people who make him feel rejected and disapproved of? That, too, should be easy to guess. In case it isn't that easy, be advised that Strawberry was 0 for 47 in Shea Stadium from July 29 to September 7.

During the '86 World Series, Mets first baseman Keith Hernandez, talking to Roger Angell of *New Yorker* magazine, said:

> Baseball is a constant learning experience. Nothing happens very quickly for most hitters, and you have to remind yourself that Darryl is still only twenty-four years old. He's played four years in the majors, but he's still a baby. It isn't often that a Gehrig or a Mattingly comes along, who can do it all at the plate right away. (Mattingly, by the way, says he's proudest of the fact that, because of a strong work ethic, he has "gotten better" since coming to the majors.)
>
> When I first came up, the Matlocks and Koosmans and Carltons of this league — all those lefthanders — gave me fits. Jim Rooker just killed me at the plate. You have to be patient and try to learn to adjust, and Daryl is still learning.

Adjustments at the plate are essential to effective hitting. Adjustments in the mind are essential to effective thinking — whether the thoughts are directed at hitting or any other element of the game. Apparently, the ego needs adjusting most: a down-toning, a lowering of the distraction level.

Family problems, financial matters, and other personal concerns also distract players. These concerns do not disappear of their own volition. The player must handle them. Responsibilities present themselves on and off a baseball field. The more effective the person/player is in controlling the many facets of his personal life, the more likely he is to be effective on the playing field, to be able to concentrate on the game as it's being played.

Internal control is always possible; external control is not. Concentration comes easier to the player who distinguishes the difference — and who acts upon that understanding. Concentration comes to the player who will first focus on his inner state and then do whatever is necessary to control his mental activity. He then is able to be sensitive to attentional cues that will direct his focus. These cues should:

Focus on the positive, not the negative.
Focus on the present, not the past.
Focus on the process/execution, not the result — or win-
   ing the approval of others.
Focus on the target! (Ball, glove, key).

Concentration comes to the player who knows what he's looking for and what he'll be looking at: the ball or the target, not the image of self.

Attention

The player knows where he wants to focus his attention before he performs. And why. Focusing on the specific task and target will allow him to "let go of the effort." The more specific he can be, the sharper the focus can be. (For example, attention to the spin of the ball is a more specific focus than just the ball.)

When the player's attention wanders, he has not so much lost his concentration as he has lost the *object* of his concentration. The object of his thought is something other than what he had intended. His distraction is really an attraction elsewhere. It becomes a *dis-*traction because it isn't what he really should be attending to at that time.

We can't be distracted without our own complicity. When we try to make ourselves pay attention, we devote energy to the task of fighting distracting thoughts. By doing this, we've contributed to our own inability to concentrate. In the process, we often don't realize we've lost concentration, because the intensity of our think-ing is high. But our thought — our attention — is inappropriate. We have turned away from our real task.

A player who can't sustain appropriate attention will not be con-sistent. Outstanding players are consistent players. Near the end of the 1984 season, former Houston and Cincinnati great, Joe Morgan, was asked if he would play again in 1985. The diminutive (5'7") second baseman, then playing for the Oakland Athletics, replied, "I've been an exception. I've been able to play 20 years (in the major leagues). And although I'm not big and strong, I have a quickness with the bat that generates a lot of power to right field. I've only hit one home run in my career that went to the left of second base . . .

Reprinted by permission of United Feature Syndicate, Inc.

My bat speed hasn't slowed, but I don't concentrate the way I should over a long period."

Morgan retired at the end of the season.

In 1983, Jayson Stark wrote of Steve Carlton in *The Sporting News*. "We are talking about a man who, more than anyone else in baseball, wins ball games through the sheer positive power of his mind." Stark was speaking to Tim McCarver, who had caught almost all of Carlton's games when the two had been teammates in St. Louis and Philadelphia, and noted that Carlton considered hitters to be "mere incidentals" when he was pitching. It did not matter who was at the plate. "There is only himself and the catcher and the plate," wrote Stark.

McCarver told of Carlton's concentration enhancement. "The nights he pitches, he'll come in after batting practice, lie down on the training table, and close his eyes. A lot of people think he's sleeping (as they did Clemente!). But what he's thinking about are lanes in the strike zone.

"He thinks outer lane and inner lane," said McCarver. He doesn't ever think about anything over the middle of the plate. And by not thinking about it, he gets himself working that way."

There are any number of things about which Carlton *was not* thinking. The key to his—or anyone's—concentration is about what he *is* thinking.

Attention is given to the inner and outer lanes. The middle of the plate, menacing hitters, screaming fans, or the day's stock market quotations were not attended to because Carlton put such strong focus on what he knew was important to his performance. And, as Stark suggested, he probably did it better than any of his contemporaries.

Pitcher Greg Cadaret is from a newer generation, but his approach is as timeless as Carlton's. When he made his first World Series appearance, in 1988 with the Oakland A's, Cadaret kept his attention where it belonged. "I knew my main job…," Cadaret said. "I didn't think outside the situation. I didn't think it was the World Series, and, 'Oh gosh, this is my first appearance.'" He got the out he was sent in to get.

Outfielder Fred Lynn told columnist Jim Murray of the *Los Angeles Times* that "over 90% of the game is concentration. It's the difference between hitting .298 and .339," Lynn said. "…When I go out to the batter's circle, and all of a sudden I can hear a conversation in the ninth row between a guy and his girlfriend, I know I am not in the game. When I go out in the middle of 50,000 people and all of a sudden it's like I'm alone, I know I am all right."

Fans, family, and friends can all divert a player's attention. So it has been; so it always will be. Fickle fate is also ever-ready to appear—and distract. Baseball can't be played without bad hops, bad calls, bad lights, bad backgrounds, and even bad times. It's as unrealistic to expect perfect conditions—internal or external—as it is to expect perfect performance. So, it's wise for a player to have a plan—be prepared—to prevent or to respond to these distractions.

Though concentration can't be forced, it can, through gentle persuasion, be coaxed. Coaxed to a point where the player's action and attention are one and the same. Identical and complete. Body and mind will work together as gently as they are told to. Some time, some patience, and lots of persistence are needed. *The player should also remember that he is aiming his attention in a desired direction rather than trying to avoid distractions.*

Many understandings escape us in the course of our lives. Many others we eventually capture. We remember, particularly, a frequent befuddlement in the primary grades. A particular teacher, with a very particular approach to her profession and her students, comes to mind. We, her innocent students, did not at all understand her dogged determination to have us listen to her directons with hands clasped in front of us on the desk tops. "Put down that pencil!" she'd bark at anyone brave or mindless enough to violate her edict. It was the bravest among us, Salvatore, who one day became our third-grade Socrates.

"Why?" Salvatore asked Miss Daly, who was an imposing figure in every sense. We all expected the worst, but Salvatore/Socrates wasn't made to drink the cup of hemlock.

Instead, Miss Daly answered his question. Her answer isn't nearly as vivid in the memory as Salvatore's word, but the theme was generally this: "Little kids can't sit still for more than a few minutes, much less pay attention to the teacher for that long. They're curious about everything and easily distracted by anything. Rolling a pencil in the hands stimulates the sense of feel (tactile sense). A little kid will pay immediate attention to that feeling and, as a consequence, no attention to the directions Miss Daly is giving."

There was more, of course, after a pause to allow us to give attention and respect to the looks of astonishment and pride on Salvatore's face.

We were then told about how our senses operate — and how they often conflict and vie for our attention. "It is something you might as well learn early, because it isn't usually learned late," said Miss Daly. Or words to that effect. Miss Daly didn't ever dwell on what we *shouldn't* do, as our previous teachers had. She gave directives, not scoldings. "Do this," not "Stop doing that." We understood later. Much later.

Miss Daly had taught divided attention and selective attention to her young students. She made us aware of our awareness; aware of the different things going on around us and of the different senses to which these goings-on were appealing. She told us that they battled for our senses' attention as we battled with our little brother or sister for the attention of our parents. She told us we had to decide which thing around us was most important to pay attention to. She told us that, in school, at least, she knew we hadn't yet learned how to decide. "Never fear," she told us. "I'll decide." And she always did.

(As great as her apparent powers were, they weren't great enough to control the mind of any student who, with folded hands and seemingly attentive eyes, used the more powerful visualization technique to escape to some exotic place like the ball field, for example.)

Selective Attention vs. Divided Attention

How many times have we read a page in a book, readied ourselves to turn the leaf over — and realized we hadn't paid any attention to the meaning of the words we'd read? Many times. We really did go over those words with our eyes. What were we thinking of as they physically moved across and down the page? The answer: Something that was more important to us at that moment. Thus, our attention was divided.

And how many times have we been reading and had someone talk to us—and have that person "snap us out of inattentiveness" to him or her? Many times. We didn't hear a word that was said. We were riveted to the words on a newspaper page. Our complete attention was given to the words' message and meaning. Perhaps they informed; perhaps they entertained. For whatever reason, they became important; we became engrossed.

Usually, we have to work at achieving that intensity of concentration. A good example is furnished in Murray Chass' comprehensive feature on Yankees first baseman Don Mattingly for *The New York Times Magazine* ("Every Pitcher's Nightmare," April 3, 1988). In the article, former New York third baseman Mike Pagliarulo provides the insight.

"On the first day of practice this spring, Donnie's in the cage and [Yankee outfielder] Claudell Washington is talking. Donnie fouls off a couple balls, and he turns around and says, 'Claudell, would you shut up? I'm trying to get some work in.'"

Chass reported that Pagliarulo was "incredulous . . ." The third baseman went on, "He told him to shut up. Claudell only said two words. It was the first day. That type of intensity is different. It's a very good thing to have."

Lapses in concentration are self-defeating Mattingly told Chass. They cost between 50–100 at-bats a season. It's a challenge "to stay tuned in," said Mattingly. "There are times that you're not; it's impossible to be tuned in for 162 games, but you really have to be ready."

Our presumption is that baseball is important to the people playing the game. Other matters are important in any player's life, of course. But as he plays the game, the player must recognize—always—to what he wants to give his attention. The ability to recognize conflicting and distracting thoughts, to choose the thought to keep, and to give mental energy and focus to that chosen thought are the fundamentals of selective attention. A problem with school work, a problem with someone's feelings, a problem with a relative's health cannot be solved on the playing field. The player has no control over them, and he must recognize that fact as well as recognize the fact of their interference with his ability to concentrate.

It often appears to a player that he *can* be doing something about performing well for a coach, or scout, or for organization "brass." After all, it's *his* performance they're watching. True. But if he's watching them watching him, he is doing the very thing to his performance he would not want to do. That approach, remember, is from the outside-in, rather than from the inside-out. He's lost control. And he has selected for his attention the people watching the performance instead of the performance itself. His awareness of them, and of whatever consequences he knows or invents, become most important. Wrongly so.

He loses the meaning of his presence on the playing field. The folks on the bench or in the stands come to mean more. The player has divided his attention. It's a losing selection he's made.

Another example of divided attention: Ricky Henderson, Tim Raines, and other basestealers often divide a pitcher's attention. The pitcher has two jobs: holding the runner and throwing a pitch. It takes mental ability to shift attention from the runner and suddenly concentrate effectively on the catcher's target. It takes practice and discipline.

Attention Span

At the end of September 1983, Cal Ripken, Jr., who had played every inning of every game that season, commented on the fact that he felt as physically strong as he had early in the season. "But there have been times when it's been tough mentally," said Ripken. "You get tired of thinking and tired of concentrating, and then as you pop up or strike out, you say, 'How did I do that?'"

Over the next ten years since he spoke those words, Ripken has played in every one of his team's games. Like the Energizer bunny, he's "still going."

Even over shorter gaps, few of us have attentional abilities long enough to span the beginning and end of our activity without interruption. Our minds need rest and diversion, and at those times the mind tends to slip away, taking concentration with it. Trying to restrain it—hold on to it—does more harm than good. Rather than do that, we should, when we start to feel it losing its task-to-task focus, give it the short break for which it's asking. We should turn if off.

If an irrelevant thought enters during the break, we should allow that thought to play itself out, rather than force it away. Then, after stretching our back or neck muscles, tightening then relaxing them, we take a deep, long breath, prolong the exhale, and gently bring our attention back on task.

There are ample breaks in action, during which the player can allow the mind its rest. Whether he's looking at the sky or hearing sounds in the environment, the player knows he is only taking the break permitted by the stop in the action. He doesn't demand uninterrupted attention of himself. He knows the appropriate time for attention, as well as the appropriate target for it.

His preparation has taught him that. The player who has established an approach founded on routine has already helped direct his attentional energy. Through repetition in practice and performance, the player has become totally familiar with his external and internal environments. He has already had the feeling — the awareness — of a maximum performance and the attentional energy that went into it, so he knows for what he's aiming. Now he has to learn the skill of consistently taking and maintaining the right aim.

Improving Concentration Skills

The thought that comes to our mind as we write this relates to our frequent amazement when talking with experienced professional players about concentration. They all seem concerned with, and interested in, improving this mental skill. They know that anyone who wishes to improve and develop a skill must practice, but they find mental practice much more difficult than physical practice. Of course, they've been practicing physically since they first played any kind of organized baseball. They've only recently learned about many mental skills.

The truth of the matter is that mental techniques are more complex than physical ones. They therefore require more regular practice. But these practice sessions can be quite short — a few minutes each. DAILY! (Part of the program of preparation, as we've said.)

The exercises suggested in the visualization chapter also serve to help a player improve his concentration. After all, the technique cannot be successful unless the player pays attention to whatever he is visually creating in his mind's eye. On whatever he feels or hears, he focuses. He's attending. So, essentially, the visualization exercises are also concentration exercises.

Use them.

OTHER PRACTICE EXERCISES

*Locate an advertising sign. Minor leaguers and major leaguers have an abundance to choose from at the ball parks. Younger players can find them elsewhere—or use pictures hanging on walls in their home, or magazine ads. (One minor league player, practicing in his rented apartment, could only find a coffee can. He said it served the purpose.)

You've seen that sign, or that picture on the wall many times. *Now really see it.* Notice, for example, the bulb on the electric company's sign in right field. *See* the color of each individual object in the illustration. Count the beads that are visible on the socket's pull chain. How many of them are above the hand pulling the chain? How many below? Is the ad's message in printing or in script? All capital letters? What did the sign painter wish to be the viewer's central focus? Is it for you? Focus on all the other details.

Turn away from the sign. Re-create it. Visualize it. Recall every element of the sign. Turn back to look. How good an observer were you?

How effective was your concentration? Did your mind wander? Did you lose interest? Did other thoughts intrude? Did you allow yourself to be aware of these intrusions—to know that they had pulled your attention from the sign? Did you give them their due, and then gently guide your mind back to its task? *Your* task!?

Repeat the process later in the day, using a different object for your attention. The entire process should not take more than 10 minutes. Of course, the more your mind wanders, the more time will be spent. After a number of days, you'll find your skill will be improving. By the end of the first week, a player should begin to gently restrain his wandering concentration — keeping it on the specific object of focus. No force, but a guiding restraint.

*Find a quiet place. Sit down, relax, close your eyes. Breathe through your mouth at a slow, natural pace. Count to 10, counting both inhalations and exhalations. *Feel* your breathing. *Hear* the count in your mind. Breathe in: one. Breathe out: two . . .

Your goal is to count to 10, eight consecutive times, without interruption. If and when you lose attention to your task, think about what interfered with your concentration. Recognize it; move it away. Begin again. See how close you can get to your goal in an allotted time of five minutes.

See how well you do tomorrow and each succeeding day. Your improvement will not necessarily move on a continuous, upwardly inclined plane. Your attitude, your physical fitness, and the environment will affect you from day to day. But after an extended period of time, you'll notice the improvement, assuming you've been conscientious. And then, you're ready to put a new wrinkle into the exercise. A challenge to your increased skill.

*Find, if you're able, a radio station that plays instrumental music. Classical music — or "easy to listen to music." Do you call that "supermarket music?" (A record or tape is fine, of course.) Play that music as you do the above exercise. The goal is the same, but you've incorporated a potential interference into the routine. The more effective your selective attention skills, the more likely that music will not be heard.

That was easy, you say? Good. After a couple of days or so, put on a favorite tape or station of yours. Find a song, with lyrics, with which you're very familiar. You know the words by heart. Same routine; same goal. Tough exercise. When you hear the lyrics — worse yet, when you hear your mind singing the lyrics — you've strayed from your course.

The song had a stronger pull on your attention than the exercise? You're not Superman. Start again. But be sure to recognize whether your goal now is to work at improving your concentration skills — or whether your selective attention is being directed at that great song on the radio. It's an important distinction and an important exercise. A very difficult one.

*Use the grid below. Sense how effective you are completing the process you're directed to follow. Note the interferences to your attention. After each interruption of concentration, resume from where you left off. After using this grid a couple of times, have a friend or relative make up a new one, scrambling the numbers.

After you've worked with a grid for a while, expect more mental discipline. Every time your concentration is interrupted, start over from the beginning: 00. You can expect a noticeable improvement.

CONCENTRATION EXERCISE GRID

Starting with 00, find numbers in sequence and, using a pencil, draw a diagonal line through each square. Be cer-

08	37	43	19	26	51	06	41	34	10
63	50	03	86	14	76	80	66	22	55
23	73	13	54	40	93	12	85	02	47
94	27	96	99	00	71	90	74	89	62
48	09	84	36	29	78	49	95	82	69
38	98	31	59	87	11	45	67	21	35
33	83	68	97	25	52	57	91	75	30
16	42	20	79	64	04	72	81	15	56
01	70	53	92	46	88	39	65	60	28
32	24	05	61	77	18	07	58	44	17

tain the line is made in the same way in each square. The second time you use this grid, draw a diagonal going the other way across the square. (If you use the grid a third time, you can draw a horizontal line; after that, make up a new grid; you know this one too well.)

There are any number of concentration exercises any interested person can find in books. They range from the use of a Yantra (a white square in the middle of a larger, black square) to mathematics exercises. All of them are useful — helpful — if the user approaches them with appropriate motivation. This, naturally, is the case with *any* exercise we've already mentioned, and with those, specific to baseball, which we will now provide.

Before presenting these concentration exercises, we would remind the reader that some players already use techniques — these or their own — to enhance their performance. They are all part of their "normal" practice routine and game strategy. But, as has become clear by now, these players are exceptions. To our mind, those interested enough to come this far in the book are also interested in joining the ranks of the exceptional players.

CONCENTRATION EXERCISES AT THE BALL PARK

*Actually, this exercise, for hitters, can be performed at local batting cages or at the field. The purpose of this simple practice is to help the hitter learn to concentrate on the ball more effectively. His goal is always to see the ball well, but somehow hitters bring distracting thoughts into batting cages. Their origins are: long ball bets with teammates; jumping in and out to get a few last swings; an on-going conversation with someone outside the cage; a b.p. pitcher whose pace doesn't allow the hitter to gather himself. And so on. Rarely, under these conditions, does a player have good concentration.

The exercise: Take the first five pitches. *Know* that you're not going to swing, so you can devote your entire attention to seeing the ball well. Follow it all the way. Look for the spin; see it as it goes by. Under conditions such as those above, the b.p. swing usually accomplishes little, if anything, insofar as concentration is concerned. Contact may be made, but a poor habit is being reinforced. Make the habit one of seeing the ball well.

Another benefit will accrue to those of you who routinely set aside a number of b.p. "takes" for the sake of concentration. You'll soon be sensitive to the difference in the quality of concentration during the drill and during games, when you're swinging. (And during your b.p. swings, of course.) You can develop a grading system based on how well you saw the ball—what kind of a "look" you had—so that after each at-bat in a game, if you use a scale of 1-5, with 5 being the best, you can grade yourself. ("I had a 4-look on that pitch," etc.) You can keep yourself continuously aware of the quality of your attention to that ball you want to see so well.

You can come early to have someone throw those concentration "takes," or you can stay late for it, if it's too difficult to incorporate into regular b.p. And remember, if you get a "take" sign during a game, *use it*. Be ready to swing; be ready to concentrate. Get a 5-look. Don't give any opportunity away.

*Another b.p. exercise: We'll start with a question: When you take b.p., is your concentration on the bunts the same as it is on the swings? Are you smiling? We are. The little guys with speed pay attention to those pitches and those bunts, because they know their value to them during a game. But what about the big hitters, the guys who say "I'm never told to bunt in a game"? Too many of them just go through the motions on that bunt.

If that's you, someday you may be called upon to lay down an important bunt, so your physical preparation for *all* possibilities is incomplete. Your mental preparation is poor. That pitch can still be used to help start b.p. off the right way by seeing the ball well. By applying some mental discipline, you're using every opportunity to help yourself. See the ball's spin. Follow it to your bat. Be exceptional.

Even when "just loosening up" (physically) by taking easy swings in his first round of b.p., there's a tendency for the hitter to pay insufficient attention to the ball. "No problem," he would explain, "I'm not even trying to really hit — just loosen up." Not a very effective pattern. The hitter could very well have "loosened up" by taking practice swings *before* he got into the cage. Allowing that he might have been rushed into the cage, we maintain that his eyes can work very well immediately. A perfect time to work at getting 5-looks at the ball.

"Ill habits gather by unseen degrees . . ." said a Roman poet many seasons ago. See the degrees of improvement in your concentration as you build the work habit of seeing the ball.

*One of the most flagrant concentration deficiencies is easily spotted during batting practice. We only have to watch the guy who runs to first after he has completed his round of hitting. He then takes his round on the bases. What's the purpose of taking that baserunning round? There are a number: the player can work on his lead; he can practice watching the pitcher's move, and go on that movement; he can practice "reading" the batted ball and respond appropriately; he can practice making his turns — and more.

We won't try to guess the number of players who do that. We've seen a few. They are practicing all of the above, and they are concentrating on their game all the while. It's called "batting practice," but each player can dictate what he gets out of it. The more the mind works, the stronger it gets.

Workouts aren't only for the body. Use the baserunning cycle for what it's meant for — and *more*. Use it to keep a constant focus. Your attention span will grow; your game will be enhanced. You'll be lifting mental weights — and getting mentally "tougher."

*Are we still talking about b.p.? Yes. Now we're talking to pitchers, however. And about them. We have never heard a pitcher say a kind word about shagging balls during b.p. Many outfielders use that time for preparation. They "read" balls off the bat; get their jumps; practice routes. "Fine," say pitchers, "But that doesn't do any good for us."

Not for outfield play. But we do see pitchers diving for balls, jumping against fences — risking their bodies, so to speak. Why? Their answer is always the same: to fight off boredom. And it's true; activity does make time seem to pass more quickly. But isn't there anything a pitcher can do to help himself as he shags?

Answer: He can work on his concentration. That's not easy, we've heard — from the pitchers themselves. We don't know if our response originally came from a Roman, or a Greek, or a Hallmark poster. Or Tom Seaver. "Don't ask for an easy life; ask to be strong."

Pitchers can pay attention to their own teammates' batting habits and patterns and techniques — and *learn* something, perhaps, about batters in general. While shagging, they can watch stances, internalize strategies. ("I'd pitch so-and-so away. There's no way he can handle that pitch with his feet the way they are in the box.") And so on.

But most obviously, shagging time can be a fine time for the pitcher to do some visualization exercises. The mind will be activated; the technique will be useful; the concentration skill will be developed simultaneously. Boredom will have a battle on its hands, depending on the strength of the player/warrior.

*Finally, this most applicable practice exercise: Whenever practicing physical skills, apply your concentration technique! Be an Ozzie Smith or Walt Weiss in the field. First, make yourself *aware* of what you're working on — your goal. You want to bear down on every ball hit to you when taking fielding drills; you want to bear down on the bases — in the batter's box — throwing in the bullpen or in simulated games.

Take an occasional break and assess your concentration. Recognize any interferences—and reaffirm your goal.

Then get back to bearing down—to concentrating on every play. How can your concentration help but improve? How can your performance help but improve?

All of the exercises given in the chapter on visualization are, at the same time, useful tools for the building of concentration. The visualization exercises for mental rehearsal are especially helpful for improving concentration and confidence, since the player gives internal focus to a well-executed performance.

Mental rehearsal can help a player develop concentration and it can help him get it back when he loses it. If, during a game, a hitter is distracted by crowd noise—a rally chant, or booing—he can step out of the batter's box, take a deep breath to relax (see Chapter 13), and gently bring his attention back by mentally rehearsing the next pitch, his seeing the ball—and hitting well.

There are many other concentration exercises that can be used and many others that can be invented. Our intention is to have the player ultimately use those exercises (behaviors, actually) specifically related to baseball. They illustrate the interrelationship and interdependency of physical and mental skills. As a player is engaged in one good practice activity, other facets of his game are being served. A bad approach does an equal share of harm. We think the player should always be *aware* of the relationship between his mind and body—and between his practice and game approach.

Four Different Types of Attentional Focus

We're fortunate to have a professional acquaintance and relationship with Dr. Robert Nideffer, president of Performance Enhancement Associates in San Diego (and previously referred-to author of *The Inner Athlete*). Dr. Nideffer is an eminent sports psychologist whose particular area of interest and expertise is concentration. After discussing four different types of attentional focus with us, Dr. Nideffer sketched an illustration.

Broad-External

As it applies to baseball, the Broad-External focus is used, for example, by the batter who looks at the infield positioning against him, who recognizes a need to move a runner over, etc. And by the relief pitcher who comes into the game, acquaints himself with the number of outs and runners on base; the situation with which he's presented.

Broad-Internal

This focus uses the information gained from the one Broad-External to develop the appropriate situational approach. For example, the right-handed batter who wants to move the runner on second over, internalizes his intention to wait for an outside pitch.

Narrow-Internal

Staying with this example, the batter, before he steps into the box, mentally rehearses — sees the outside pitch and sees himself hitting it hard on the ground where he wants to — from the middle of the diamond to the right side. He takes his deep breath for relaxation, and steps into the box.

Narrow-External

The batter tells himself, in a relaxed tone, to see the ball. He knows where he wants it, now he cues himself onto the object of his attention — the ball.

Let's take a pitcher through the sequence. *Focus must be sequential.*

Broad-External:

The pitcher checks out the situation: where the baserunners are, whether a left-handed or right-handed batter is coming up.

Broad-Internal:

He decides he wants to come inside on this batter (because of situation and/or batter's weakness). He sets up in his mind a possible sequence of pitch selections and locations.

Narrow-Internal:

Not yet on the pitching rubber, he sees himself throwing the first pitch (he never gets ahead of himself; one pitch at a time) how and where he wants it.

Focusing on the target.

Narrow-External:
He steps onto the rubber, takes the catcher's signs and focuses on the target.

What Bob Nideffer stressed was the fact that athletes have to shift their attentional focus frequently, and should therefore be aware of the direction of those shifts. We strongly remind the player to understand *when* each direction should be followed. The player will learn the order as well as the directions for his attention. He'll settle into a mental rhythm, just as he establishes a physical rhythm. He does not want to hurry his thinking any more than he would want to rush his physical approach. The two should be—and will become—comfortable and *consistent.*

Many times in the earlier chapters of this book, we've brought up the importance of approaching "the task at hand"—the job/business at hand—whether it be to pitch the ball, hit the ball, field the ball, run the bases. *One pitch at a time*—all the great players know that's the only way to play the game well. Ultimately, we have come to the major rationale for that approach. Simply, the only way to have good concentration is to pay attention from moment to moment, only as each moment presents itself.

Dave Dravecky, pitching for the San Diego Padres in 1983, made five starts after having won his 12th game on July 3, and was 0-3 with a 8.02 ERA in those games. On August 3, he won his 13th game, after surviving a first inning in which he allowed three hits and a walk.

Said Dravecky after the game, "You tend to think about it (when you'll win the next game) a little too much, and maybe that's why I had a shaky start today. After the first, I concentrated on taking every pitch—one at a time."

Many baseball people believe that 1984 was the year Gary Carter finally put his approach to hitting on the right track. Billy DeMars, the hitting coach in Montreal when Carter was still playing there, offered his view of the change.

"I tried to impress on him (Carter) the importance of taking one at-bat at a time," said DeMars. "If you take a bad cut one time, or just get under the ball, or maybe miss the chalk by a fraction for a foul ball or the umpire gives you a bad call—forget it. Just concentrate on the next at-bat."

And once in the box, the next *pitch*, narrowing the focus, remember.

On June 25 of that season, Carter was robbed by outfielder Lonnie Smith, then with the Cardinals. Carter's apparent extra-base hit was turned into an out.

"In the past," said DeMars, "he (Carter) might have been a basket case after that first at-bat. This time, he stepped in there concentrating on what he had to do and hit the ball out of the park."

Anyone watching Carter's performance with the Mets in 1986, through the World Series, saw a mature hitter.

Toronto's John Olerud had the reputation of being a mature hitter when he came right to the major leagues from Washington State University. During the 1993 season, the media was relentless in its pursuit of Olerud's projected views on his 25-game hitting streak and .401 batting average. But Olerud refused to have his focus changed: "I don't think about the streak or .400," he said. "I just try to hit the ball hard somewhere."

Dravecky concerned himself with the possible future, Carter with the unacceptable past. In each case, a player is distracted from the functional present. Not that the present is free from distraction, as we've mentioned. Fans, friends, and foolish thoughts all do the job. And, as a player gets older, so do the media.

When Don Mattingly went through contract negotiations before the 1986 season, the men of the press hounded him with questions. Mattingly answered them by saying, "I can't concern myself with what's going on with the club or what the media is writing. If you pay attention to those things, that's when you get yourself in trouble."

Mets outfielder Ryan Thompson was projected as a potential Rookie-of-the-Year candidate before the 1993 season, but he was sent down to the minor leagues inside of a month after the season had begun. He couldn't handle the reality of it. His play in AAA Norfolk was awful. He had told himself he couldn't be there in Norfolk—that this couldn't have happened to him. "I was playing," Thompson said. "But I was not there. I swung at anything. I had 11 strikeouts in four games. I couldn't put anything in perspective. Everything had gone wrong."

Because of pre-occupation with the Broad-External, Bob Nideffer would say.

So, simply put, we now come to this:

1. Self-doubt, self-blame, people who would distract, perceived stress and the like all interfere with concentration.

2. Distractions arc dysfunctional to performance. They divide attention.

3. To effectively pay attention to the task is to have overcome all types of distractions.

4. Players who develop their concentration skills will find them to be dominant—prepotent—over pressure, pain, anxieties, anger, noise, and the like.

5. *The ability to concentrate will put the player in control of his attention.*

Players—people—with that kind of control are most likely in control of most situations, because they are most likely in control of their thoughts and feelings.

The expression of that control is a key to all effective behavior, we believe. It's the discipline of mind and strength as it combats emotion and weakness. Many speak of "mental toughness." We choose to identify it as *mental discipline*. It is an expansive subject, as the following chapter will reveal.

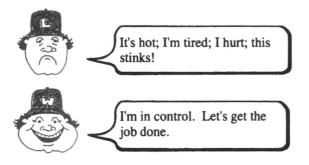

12
MENTAL DISCIPLINE
The Control of Thoughts and Feelings

It may seem to some that, by treating the control of attention before the control of thoughts and feelings, we've put the cart before the horse. We would strongly dispute that view, as we very strongly support Bob Nideffer's belief that the ability to pay attention to the task, *is* the ability to *control* the self. After all, what do we control when we're able to attend completely to a given task? *We control our mind and emotions.*

Concentration, then, is synonymous with mental control—mental discipline. It is, as we've said, prepotent, meaning that if a player has developed all the skills of concentration, he needn't concern himself with identifying all the distractions that can get in the way—because they will *not* get in his way. His concentration will have power over outside—and inside—interferences. It is prepotent.

This chapter would be unnecessary if, ideally, every player who read the preceding one had developed that prepotency; every player had easily learned how to concentrate effectively and consistently. But we all know better. (It would please us, though, if some players had already improved their performance by using and integrating into their approach the material presented thus far.)

The value of mental discipline is acknowledged in sporting and political arenas, corporate meeting rooms, military camps, even Hollywood studios. Though most everyone seems to recognize it as a necessary ingredient in personal and professional effectiveness, not everyone uses the same term or definition. "Mental toughness" and "mental stamina" are the most common terms we hear. We choose the word "discipline" because its multiple definitions seem so appropriate to what we advocate for a ballplayer who wishes to maximize his talent.

Discipline: "training to act in accordance to rules; instruction designed to train to proper conduct or action; the training effect of experience, adversity, etc.; a branch of instruction or learning." (*The Random House Dictionary,* 1980).

We emphasize this definition (though in a verb form here): "to bring to order and obedience by training and control."

Training and Control

Mental discipline, then, for our purposes here, is the ability to sustain effective and consistent concentration on task — specific performance task — according to what's required within the given situation (i.e. seeing/hitting the ball; seeing the target/throwing the pitch). This is accomplished through controlled attention to relevant information and cues, followed by appropriately controlled behavior. (As discussed in the preceding chapter.)

We've learned what direction we *want* to take and *how* to take it. Now we discipline ourselves *to take it.* Over and over again. Despite pressure and pain. Despite adversity and failure. We reject, rather than accept, pressure. We control pain, rather than be controlled by it. We grow, rather than shrink, through adversity. We become further motivated, rather than defeated, by failure.

We can't be distracted because we recognize distractions for what they are; we deflect them and turn our attention elsewhere, where we know it belongs. We control it; we control ourselves.

Yes, we control ourselves. We realize that some conditions, situations, and problems are uncontrollable. But when we control our reactions to problems and adversity, we are controlling their effect on us. How we act and react will illustrate the degree of our self-control — our mental discipline.

Mental games are won through being aware of what our goal is,

"OK, now, good low strikes."

knowing what it takes to achieve it in a given context, and dedicating ourselves to that end. We've said it before; we'll say it again. To have the skill for such specific and directed concentration is to have mental discipline and control. The more consistent we are, the more mental games we are winning — and have already won.

The Cycle of Control

Let's construct a series, which become a cycle:

> *Control through awareness:* The control of ability to recognize and evaluate what we're thinking, feeling, and doing — and what is happening to us. This control gives us the understanding of where our attention is directed and, if it isn't where we want it to be, the reason it isn't. We are then able to follow the procedures we know for effective concentration.

> *Control through thoughts:* Exerted after concentration breaks down or has been "given a break," these thoughts should be rational and relevant to the task of the moment. These controlled thoughts get our focus back on task.

> *Control through self-talk:* If the quality of our thoughts has deteriorated and become dysfunctional, we control the words we speak to ourselves — internally or externally. These words are directives to get us back to a general positive attitude and to concentrate on positive function.

> *Control through behavior:* Physical behavior guided by rational, rather than emotional, directives; the "final instructions" — given through self-talk, which is the goal, after all (e.g., "See the ball."). Regardless of how we feel, we act out what we know, what we've been reminded. And after the action, we assess our body's behavior — we're again aware of it — and of the quality of the thoughts and words that directed it. We come full cycle and anticipate greater success in the next cycle.

The Responsibility for Control

The abilities to direct attention and act on what we can control enhances our effectiveness as people and as athletes. To focus on matters beyond our control is to misdirect energy, waste time, and doom us to frustration and failure. The kind of failure that doesn't inspire us to have better efforts.

Winning games, hitting .300, pleasing fans and the like are, as we've said many times, poor goals, because we have no control over their attainment. The past is beyond our control; the future is not yet within the limits of it. The opportunity for control lies in the player's present, in the matter of the moment. And, essentially, it lies within the player himself as he moves through the cycle discussed above.

Responsibility begins with a willingness to acknowledge who we are and what we are — and what we want to become. We said that in Chapter 5. We referred to writer Jim Newman, who wrote in *Release Your Brakes,* "People are responsible/accountable for everything they think and do, whether they like it, accept it, or even know it."

The chapter on responsibility was intended to give the reader the notion that he should gain as much self-control as possible. The chapter on concentration was intended to help the reader (as baseball player) to establish control of his attention as he performs. So by now, the reader does "know it." He not only knows that what he thinks and what he does are his responsibility, but he knows there are techniques he can practice and employ to control his mind and muscles. He knows he is responsible for dedicating himself to whatever it takes to reach his goal.

Those who do *know* — who see control as being in, rather than out, of their own hands — are said to have a "locus of control." So it comes down to having that aspiration, that vision, that acceptance, as Newman would say. It's the only proper way to see it, we believe. Studies show that through this acceptance, we become more able to regulate our problem-solving behavior. And we enhance our ability to recognize rationally what is and what isn't within the limits of our control.

Negative experiences from our past have a way of moving with us as we move through time. They disrupt the striving for control.

Also, we often believe we are who we used to be (still an insecure 10-year-old, for example), rather than who we are now. This mistaken belief, and the distorted self-image from the past, commonly lead us to false conclusions — irrational beliefs — about our world and about ourselves. These beliefs become a source of self-imposed stress and anxiety.

For the player, the result is a loss of control and an inability to perform effectively. Why? Because he fails to recognize what can and what cannot be controlled. He therefore fails to recognize to what he must pay *undivided attention*. His performance task becomes part of a maze of personal disruptions and distractions.

Albert Ellis (1977) presented 10 irrational beliefs that he found to be common in our society. We note them below as they would apply to baseball players in particular:

1. You must have approval all the time from the people you find significant. (Teammates, fans, manager, organization "brass," et. al.).

2. You must be thoroughly competent, "producing" every time, all the time.

3. Things must go the way you'd like them to, and it's terrible if they don't.

4. Others, particularly superiors in rank (coach, manager, farm director, general manager), must treat you "fairly" and "justly," and it's terrible if they don't.

5. When threatening and/or "clutch" situations present themselves, you must become preoccupied with them and the consequences (as *you* perceive them).

6. It's terrible if you don't immediately find solutions to your problems, on and/or off the field.

7. Your emotional misery comes from external pressures, and unless these pressures change, you can do nothing to make yourself "better" (i.e., more effective as a player and/or person).

8. It's easier to avoid responsibility (be passive or *quit*) than to take charge of your life and/or a situation.

9. You are helpless to cope with the overriding influences of the past.

10. You can gain happiness and/or effectiveness by inertia or by uncommittedly "having fun" and waiting/hoping for the right things to happen to you.

If you reread the above list, you can easily recognize how many (ALL!) of these irrational beliefs had already been brought to your attention in the chapters preceding this one. They march through our lives under many banners. As we reject—and change—each of these beliefs, we are learning how to gain greater control.

As we do that, we reinforce the learned techniques of concentration. We are more easily and consistently able to disregard irrelevant cues, whether they're external or internal. The degree to which we can do this is, of course, in direct proportion to the degree of our control. If the most relevant cue for concentration control is, for example, the ball or the catcher's target, what are the most irrelevant cues? What is it that most often divides or controls a player's attention?

We've previously mentioned many distractions: crowd noise; the expectations of others; poor attitudes; lack of confidence and resultant doubt; fear of the consequences of "failure"; awareness of inadequate preparation; opponent intimidation; "clutch" situations, and the like.

There are other sizable obstacles on the road to effective mental discipline and control: emotional swings; negative thinking; pressure and anxiety; slumps; pain; anger. These obstacles will now be individually examined, and, we trust, pushed off the road by some pretty "heavy equipment": a sense of balance; positive thinking; positive self-talk; rationality and more.

Obstacle One: Emotional Swings

Gary Carter, coming to bat for the fourth time, after three previous hitless at-bats, used to say, "I gotta get a hit." Ray Knight, coming to bat for the fifth time, after four previous hits that game, said, essentially, "I gotta get a fifth hit." Each player lost his sense of control. His approach was a departure from "typicality." Each forfeited his sense of balance. Carter's emotional swing came from a negative stimulus: a desire to avoid failure. The anxiety interfered with his performance. Knight's swing was triggered by a positive desire. He was anxious to get his fifth hit and have a perfect day. "Anxious." In Knight's situational context, that word sounds innocent. It isn't. It still causes a form of tension. It did for Knight. He popped up weakly: a terrible at-bat. He knew it as soon as it was over.

Each hitter's emotions took a swing before and during the at-bats. One swung to a "low" state; the other to a "high." Each hitter swung away from the state of balance.

During the 1983 season, while Bruce Hurst was working hard on his mind games and winning them more consistently, his Red Sox team traveled to Anaheim to play the Angels. Hurst was to pitch against Tommy John. He had a positive anticipation of the confrontation — the challenge. The game was scoreless at the end of seven innings. In the top of the eighth, Boston scored three runs. Hurst, who had been pitching by focusing on one pitch at a time, became excited when the Red Sox gave him the lead.

"I went out to pitch the bottom of the eighth thinking, 'Two more innings and I've got a shutout, a win over Tommy John.' I came off the even keel I'd been on. I thought too far ahead. My concentration broke down."

California scored three runs in the bottom of the eighth to tie the score and knock Hurst out of the game.

Tom Seaver credited Mets manager Gil Hodges as being the most influential man in his career. Seaver said that Hodges taught him how to be a professional.

"I remember a game in 1968 when I was ahead, 7–0, and got very giddy and wound up losing my concentration. Before I knew it, the score was tied, 7–7. Gil called me into his office after the game and said, 'You can't let yourself down at any point in the game because there's no guarantee you can get back up emotionally.' I think I've benefitted from that every year since then," said Seaver, shortly before he won his 300th major league game.

Why was it so hard for Hurst and Seaver to get the outs they wanted? Because they failed to concentrate on "business." They stopped planning and focusing on their targets. By "giving in"— each in a different way, when things were going *well*, not poorly, they showed a lack of mental discipline.

The tendency is probably more common when a player is having trouble. He starts to concentrate on what the opponent might do; on what is happening to him, rather than on what he wants to make happen.

Control is lost when a player's feelings and thoughts focus on consequences—whether they be catastrophe or conquest.

John Denny pitched for St. Louis and Cleveland before going to the Philadelphia Phillies and winning the Cy Young Award in 1983. Claude Osteen was Denny's pitching coach in both St. Louis and Philadelphia. Everyone noticed the difference in Denny's performance. Osteen noticed the difference in Denny.

"He's got things straightened out now," said Osteen in the summer of '83. "Most of the games he'd lose (in the past) were ones in which he'd lose control of himself. He'd start fighting with umpires over a simple call, disagree with a manager's decision to take him out. It was all those things that go along with a pitcher who is immature as a person."

Denny spent much time with teammate Steve Carlton, who helped him understand the importance of balance, control, and concentration.

In 1986, pitcher Bob Walk completed his first full season in the major leagues since 1982. At the age of 29, Walk knew he still had much to improve upon, if he wanted to prolong his major league career.

"I have to stop getting hyper when I give up a big hit in the late innings. I lose my concentration. I know I can't continue doing that."

Players at every level continue to allow situations to push them to emotional extremes during ball games, whether the state be elation or depression. Either feeling gets in the way of peak performance.

Wade Boggs had been criticized in 1983 for being "just a Judy-hitter." After hitting his first home run of the season on July 14, he was asked if he'd change his swing now that he "felt the good feeling of hitting a homer."

Boggs replied, "Of course not."

Mark McGwire, the American League Rookie of the Year in 1987, most impressed teammates and opponents, veteran Don Sutton included, with "his ability to stay on an even keel no matter how good things are going."

Bad feelings are, perhaps, harder to control. Even the tough can't always get going very easily when the going gets tough. "You want to quit," Tom Seaver admitted. "You feel it is all hopeless. You have to force yourself to forget and start over as if it never happened. Some guys can't do that (at all). They are always fighting things beyond their control."

In 1982, Montreal pitcher Ray Burris was one such guy. He lost his first three starts of the season by the scores of 1-0, 1-0, and 2-1. Though his ERA was the best in the National League, his record was 0-3. He began to press, and his performances deteriorated. He then lost his spot in the starting rotation.

"I began losing my concentration," said Burris, "and worrying about things over which I had no control."

Burris finished the season with a 4-14 record—0-11 as a starting pitcher.

Whether a player tries to hide his depression, or whether it is so deep and controlling as to be visible to most anyone, the effect is negative. Just the degree varies. "Caving in" part way or all the way hurts the player's game and the player himself.

Every pitcher, batter, fielder, baserunner faces tough situations. None of them *always* comes through. Everyone has emotional reaction. Everyone fails. The manner in which we approach and cope with these situations—the manner in which we control our emotional reactions to them—will indicate the quality of our mental discipline.

The Heavy Equipment Needed: Balance

Trying harder when things are going poorly may be a good sign of character, but it is *not* the right way to improved performance. The player who maintains the same, solid approach regardless of adversity or good fortune, best controls himself and the situation. He is the real "gamer," because he lets nothing take him out of his plan. He lets nothing throw his emotions off balance. He comes through in the clutch, because he knows that what he wants to do in the clutch is what he wants to do *always*: To maintain *control*. To keep that even keel. He is the "steady" ballplayer. His mental discipline — "toughness" — lies in the consistency of his good approach, his ability to "grind it out," day after day, situation after situation. Every pitch; every play. The same way. He "keeps his lows high and his highs low."

The player with mental discipline has control and balance — whether ahead or behind; whether starting the game or finishing it; whether the situation is critical or seemingly meaningless. The mentally tough player controls his emotions by focusing on what he knows will get the job done.

Joe Garagiola once said that winners are those who can erase everything except the factors that determine their immediate performance. We've said that quite a few times, we know.

A player with mental discipline doesn't allow his emotions to be affected by situations, people, or his own past mistakes. If his emotions are affected, his thoughts will be. He will make faulty judgments, because he'll tend to perceive situations emotionally, rather than rationally.

In his book *The Science of Hitting*, Ted Williams mentioned the nervous energy he noticed in Carl Yastrzemski when Yaz was a rookie. "I think it is good to be a little nervous," wrote Williams. "My impression when I first saw (him) was, 'Gee, what a twitchy guy this is, all coiled up like a spring, ready to pop, just can't wait to hit.' Naturally, if you are so nervous it affects your control at the plate, then you've got a problem, but that won't happen very often if you've got your mind on the business at hand."

The "nervousness" Williams observed in Yaz was a positive anticipation, which is good for a player to have before performance.

Almost every athlete feels it. It's an energy that arouses the athlete and stimulates his readiness system. He arouses himself to the point of balance that allows him to be effective. Effective athletes gain and maintain their balance by, as Williams said, paying attention to "the business at hand."

It can be learned early. Texas Rangers pitcher Edwin Correa, a rookie at 20 in 1986, takes pride in "keeping his cool" at all times.

"I just stay the same temperature all the time, believe it or not," Correa said. "One thing about getting too pumped up is that it makes you forget your tempo and the things you have to do."

Correa's pitching coach, Tom House, appreciated the pitcher's competitive approach. "He's intense but with no anxiety. That spells winner in any field of endeavor," said House. "You see it in corporate executives, surgeons, and pilots. In any high-pressure existence, it's the perfect profile."

Atlanta pitcher Tom Glavine, having completed his third consecutive 20-win season in 1993, is perhaps the best current example of one who performs with controlled intensity. Admittedly, Glavine has his times of struggle on the mound. "But I try not to show the other team I'm uncomfortable," he said. To observe him is to believe him.

Not too high, not too low. Not too fast, not too slow. "Nothing in excess," said the Greeks. Moderation. Balance.

There's an interesting exercise that can help you understand balance and appreciate its importance:

*Force yourself to approach a physical activity (other than baseball) *out of balance* (ping-pong, tennis, racquetball, golf). If you have a tendency to slice when hitting a golf ball, play every shot as if you want to hook. Exaggerate it for the hook always. Play at least four holes that way one day.

*If you're an aggressive ping pong player, play a game in an extremely submissive way. Be defensive. Play over-cautiously, rather than aggressively.

*Devise your own activity. Use an approach that's counter to the one you typically use. Pay attention to how you feel as you perform. And to the results.

Certainly, you'll feel strange as you act out those unusual approaches. But it's easier to know, feel, and understand balance after you've fallen off *both* sides of the "balance beam."

If you lose your balance when playing baseball because you tend to be too excitable, then learn the feeling of extreme passivity. It will help make you aware of the other way to lean on the beam, in order to regain balance.

If you tend to be an unaggressive player, you'll get the strange feeling of unnaturalness by forcing yourself to act in an overly aggressive way, but you'll more easily understand that it's just as unnatural to be a submissive athlete. And, we hope, that understanding will guide you in whatever direction you need go, toward a more balanced and controlled approach.

Obstacle Two: Negative Thinking

In Chapter 4, we briefly spoke of negative and positive attitudes, of pessimism and optimism. The essential point to reiterate here is brief: one of the best ways to make something happen is to say it will happen.

"Man is what he believes," wrote Anton Chekhov. Our beliefs influence our behavior. Our thought becomes father to our deed.

We've heard this from faith healers and motivational speakers and mothers for years. Now, work in a "new" science, psychoneuroimmunology — PNI — has helped to confirm that the nervous system and the immune system are "connected." What happens to one affects the other. Scientists have found that the positive thoughts, optimism, and strong-willed aggressiveness help the body manufacture antibodies to fight disease. Many cases of cancer patients outliving doctors' death sentences or beating the disease completely have been studied and documented. The thoughts and attitudes of these patients affected their internal chemistry. Other studies showed that negative thoughts, hopelessness, loss of control and will affected the chemistry of cancer patients who succumbed swiftly or immediately to time-table predictions of death.

This is noted here for a definite purpose: to convince the reader that negative and positive thoughts determine the quality and length of our lives, which is most important. They also determine the quality of athletic performance. The belief system isn't just a state of mind.

The belief system is a psychological reality that greatly affects physiological realities.

Norman Cousins applied this principle to his own circumstance, and he defeated a "fatal" disease. Cousins wrote, "Nothing is more wonderous about the fifteen billion neurons in the human brain than their ability to convert thoughts, hopes, ideas, and attitudes into chemical substances. Everything begins, therefore, with belief. What we believe is the most powerful option of all (we have)."

One non-medical example related to our belief system we draw from Dr. Bernie Segal's book, *Love, Medicine & Miracles*:

> Shlomo Breznitz, a psychologist at Hebrew University in Jerusalem, recently demonstrated that positive and negative expectation have opposite effects on blood levels of cortisol and prolactin, two hormones important in activating the immune system. Breznitz had several groups of Israeli soldiers make a grueling forced march of forty kilometers, but varied the information he gave them. He told some they would march sixty kilometers, but stopped them at forty, and told others they would march thirty kilometers, then said they had another ten to go. Some were allowed to see distance markers, and some had no clues as to how far they had walked or what the total distance would be. Breznitz found that those with the most accurate information weathered the march best, but the stress hormone levels always reflected the soldiers' estimates rather than the actual distance.

What the soldiers *thought* dictated how their bodies *reacted*. There should no longer be any question in our minds about the significance of that connection. And there should no longer be a negative control in the mind of anyone who wants to reach his peak.

We've already mentioned that many people carry their childhood perceptions forward with them. They're still "victims" of negative warnings, scoldings, and punishments administered to them as young children. They think they still are those children, and that often is why so many of them think more in negative terms than in the positive. Fortunate are those people who grew up in an environment of positivism, encouragement, and support. They are rare, from our experience, sad as it is to say.

But children became adults, and adults can learn to free themselves and take control of their own attitudes, thoughts, and behavior. Whatever the historical and personal reasons may be, too many of us take too long to become aware of the negative thoughts that become the energy to fuel our behavior. Change starts with awareness.

Listen to yourself. Catch yourself. Change your thoughts—and yourself!

It's easier to be aware of the flaws in others, so begin or resume now by listening to a few words spoken by major league ballplayers during recent seasons. (The team noted is the team the player was with when he spoke the words quoted.)

Frank Viola, pitcher, Minnesota Twins (quoted in an earlier chapter):
"I know my insecurity stemmed from not really thinking
of myself as a pitcher."

John Tudor, pitcher, St. Louis Cardinals (the first statement during a television interview before pitching—and losing—the final game of the 1985 World Series; the second statement during the following spring training):
1) "If I get beat, I hope this isn't the game people will
remember."

2) "That was unlike me. I'm not usually negative like
that before a game, or a season. I don't know why I said it."

Addenda**

*Steve Freyer, Tudor's agent, quoted in the November 11, 1985, issue of *Sports Illustrated*:
"His (Tudor's) fears became a self-fulfilling prophecy. He
knew that if he had to pitch again after the fourth game
that the Cardinals were in trouble."

*Dave Bettencourt, Tudor's good friend, quoted in the same magazine, same issue:
"You could sense before the game that he (Tudor) was talk-
ing himself out of it. It wasn't that he couldn't handle

the pressure. It was that he was afraid of letting his teammates down."

Tony Phillips, infielder, Oakland Athletics (after his team had been two-hitted by Bert Blyleven):
"He kept me off-balance all night . . . I knew he was going to strike me out the last time up. I didn't have a prayer."

Bruce Berenyi, pitcher, New York Mets (after he had pitched a four-hit shutout against the Los Angeles Dodgers and admitted he allowed negative thoughts to interfere with his pitching):
"Tonight, however, I had a positive attitude . . . I've had negative thoughts my whole career. I've thought the worst, and the worst would always happen."

Bill Gullickson, pitcher, Montreal Expos (explaining a sudden improvement in his performance):
"I don't pretend to understand it completely. [The problem] could have been indecision — not knowing really what to do. You start thinking, 'I want to do it this way, but maybe I should do it that way.' I have better positive concentration now."

Cory Snyder, infielder/outfielder, Cleveland Indians (near the end of his outstanding rookie season in '86):
"I keep wondering when something's going to go wrong. But I'm learning to leave that out of my thinking."

The sooner that lesson is learned, the sooner any player puts himself in control.
One warning, before we offer some contrasting remarks to those above. Some *positive* thoughts can have *negative* effects. For example, a player may go up to bat thinking, "I'm gonna win this game for the guys by being the one to hit the three-run homer we need."

Positive, yes. But a thought such as that creates an excessive emotional arousal, muscular tension (see next chapter), and is an approach more likely to distract the player from, rather than help him concentrate on, his specific performance function.

Thoughts or self-statements such as, "I'm going to pitch a shutout," or "I'm going to get four hits today," are positive, to be sure. But they are thoughts based on *result goals* — which are beyond the control of the player—and therefore likely to provoke feelings of pressure, not confidence. They are seemingly positive means which lead to negative ends.

Beware! Be aware of the *quality* of your thoughts. *Always!*

The Heavy Equipment Needed: Controlled Positive Thoughts

First, let's listen to a few more players:

Tom Hume, pitcher, Cincinnati Reds (who manager Pete Rose said had "regained his lost confidence" and effectiveness):
"Yes, somewhere I lost my confidence. Where? Don't know. Somewhere. But, yeah, I've found it. This winter I completely rested my mind, and I've forgotten all about 1983 and 1984. I'm remembering back to the good old days. If you want good things to happen, you have to think about good things." (Advice he had gotten when he sought out teammate Tom Seaver.)

Ron Kittle, outfielder, Chicago White Sox (who won Rookie of the Year honors in 1982 [35 homers, 100 RBIs], then struggled in 1983 [67 RBIs, .215 BA]):
"The biggest part of it is believing in yourself. I hit for average in the minor leagues, and I'm capable of hitting .270 in the major leagues and still get my home runs."

Jesse Orosco, pitcher, New York Mets:
" . . . When I get on the mound I have all the confidence I can do the job. And if I don't do the job, I know I'm going to come back and get them."

Scott Fletcher, shortstop, Texas Rangers (who had a .245 lifetime batting average and was labeled "utility infielder" when the Chicago White Sox traded him to Texas. Fletcher hit .424 in his first spring training for the Rangers [1986], but didn't become the regular shortstop until May, hitting .300 for the season):
"I never thought of myself as one (a utility player), and I wasn't going to let myself start thinking that way. I believed, really believed, that by doing everything I could to improve myself, I would be totally ready once my chance came along."

*Addenda***
*Bobby Valentine, Texas manager (who was well aware of Fletcher's weight workouts, extra batting and fielding practice, and videotape viewing of his hitting stroke, despite being a "utilityman"):
> "He has worked harder than the next guy to get himself to this level."

*Tim Foli, former Texas coach (who was watching Fletch taking batting practice):
> "What discipline and concentration he [Fletcher] has."

Kirk Gibson, outfielder, Detroit Tigers (who spent some time at the Pacific Institute after the 1983 season):
> "...You have to set goals and reset them. We hold certain pictures. If you're holding a negative image, you will perform accordingly."

*Addendum***
Dick Balderson, general manager, Seattle Mariners (who brought in the Pacific Institute program for a three-day seminar for players, coaching staff, and front office personnel before the 1987 season):
> "We are simply trying to utilize another avenue in preparing to play the season. Physically, we get ready to play in spring training. This is mental conditioning, a reinforcement of positive thinking and an attitude adjustment."

Many major league teams now employ sports psychologists.

Jim Frey, when he was managing the Chicago Cubs, recalled the Hall of Famer Stan Musial. "I remember standing next to him one day when it was around 100 degrees out, and somebody was groaning about having to play a doubleheader in the heat. Musial turned to me and said, 'Little guy, do you know what this doublheader means today? It means Stanley has a chance to get 10 hits today. Ten hits!' Here the other guy is griping and Musial's thinking 10 hits."

Recalled regularly, by many, is the ever-positive Ernie Banks and his now-famous, "Let's play two today." A far cry from the attitudes (Chapter 4, "Dedication") that Montreal pitcher Steve Rogers found in his teammates on a particular night during the 1983 pennant race.

Marcus Allen, the very talented running back for the Los Angeles Raiders, is another of the many exemplars in other sports. Said Allen to a *Sports Illustrated* writer, "My whole game is attitude. You've got to think positively to achieve the impossible, to be what you expect to be. If you seek mediocrity, that's what you'll get out of life."

Research supports Allen's philosophy. Beverly McLeod, in the October 1986 issue of *Psychology Today*, wrote of Stanford psychologists findings, which supported the view that people are influenced "by how (they) size up their capabilities and their situation — what they are thinking."

Control All Your Thinking Patterns

Most players are aware of the "power of positive thinking," but few realize that consistent thinking patterns prior to performance are essential to consistent peak performance. The great players control their thinking; the poor ones are controlled by theirs. Thinking patterns may be thought of as "mental wind-ups."

Thinking patterns consist of the:

1. Nature of thought (What you are thinking)
2. Process of thought (How you think)
   a) Words/Self-talk (Sometimes even thinking out loud)
   b) Feelings (We can imagine what something may feel like or what we want something to feel like.)
   c) Pictures/Images
3. Speed of thought (Sometimes they just flash through our minds.)
4. Sequence of thoughts
5. Timing between thoughts
6. Place (location) where thoughts occur

Changes in thinking patterns influence performance. Some changes are:

1. Thoughts added
2. Thoughts left out
3. Thoughts in a different sequence
4. Thoughts at a different pace (changed timing)
5. Thoughts not completed

Adding thoughts is the act that gets in the way most often. Whether the thoughts are negative *or* positive, thoughts about the situation, thoughts used as self-coaching or thoughts trying to get the player to do a little more can be great distractors from the concentration process. Additional thoughts can be about possible consequences of success or failure, about mechanical reminders. Whatever they are—no matter how well-intended they are—they alter, for the worse, the player's mental wind-up.

Timing and pace of thinking are very important, having an immediate effect on the player's state of arousal. When you, as a pitcher, for example, change your mental timing, the same effect results as when you change the timing of your delivery—your physical wind-up.

Timing is important because our minds are at peak efficiency for approximately six seconds, and then we must refocus our attention. When we rush our thinking, sometimes not even completing thoughts, the effect will be the same as a rushed delivery, approach to a ground ball, throw, or swing. We will not have physical or mental control.

In learning to control your thinking, first determine what it is you were thinking about prior to and during your best performances. (Hitting, fielding, pitching, etc.) Once you become aware of the nature of those thoughts (the best "mental wind-up"), you should consistently follow that pattern. Whenever you deviate from it (unless making a conscious adjustment for improvement), *you should stop your thoughts and begin again at step one.*

After each play that a player is involved in (a pitch, a swing, a play in the field or on the bases), he will evaluate his performance. When the evaluation is positive, the thought will usually pass through his mind rapidly (sometimes almost out of consciousness). But when the player—or any of us, for that matter—is not satisfied with outcomes, he tends to dwell on it.

Be aware of this if it happens to you, and give yourself time to let those thoughts leave your mind. You can replace those thoughts with constructive ones. Think about what you will do next time, in order to get the outcome you desire. Then, anticipate the possibilities for the next play/pitch. (Step off the mound/out of the batter's box.) The evaluation and anticipation steps are to be completed before you begin the "mental wind-up."

Step by step, the process—the mental wind-up—can be as follows:

Reprinted by permission of United Feature Syndicate, Inc.

1. Evaluation and "fixing" previous play
2. Anticipation
3. "Keying" up or down (whichever adjustment your arousal level requires)
4. Giving yourself instructions (visualizing what you want to do)
5. Narrowing attention to immediate (external) function (seeing the ball or target, etc.)
6. Being "quiet" (relaxed) as you switch over to "automatic pilot" (muscle memory)
7. *Doing it!*

   Through the use of the above strategies, a player can be greatly assisted in establishing control of his emotion and tension levels (arousal states); instructing his body as to desired behavior (through visualization and imagined feelings); focusing his attention on specific targets.

   The strategies are based on a functional, *positive* approach. A player whose major "contribution" to his performance is negativism is contributing to his probable failure.

The player who belittles himself and curses his situation establishes his incompetence and brings his past failures forward. The player who assures himself is freeing himself to learn, to concentrate on what he wants do. He is moving toward success.

Most of us want to succeed. But few realize how much we get in the way of our own abilities to do so. The more we commit ourselves to the choice of *mind over emotion*, the more likely we'll reach our goals.

In his book, *The Psychology of Self-Esteem,* Nathaniel Branden writes, "To think or not to think, to focus his mind or to suspend it, is man's act of choice, the one act directly within his volitional power . . . To the extent that man characteristically makes the right choices . . . he experiences a sense of control over his existence — the control of a mind in proper relationship to reality. Self-confidence is confidence in one's mind . . . "

We've never met a self-confident person whose mind wasn't filled with positive thoughts. And those whom we've watched become self-confident before our eyes have acted out positivism — and encouraged their minds to catch up to their behavior. Their behavior is a clear example of the conscious movement toward the development of mental discipline. Toughness.

Whether mind or behavior is fueling the machine, positivism must be in the driver's seat.

Obstacle Three: Pressure

An obstacle interferes with one's movement and progress. But obstacles can be hurdled or removed. At least *real* obstacles can. Imaginary obstacles — imaginary problems — slow us most and cause the most frustration and anguish.

Imaginary problems are insurmountable. How, after all, can people solve a problem that doesn't really exist? During the process of creating these "problems," the imagination and emotions most dramatically get in the way of rational thought and behavior, in the way of peak performance. When this happens, people tend to ignore Julius Caesar's wisdom and find fault in their stars, rather than in themselves. As they bemoan their fate, they blame the "star" called pressure. Their anxiety, they complain, is a result of "all the pressure that has been put on" them.

We refuse to grace "pressure" with lofty discussion. We recognize the "feeling" of pressure; we've referred to it many times in the preceding pages. But our most powerful reference—and belief—is what we wish to emphasize. We heard Al McGuire express it strongly. He said, "I really think pressure is something you put on yourself and it's a sign of incompetency. If you don't have faith in what you are doing, it's probably because you are not properly prepared."

Preparation. That is the emphasis, really, of this book, because everything we advocate leads to—prepares for—performance. The player who feels pressure has not reconciled himself to the fact that he can't please everyone, he can't be perfect, he isn't a failure whenever he doesn't achieve his goal; his fears that the quality of his self and his life are at stake when he performs are distorted and irrational.

Again, such thoughts are common hurdles for competitive athletes. But the exceptional athletes recognize the barrier for what it is: an invention of an undisciplined mind. It's then easy for them to run through what isn't there.

Jack Nicklaus again: "When fear starts to hit me, my best chance of overcoming it lies in facing it squarely and examining it rationally. Here's what I tell myself. 'O.K., what are you frightened of? You've obviously played well or you wouldn't be here . . . Well, go ahead and enjoy yourself. Play each shot one at a time and meet the challenge.'"

Challenge, not danger. Those who enjoy the challenge enjoy it because they *interpret it as a challenge, not as a threat. They* create their reality. The crowd does not; the coach does not; the conditions do not. *The game does not.* The individual applies internal control and mental discipline.

That individual is clearly winning his mind games. He understands all the elements that can have him apply pressure to his existence and his performance, and he understands that only his own interpretation and acceptance of pressure is responsible for his freedom or his bondage.

The exceptional athlete, with a disciplined mind, makes his own choice. The choice is responsibility; the choice is freedom. The choice is to enjoy — *to love* — the challenge.

As we've said, it isn't our intention to dismiss the reality of pressure. We talk with people of all ages and pursuits, certainly with many professional baseball players, who battle pressure/stress/anxiety on a daily basis. Our intention is to identify the origins of pressure and to reiterate the fact that people create their own internal realities. Almost all of the ballplayers we talk with admit that their pressures are "self-inflicted."

These ballplayers learn that they create their own pressure by looking at a circumstance in a particular way and by making a particular interpretation — in other words, by how they look at a situation and by what they say to themselves about it.

The following was said by Joe Garagiola: "Baseball gives you every chance to be great. Then it puts every pressure on you to prove that you haven't got what it takes. It never takes away the chance, and it never eases up on the pressure."

We feel Garagiola gives too much credit for control to the game and too little responsibility to the player.

A packed Yankee Stadium is not the same physical environment as a familiar hometown baseball park, packed with familiar faces. The major difference, though, is usually the mental environment of the player. His tasks on the field remain the same. Does his approach?

We often take a three-foot plank and place it on the ground in front of a group of ballplayers. We walk across it easily, confidently. Every player is just as confident that he could do the same. We then say, hypothetically, that we're placing the plank over an alligator pit. It becomes clear to everyone with an imagination (and they've already imagined many more realistic horrors during their careers) that our approach to walking the same plank would change. It's the identical change that comes during athletic competition, for a number of reasons.

Bob Nideffer would say this: "The ability to attend (give focus) to relevant external cues would preclude that pressure."

Relevant external cues. The relevent external cues as we walk that plank are the plank itself and the movement of our feet. Muscle memory would take care of our feet; we know how to walk a straight line with ease. Relaxed. But we focus on the alligators. And on the consequences of taking a misstep, a fall. We visualize the eager jaws snapping shut . . .

We are concentrating on irrelevant external *and* internal cues. Our breathing shortens or stops; our muscles tighten; our mind and body succumb to the dreaded pressure. To the alligators? To the plank? Or to our own reactions? Our nervous reaction?

What's commonly called nervousness is a state of the brain in which its activity is being exhibited in a chaotic and disorganized way. Nideffer's message is simply that by training well at paying attention to the appropriate cues and tasks at hand, nervousness would be prevented. Thorough preparation, as Al McGuire suggested, is the solution. But we're not yet finished with the problem.

HOW DO PRESSURE AND TENSION DEVELOP?

1. Forced intentions become awkward actions. Players often try to force things to happen. A great percentage of the so-called "choking" in sports is the result of trying so hard that a player's tension level "shoots sky high." He gives more effort than the task requires. He becomes the proverbial bull in a China closet or the "golfing gorilla." The tension level gets so high the player freezes (stiff movements or none at all). Many times a player doesn't even realize what's happening to him.

In the 1981 World Series, New York Yankee outfielder Dave Winfield was one for 22, a batting average of .045. Even in the first game of the Series, it became clear to many baseball people that Winfield was pressing, trying to force things "to happen." After the Series, Winfield was asked, "Did you choke?" He answered, "No, I was trying too hard."

Players in such situations must *learn* to recognize and realize the mental and physical effects of trying too hard. They must have a "game plan"—a strategy—for handling "clutch" situations. With one, they'll be able to maintain their control when matters that mean so much to them seem to get out of hand. The more it means to a player, the more mental discipline he'll be required to have. The very determined, highly motivated players who always seem to put meaning into their game are the most frequent victims of "forced intentions."

Remember: When a player perceives that it's dangerous to make mistakes, mistakes will increase. A player trying hard not to make mistakes usually makes them, because what he is trying *not* to do becomes his dominant thought and focus.

2. Many thoughts in rapid succession tend to create pressure and anxiety. The mental rush just before a player is ready to perform has the same effect as rushing around doing last-minute chores while getting ready to go somewhere. The tendency is to get nervous and tense—and ineffectual.

3. Setting unrealistic goals, as we said earlier, causes players to expect too much of themselves. They put pressure on themselves to live up to the expectations of others. When they fail to reach these goals, they tend to become tense with anger, resentment, and frustration.

When outfielder George Foster signed the now-infamous large contract with the New York Mets in 1982, after having come to them from Cincinnati, he felt great pressure and attributed it to the expectations of the New York fans.

"You're always on trial," Foster said. "If you do the job today, they'll want you to do it tomorrow. If you don't do it, they want to know why . . . You can't rest."

Note: Foster batted .247 for the Mets in '82, the first season of his multi-year contract. He hit 13 homers and had 70 RBIs in 550 at-bats, the second lowest RBI full-season total of his career before or after. (He had hit 30 homers and knocked in 98 runs with only 440 ABs in 1979.)

4. Social pressure leads to trying to please or impress others; it creates a distinct feeling of stress. Worrying about how and what "they" think, as Foster also did, creates a misdirected focus and a misguided approach.

These are common products of such thinking and feeling:
A. "I want to show them just how good I am."
B. "I'm going to make them proud of me."
C. "I don't want to embarrass myself in front of all these fans."

Mike Schmidt, after winning his first MVP Award in 1980, said, "The biggest thing I had to learn was to define my audience. When I walked up to home plate, who was I trying to impress? The fans? My teammates? Management?

"In 1978, I had to come to grips with the fact that I couldn't try to impress 50,000 people. I had to stop saying, 'I'll show them.' For one thing, they are too loud. For another, the more you try to impress them, the less chance you have to succeed. The more you try to impress, the more you press. The more sawdust you squeeze out of the end of the bat."

5. Fear of failure and the imagined consequences create pressure. What are the sources of this fear? Usually, the source is a person close to the young player (coach, parent) who has punished the youngster for his failure to achieve a desired outcome. The punishment may be, in rare cases, physical (George Brett was booted in the rear), but it is almost always psychological. We have dealt with any number of professional players whose real and damaging anguish has been caused by the mental abuse of a so-called "well-intending loved one." (Most often this person was a father or a wife.)

Because the "punishment" and the resulting loss of self-esteem are so distasteful and/or upsetting, the player may come to fear the continuing possibility of failing. His performance on the field suffers, and so too may his behavior off the field. We know of minor league players who have lied to parents on the phone, in regard to their daily performance, in order to avoid the ridicule with which their nonproductive performance is met. Such irrational behaviors can be habit-forming. They are sad, but understandable.

There is no rational reason to feel such pressure. It's important to recognize the different sources of pressures that can so dramatically affect our hearts and minds.

When fear of failure dominates a player's mind, he's in trouble. The feeling of pressure is real enough. For example, Cal Ripken, Jr., speaking of his first year in the big leagues (his Rookie of the Year season), told *Baltimore Sun* reporter Kevin Cowherd, "I was hitting defensively, not wanting to look bad. I was putting so much pressure on myself, that I wasn't thinking clearly. I was down and all I could think about was that I might be going back to Rochester (the Oriole's Triple-A team). I would be OK when I first got to the ballpark, but gradually I would get depressed. And when I went hitless again, I just couldn't wait to get out of there as quickly as I could. I had to get away."

When fear is strong in us, our thoughts reflect the feeling. A fearful player may say the following:

"If I don't get a hit, we'll lose. It will be my fault, and I'll let the team down. I might even get benched tomorrow." "The background is bad; the ball is hard to see. I don't want to strike out."

"I don't want to blow this lead. They have the best hitters coming up. I wish I had better control today. If I don't make good pitches, they'll kill me. And then everyone will think I can't pitch in this league."

"The last time I was in this situation, I didn't get the job done."

We've now examined the most common causes and sources of pressure. It's also important to mention some specific effects created by tension. Positive tension, we must note, is a prerequisite for achievement. We all need some emotional excitement to stimulate us, to make us reach for our personal best. Some excitement makes us more alert, improves our reactions, gives us additional strength.

Emotional excitement (being "up," aroused for competition) is good for an athlete—until there is too much. Balance is lost. That even keel is lost. Whenever more is in the mind than what the job calls for, a negative influence on performance results. The excessive excitement and tension create an overload on the central nervous system. Nervousness becomes a distraction from task. We then do not function well mentally or physically.

MENTAL EFFECTS FROM OVER-EXCITEMENT

1. Messages from our eyes and ears become unclear and distorted.
2. Our judgments are not as accurate.
3. Indecisiveness sets in.
4. Our minds jump from one place to another—out of control.

PHYSICAL EFFECTS

1. We hyperventilate, not exhaling enough air.
2. Blood flow is adversely affected by our tightness.
3. General muscular constriction results.
4. We have a reduced range of motion.
5. Movements become less smooth or fluid, often becoming tight.
6. Our ability to see clearly may also become impaired.

Trying harder doesn't get it done. Many times after a player has hit a ball as well as he can, or has thrown a ball as well as he can, he thinks, "If only I would have tried a little harder, I could have done even better." Whatever the pressure—to do better, try harder, accomplish more, be perfect, not fail, whatever—the player should not fool himself: *He will be at his best in baseball when his performance is effortless.*

Pressure demands greater effort. It is an unreasonable and counterproductive demand, and the player should not meet it. He must understand the elements of pressure. He must remind himself of the difference between "challenge" and "threat."

The difference between clutch players and mediocre players becomes clear when they define tight game situations. A clutch player sees an opportunity for success; the other sees a risk of failure. It's bad enough when the results of a player's performance become his

Positive self-talk: "keep it up"; "one pitch at a time; go at 'em."

focus. But when they also become a matter of personal survival, the activity has lost its proper meaning for him.

The Heavy Equipment Needed: Rational, Positive Self-Talk, and Effective Breathing Techniques

Once again, we express emphatically that the "heaviest equipment" a player can utilize is his preemptive powers of concentration. Knowing *what* to focus on, and *how* to focus on it are all-powerful.

But the most skilled among us are far from perfect. It's essential, after all, for even the best navigator to know how to get back on course, should he sometime lose his way. For a ballplayer, knowing *what* to say to himself and *how* to say it when feelings of pressure distract him are essential for his "getting back on course."

Having read this far, the reader knows that the establishment of goals, a work ethic, a routine, a good attitude and so on all guide a ballplayer toward the development of his ability to concentrate well. When pressure becomes a problem, the player should review and reaffirm his philosophy in a quiet, private setting.

When pressure is felt as the player is performing, his task is to be sensitive to his feelings — be aware of the pressure — and put into action the strategies he believes in, act out what he knows, in other words.

The "great awareness," of course, is to recognize and accept that the pressure is being created and/or accepted internally. To deal effectively with pressure, we must acknowledge that it doesn't exist within the circumstance or situation, but rather comes from how we look at it and what we think of it. Our perceptions create our reality. It isn't "they" or "it" that makes us tense: *we make ourselves tense*.

The great players create the reality of joyful anticipation when they're faced with pressure situations. Regardless of talent, everyone has the ability to create that inner environment. That inner control allows players to produce more consistently in those situations. Being in control of their thoughts and tension level allows them to maximize their talents, to move to the top — where the pressure and rewards are the greatest.

Al Oliver played just under 20 years in the major leagues and had a lifetime batting average just over .300. He was recognized as an outstanding hitter in the clutch. His attitude very apparently was responsible for his approach.

"I am the same in every situation," said Oliver. "Whether it's an at-bat in a spring training or a World Scrics game, I think the same and I feel the same. I will be the same person if I get a hit or if I make an out. I'm good when the chips are down, because a lot of players tighten up and aren't as good. I take advantage of them, because I'm just me."

Positive thinking alone is not the answer to the problems of feeling pressure. Recent studies have shown that many mediocre performers employ the same amount of positive self-talk as the top performers. The difference is that mediocre performers mix in large doses of statements containing doubt and difficulty.

This suggests that much of the power in our thinking is actually in non-negative thinking. But just telling ourselves to stop that thinking — or to relax — won't solve our problem very often. "Keying down" requires specific techniques, though the individual player, as always, must be selective and find what works best for him.

The next chapter will treat relaxation more comprehensively, but it seems necessary here to note the following techniques, because they are very useful, particularly to players feeling stress during a game. The procedure below should be helpful as a "gathering process":

1. *Getting away from the source of the pressures:* Leave the batter's box, step off the mound, etc.

2. *Moving/stretching:* Make movements that are the same as those you make when you're relaxed — perhaps even slower and looser movements. Stretch slowly, as you might if you were yawning.

3. *Visualizing:* Visualize yourself relaxing or seeing something that relaxes you (fishing, lying on the beach, etc.).

4. *Tensing and relaxing:* Tense yourself for a few seconds, and then completely let go. (Gary Ward squeezes the bat as tight as he can and then relaxes his hands a few seconds before the pitcher delivers.)

5. *Talking out loud:* Give yourself positive, functional directives out loud, either mumbling or speaking under your breath at a slow pace, in a relaxed tone. (Many players make the mistake of using angry tones. Few know how to use anger effectively. As a general rule, the harsher your tonality, the tighter your muscles become. This is not to say that your physical approach should be passive or weak. We always advocate aggressive action.)

6. *Controlling breathing:* This is one of the most important — and neglected — performance techniques. Simply being aware of your breathing can help relax you when you are "keyed up." (Goose Gossage said, "When I'm throwing good, my breathing is the same all the time. I guess it's like shooting free-throws: if your breathing is different, you'll shoot different.")

A) Breathe in slowly until the lungs are comfortably full.
B) Hold for a couple of seconds.
C) Let the air slowly and completely fall out, without forcing.

Self-talk is also one of the most effective tools in shaping performance. It's extremely valuable when properly used during pressure situations. Effective self-talk assures the player that he is aware of the need to focus his attention on function. Appropriate focus, by definition, excludes anxiety, therefore eliminating it as a problem. The best mental discipline is applied when the best commands (self-talk) are spoken and enacted by a player. The dedication to employing these techniques is a part of mental discipline.

Los Angeles rookie Tim Belcher was his team's opening game pitcher in the 1988 World Series. Belcher struggled dramatically before giving up a grand slam home run to Jose Canseco of the Oakland Athletics.

Belcher, who had spent a number of years in the Athletics minor league system, said of his unimpressive Series opener, "I wanted to do well against Oakland, but you can't think that way. You have to take it like any other game. I was keyed up and anxious. Usually I walk behind the mound and relax. But on Saturday, I stayed on the mound. I toed the rubber. I started thinking I can't walk Canseco or I can't hang a slider to him. I thought too much. I just went crazy."

The quality of Belcher's thoughts were more damaging than the quantity. Belcher realized it — too late to fix that performance. But he made the adjustment in his second appearance of the Series.

"In Game 1, I was muscling up there trying to throw the ball 900 miles an hour. I might have been throwing 95 miles an hour, but I was missing the plate," Belcher explained. In his next appearance, an impressive World Series victory, Belcher again employed the techniques that had made him so successful during the regular season — a very successful one for the rookie pitcher.

"I used more self-talk than I've ever used in my career . . . reminding myself of mechanical checkpoints. Talking out loud is a great tool," Belcher said.

It's easier to ride the wave than to swim against it. When we anticipate the wave of pressure, we must be willing and able to first keep ourselves afloat and then move in the right direction.

The learning process contributes to dealing with pressure. Players can learn how to deal with the "big play," the "big game," everything that "is on the line." They learn from experience. Every time they fail to control their emotions, they have an opportunity to learn, to figure out what mental adjustment they must make to help themselves. Many of these adjustments are made through the use of self-talk.

Self-talk serves a player best when used as follows:

1. *Learn*, through asking questions, such as:
A. "What's stopping me from . . . ?"
B. "What can I do differently to get the results I want?"
C. "To get this right, what has to be different?"
D. "If I could do that the way I want to, what would it be like?"

2. *Anticipate* situations and plays.

3. *Direct your intentions*, such as:
A. A batter: "I'm going to hit the ball on the ground between the first and second baseman."

B. A pitcher: "Fastball, low and away."
C. An outfielder: "I'm going to hit the cut-off man if the ball's hit to me."

This self-talk focuses on what you will do when a play develops. It provides control; you become the actor, rather than the reactor. Talk is not an exclusive tool used when preparing for physical action. Pictures and images help. Use the words to trigger the previews of coming attractions. See yourself making the play.

4. *Assist yourself in your readying process.* Ready yourself for what you *know* will be happening (a pitch will be delivered to a batter or thrown by a pitcher) and on what you *want* to focus (e.g., "See the ball/target."). Use your statement to control this focus.

Remember, self talk helps you *get ready* to perform. Thinking (self-talk) and doing (hitting, throwing, fielding, etc.) are separate activities. It's difficult to do two things at the same time. Just as we think best when we aren't active physically, we "do" best when we aren't thinking. (Yogi Berra: "I can't think and hit at the same time.") Know when you're readying — and know when you're ready.

There's a story told concerning Hall of Fame pitcher Warren Spahn. As the story goes, Spahn was pitching for the Milwaukee Braves in the opening game of the 1957 World Series against the New York Yankees. The Braves were ahead, 4-1, in the top of the ninth inning with the Yankees at bat. They had two men on base. As Yankee catcher Elston Howard was coming out to bat, the Braves manager went to the mound to talk to Spahn about this pressure situation. He told Spahn of the "dangers" of an extra-base hit, "So don't give him anything up and out over the plate."

Spahn's first pitch was "up and out over the plate," right where it wasn't supposed to be thrown. Howard hit an opposite-field home run to tie the game. (The Braves — and Spahn — won the game in extra innings.) After the game, Spahn was muttering, loud enough to be heard. "Why would anyone ever want to give you a *negative* command?" He was puzzled and frustrated because, though he eventually won the game, he had been led away from his own strategy of giving himself functional, positive directions. Apparently, the manager felt more pressure than Spahn had. Yet Spahn pitched with the image of the manager's direction in his mind. He thought of what the manager didn't want him to do and increased the probability of doing it. His muscles responded to his mind. Even though Spahn was a veteran, he still learned a valuable lesson.

Now, a sampler of other voices from the "pressure corner" of major league baseball. Consider the players' statement carefully. What direction did each come from? More significantly, in what direction was he likely to be headed? Compare these remarks and experiences to your own. You be the judge. Which, if any, of these mental games can serve you best?

Von Hayes, feeling the pressure of a five-for-one trade from Cleveland to the Philadelphia Phillies (He was the "one."):
> "The team was going bad, and I was pressing . . . I was afraid everyone was thinking it was my fault."

Mike Schmidt, as a rookie hitting .201 with the Phillies, anticipating being sent back to Double-A, and gladly accepting a switch from third base to second base, hoping the new position would occupy his mind and allow him to relax at the plate:
> "I started playing second and it seemed like I totally concerned myself with my defense and just forgot about the pressure that was on me to learn to hit. I started hitting like crazy. I ended up hitting over .290, which means from that point on I had hit a good .350 or .360. I hit 26 home runs and I had 90-some ribbies."

Dave Righetti, after a Fourth of July no-hitter against Boston in Yankee Stadium:
> "They gave me the ball in spring training and told me I was in the starting rotation. That gave me the self-assurance to stop worrying about who I'm facing. I just have to throw my stuff. It's almost the same philosophy Yogi Berra has — why think?"

Ron Kittle, after having admitted to days of not wanting to go to the ball park during tough times with the White Sox, and getting advice from his friend and agent, Jim Bonner:

> "He told me, go out these last 60 or whatever games and have fun, have a blast, and he's right. I know I can hit a ball as hard and as far as anybody in the big leagues. If somebody boos me for throwing a ball in the stands, I'll brush it off . . . I'm one of 600 people playing major league baseball, and if I quit tonight, I will have had the highlight of my life—wearing the big league uniform. You can't think yourself to death in this game . . . "

Dale Murphy, discouraged after a tough July in a streaky 1986 season:

> "There have been times when I haven't driven in runs. Then the guys get out there again and you press and start thinking, 'I haven't done it in so many times.' Then you really press instead of just relaxing and playing the game . . . I have to go out and have fun and not worry so much about what might happen . . . "

Willie Stargell, a coach on Murphy's Braves team at that time:

> "It's a constant battle and constant work. It took me 10 years to know me. He (Murphy) can't worry about anything. I've seen improvement. It can be embarrassing and frustrating, but he has to stay aggressive."

Jose Canseco, as a rookie with the Oakland Athletics, unhappy at being written about as "a mixture of Roberto Clemente, Dale Murphy, and Reggie Jackson:

> "Fans say, 'Yeah, hit a home run every at-bat.' I just wish the fans could come up and get an at-bat and see how difficult it is. Especially for a guy like myself, a 21-year-old who's never seen the pitching in this league. It's doubly tough for someone like myself."

Darryl Strawberry, earlier accused of "giving in" when things got tough by his Mets teammate, Keith Hernandez—and later accused of "inconsistency" by many observers:

> "People are always talking about me hitting 50 home runs. The pressure has been on me since the day I ar-

rived. Maybe they expected me to hit 50 right away. When they talk about me, they say I should hit .300, 50 homers, drive in 125 to 130 runs, and steal 50 bases. That's what they say. It adds pressure."

During the summer of the Mets' 1986 championship season, Strawberry was being booed at Shea Stadium. He was hitting 100 points higher on the road and said:

"It's disgusting the way the fans treat me in New York. They like to point the finger at one particular player and say he's not doing well. It's not fair for a player to suffer through that . . . "

Cory Snyder, before his second season in the big leagues with Cleveland:

"I feel a lot more relaxed this year. I know what's expected of me, and I'm not putting as much pressure on myself."

Carl Yastrzemski, at age 39, during the year his mother had died of cancer:

"I used to take every game as life and death. I was extremely nervous, uptight. I took aspirins before games, drank a lot of coffee. I'd get sick to my stomach . . . I said to myself, 'Why the hell should I worry about going 0 for 4?' At first [after his mother's death], baseball seemed almost trivial for a while, then it seemed something to enjoy, take as it comes . . . "

Don Mattingly, after signing a contract that would give him $1,375,000, and after Yankee owner George Steinbrenner made a public pronouncement relating to the performance "demands" of such a contract:

"All of a sudden, I wanted to prove I deserved it. I was trying too hard. I finally told myself, 'Hey, Donnie, just go out and play the game.' I realized that I can never do enough for the fans to say that I'm worth a million dollars, no matter what kind of season I have. I'm hitting .345 and I'm 1 for 2, but a guy yells at me the other day, 'You haven't done anything tonight. If you can't take the pressure, get out.'"

Eric Davis, opening the 1987 season as Cincinnati's centerfielder and cleanup hitter, and having heard that the Reds general manager "couldn't accept a slow start from Davis":
> "I think the Reds feel more pressure than I do. They're already talking about 40 home runs and 130 stolen bases. Those are astronomical numbers. But see, they believe it. I'll just try to do my own thing."

Eddie Murray, being spoken of as a future Hall of Famer by Baltimore manager Earl Weaver, and praised for his consistency in pressure situations:
> "I love being on the spot when the game is on the line. Some guys don't like the pressure, but I do. Sometimes, before I get to the plate, I know what the pitcher's going to do."

Pete Rose, while chasing Ty Cobb's record of 4191 career hits and being called by Mike Schmidt, "the best pressure ballplayer I've ever played with or against, and that's the highest compliment I can give":
> "The closer I get to the record, there's not going to be pressure . . . The closer I get to the record, the more revved up I'm going to get."

Wade Boggs, being questioned by reporters about the pressures of his race for the American League batting title with Rod Carew:
> "Never enters my mind. I only think about seeing the ball and hitting it."

Finally, a few words from a football player about the pressures athletes put on themselves to be the best. Says Marcus Allen, "You've got to think positively to achieve the impossible, to be what you expect to be. If you seek mediocrity, that's what you'll get out of life. I have a burning desire to be the best. If I don't make it, that's OK, because I'm reaching for something so astronomically high. If you reach for the moon and miss, you'll still be among the stars."

That kind of philosophy is helpful. So is the view of Dr. Robert Eliot, a cardiologist at the University of Nebraska. Speaking on the topic of pressure and stress, Dr. Eliot said, "Rule Number One is, Don't sweat the small stuff. Rule Number Two is, It's all small stuff."

If the athlete feels his philosophy — and his performance — is slipping away from him during competition, he can work toward recovering both by taking control of his internal communication. He should talk to himself in the manner that has helped him produce his best performances in the past.

Obstacle Four: "Slumps"

"When I'm not hitting, I don't hit nobody. But when I'm hitting, I hit anybody." So said Willie Mays, and, in their own ways, so say many other players. Slumps (and streaks) are a real part of the game of baseball. As a subject, "slumps" have been frequently written about and discussed. The term, like "pressure," begs definition. The media and fans are quick to identify a slump and just as quick to define it. If a player buys into their definition, he is at risk. That's why we put the term "slump" in quotation marks above. Let the player/definer beware.

We mentioned in an earlier chapter our conversation with Wade Boggs, who heard about his own slump — identified and defined by the host of a radio talk show Boggs was listening to, as he drove home from the ball park after a game. Boggs was in the midst of a nine-game hitting streak early in the season, but his batting average was "only" slightly higher than .300. The Red Sox third baseman knew he was seeing the ball well and hitting the ball hard. He turned the radio off.

In July of 1983, a sportswriter for *The New York Times* called Hall-of-Famer Joe Morgan, who was playing for the Philadelphia Phillies at the time. Morgan had gone 0 for 35. The reporter asked the player about his "slump."

"But I'm not in a slump," Morgan replied. "I'm just not getting hits. There's a difference. A slump is when you're not hitting the ball and striking out. I've been hitting the ball; they're just making great catches."

Bill Giles, the Phillies president called it a slump, and said he would replace Morgan if he didn't soon produce.

"Produce" results. Morgan was talking about the litmus test called "approach." Fans, media people, and presidents whose teams are in the middle of a pennant race talk about results. We made the distinction between those two terms early in this book. Slumps are real enough, but, once again, whose reality and definition do we accept?

The most common use of the term is based on results. Did the batter get a hit? Did the pitcher win the game? O for 14? Six straight pitching losses? A slump. This is the popular definition — the very one every player should reject. But players grow up hearing the word bandied about and many never make the adjustment to a more valid and appropriate definition, as they play the game themselves.

Sports psychologists Bruce Ogilvie and Maynard Howe define a slump ("Beating Slumps at Their Own Game," *Psychology Today*, July 1984) as "a prolonged performance decrement that causes an athlete or team to suffer a serious loss of self-confidence. This is accompanied by a feeling of powerlessness as the physical skills that were once taken for granted fail to win the day . . . As (athletes) fail to produce, fan and press attacks intensify, increasing anxiety and making it harder to break the destructive pattern of pressure, stress and failure."

"Feeling of powerlessness." Loss of control. "Failure." Ends, rather than means. The familiar trap. As we said, *beware!*

Every player who has ever played the game has had good days and bad days. Hot streaks and slumps. Hitters go through periods when they "just miss" pitches they usually kill, hitting two-hoppers to infielders instead of drives between the outfielders. They start chasing pitches they usually take and taking pitches they usually hit. Every pitch seems to "have something on it" and is right on the corner. The hitters don't hit many balls hard, and when they do, someone makes a fantastic catch. Classical signs of "a slump."

Statistics do not tell an experienced, confident hitter that he's in a slump. The quality of his at-bats and how often he hits the ball hard tell him.

In 1983, as Pete Rose chased Ty Cobb's total hit record, a *Sports Illustrated* article appeared entitled, "Is the Bloom off the Rose?" The subhead read: "Unless he picks up the pace, Pete Rose, 42, may not tie Cobb after all." Rose, on the other hand, had no such concerns. "I know I'll get it," he said.

He also explained his "slump" that season. "When I went 0 for 20, I wasn't swinging and missing. I just wasn't getting hits. When I go into a real slump, I start topping the ball. I wasn't doing that, so I wasn't worried. I never struck out and I wasn't tentative in my swing. I could easily have had six or seven hits."

Rose may have been frustrated at times during those 20 at-bats, but he didn't allow his feelings to change his approach. He knew he wasn't in a slump. He was patient, kept his cool, and his concentration. He knew there was luck involved — over which he had no control — and that during the course of a season he would get his share of "cheap hits" to make up for the line drives that were caught.

Every player should know that. But inexperienced and immature players tend to panic. A hitter will think, "I'm 4 for 25; I'm in a slump. I have to do something different. I have to change." If they don't fall into this trap, they may be pushed in by others, well-meaning as those others may be.

Dave Winfield now understands this well. "Everybody tells you something else you're doing wrong." he said. "You go up to the plate thinking about all these things. Then Scott McGregor throws one down the pipe that you should hit over the fence and you're so screwed up, you pop it straight up. Then you decide, to hell with it, and you go back to swinging naturally."

Hitters can't guide the ball through the holes. A player who is aware of pitfalls is most likely to avoid the pit.

Pitchers included. Tom Seaver, in his book, *The Art of Pitching,* writes: "Even a talented, dedicated pitcher who learns from his mistakes and tries to correct them will inevitably have to endure a slump . . . (A)nother challenge of pitching is to accept them [slumps] and battle your way through them. One game or one inning will not get you into a slump, and one game or one inning will not get you out of a slump. But if you constantly monitor your performance, pitch by pitch, you can limit the severity of a slump. In trying to conquer a pitching slump, don't panic and overhaul your mechanics. The problem is almost always minor and needs only a small adjustment."

For many pitchers, a minor mechanical problem becomes a major mental problem.

Many players don't know what to say about a slump. "I feel it's hopeless to talk about it, because I don't have the slightest idea what's wrong," said first baseman Cecil Cooper in 1983, when he was with the Milwaukee Brewers.

But most players can less explain a hot streak. They "just happen" is the most common explanation. And they can lead to trouble. A hitter can do anything, yet still "hang out ropes," and he knows it, he feels it. He starts thinking, "I've got it together; I've found it. This is easy." His confidence may lead him to complacency. He loses his mental discipline in batting practice, because he can have some fun and back off. Play some "long ball." In the game, he starts thinking more about how they are going to pitch him and starts trying to hit "cookies" a little harder, maybe much harder.

The hot hitter can get away with fuzzy thinking and trying to do more for a while, because the physical and mental habits he developed while working his way out of a slump have a carry-over effect. This effect is the reason it's so difficult to figure out how real slumps start — and what is really the problem.

Batting slumps actually begin while the hitter is "going good," while he is hot, feeling secure, unbeatable — and becoming undisciplined mentally.

The great Rod Carew understood that going good was kept good by sticking to the good habits, maybe even developing *better* habits. He would come to the ball park and take extra batting practice despite the fact that he was hitting .340 or .350. Roommate Tony Oliva, himself a three-time batting champion and now the hitting coach of the Minnesota Twins, said of his roomie in those days, "He knows you can lose your timing overnight."

Generally speaking, hitters build hot streaks over a period of time. Likewise, they "cool off" over a period of time. Quite often though, after one very poor at-bat or one "bad game" (pitching performances as well), some doubt creeps in. They lose some confidence and begin to wonder, "What's wrong, am I losing it?" And they lose it. The hot streak is over.

Darryl Evans had "been there before." He explained, "What happens is you hit the ball good for a while and find you're not getting any base hits. Then you start worrying about the hits; you become frustrated and soon you're not hitting the ball so well. The big thing when you start swinging at pitches out of the strike zone is getting back to reality."

Reality should not include the continued process of analysis that creates paralysis. "What's wrong; am I opening up too soon?" "How about my stride?" "Am I dropping my hands?" As Dave Winfield noted earlier, people will be more than happy to provide answers — even for questions you didn't ask. What we hear most from players who are truly slumping is, "I can't seem to get comfortable."

Most of the time, for hitters, "not being comfortable" is a direct result of not seeing the ball well. Pitchers suffer from the same type of poor concentration. Their location suffers and the results make them suffer. The discomfort felt is the body saying, "I can't do the job, because I'm not positive where the ball is going (or where it is)." The *player* doesn't seem to realize he's not seeing the target or the ball as he should, but his *body does*.

Only a person confident of seeing the ball well can stand in the batter's box relaxed and comfortable, knowing a baseball will be coming at him at the speed of 80-plus miles per hour. Only a person confident that he can knows exactly where he's going to throw the ball can stand on the rubber and allow his body to be free to "let it all out" easily.

George Brett has said, "I can't hit if I can't concentrate." He thinks it's that simple, and so do we. How can a player be comfortably prepared if he's worried/concerned/thinking about anything but the ball or the target?

Don Mattingly has gone 0 for 18 a couple or so times in his career. He explained, "Most of the time in those slumps, it was because I just wasn't 'locked in' mentally. I'd try to concentrate but it seemed like I just wasn't there for about four days."

"Trying to concentrate" focuses on the *act* of *concentration*, rather than on the ball itself. It's a common attempt, made particularly by players who are "slumping," pressing — trying everything they or others can think of, all the while becoming more uncomfortable in the batter's box, on the mound, in the field.

Discomfort often occurs in players who feel they must have "the perfect stance" or "the perfect pitching motion," and who consequently tighten up as they search for it during their performance. "Slump"-inducing, to be sure.

What Causes "Real Slumps"?

First, let us say that we define a "real slump" as an *extended breakdown in a player's typical approach,* be it hitting, pitching, or fielding.

A poor approach leads to a poor result. A non-typical approach leads to a non-typical performance. The slumping player who concerns himself with the result is fretting over the symptom, not the problem. His slump is likely to last much longer than the player who understands and tries to get himself out of his slump by finding a remedy for the problem. (Wade Boggs won't even use the word "slump," in any context. He calls his difficult times a "reconstruction period," and rightly so. It's a time he works on reconstructing his typical and effective approach.)

The most common slump, the hitting slump, has two basic causes. One is mechanical; the hitter is doing something "wrong" at the plate (stance or swing). The other relates to the hitter's mental "stance." More often then not, the player's mental approach is the source of the mechanical breakdown.

The following are some of the elements that contribute to a hitting slump:

1. *Seeing the ball is taken for granted by hitters.* They think more about statistics, mechanics, situations or whatever, rather than seeing the ball.

2. *Hitters begin to chase pitches that they ordinarily take.* In the midst of a good streak, they think, "These pitches look fat, and I can hit anything they throw now." As a result, they lose their mental discipline and bad pitches lead to bad swings . . . and so much for the "hot streak." Now, they're flailing at everything and getting nothing. The pitches don't look fat any longer.

3. *Hitters overswing, trying to do too much with the ball.* This can start in batting practice, playing some "long ball." Doing that, the player is practicing overswinging. Loss of a disciplined swing will cause problems.

4. *Hitters think more.* This may happen any time to a player, for whatever reason, begins to think of things in the batter's box that should have been thought of before — or not at all.

5. *A hitter tries to repeat a swing.* "I'm going to try to hit it just like I did that last one." With this type of thinking and approach, he's trying to control the swing, not his thinking. Good swings are free and natural. There's a world of difference between a free, natural swing and one consciously controlled by the hitter — as he hits.

6. *A hitter analyzes how he's doing it (hitting).* He thinks, "If I figure out what I'm doing now (during a good streak), I'll be able to keep doing it." The natural and unconsciously resulting stance and swing become unnatural and conscious. These movements are seldom as free and smooth as unconscious movements. A decrease in the accuracy of hand-eye coordination may also result.

7. *Hitters begin to wonder, "How long can it (good streak) keep going?"* Or a hitter will think, "I hope I don't lose it." Thoughts of "hope," "I wish," and "I wonder," are brought up by an underlying doubt or fear, and therefore are negative thoughts, which most likely will cause negative results.

The Heavy Equipment Needed: The Same Old Equipment, The Approach That Works

Pressure of all kinds lead to strategies that cause slumps. The "cure" is the same: *mental discipline* — going back to all the approaches the player knows have worked for him in the past. It's the same old story — the same old "equipment." But the old "equipment" is still around because it still gets the job done best. Trust it and get back in the driver's seat.

Great hitters, when asked about getting out of slumps, mention the same type of approach again and again:

Concentrate on seeing the ball.
Drive the ball up the middle.
Stay within yourself. (Swing easy, just meeting the ball, as opposed to overswinging.)
Keep things simple and don't rush yourself.
Swing at pitches you can hit. Take bad pitches.
Control the emotional and tension level with a regular breathing pattern.
Discipline yourself in batting practice.

Outstanding pitchers offer the following advice:

Concentrate on seeing the target.
Know the situation and the opposition.
Have a purpose with every pitch.
Control the emotional and tension level with a regular breathing pattern.
Warm up properly.

Discipline, always. *That is mental toughness*, as we've said a number of times. Through a disciplined mental approach in practice and in games, the behavior becomes habituated. The approach becomes consistent. Good pitches, good fielding plays, and good at-bats become more frequent. As physical and mental habits become stronger, confidence builds, until it gets to a point at which he feels he is master of his game. First, he becomes master of himself.

Remember your goal, no matter how things are going. One of the first topics discussed in this book was the setting of goals. Whatever is thought most about, we said, will function as the player's goal. During a slump, the slump itself becomes the preoccupation of the hitter. His primary goal is "instant recovery." That goal won't help him out of his slump; those just mentioned above will.

Hall of Famer Billy Williams, a great player with the Chicago Cubs and a major league hitting coach, said, "A hitter has to know himself. He has to know his strengths and weaknesses. He has to know what to look for mentally and physically. And he has to remember how he has gotten out of slumps in the past!"

Williams warned, "All of the well-intended advice and tips from other players, family, friends, cab drivers, barbers, etc., that every player receives when he's in a slump compounds the problem. Those that listen to and think about what everyone else has to say will become deeply confused. A hitter should have one, no more than two people he can turn to for help. It will usually be someone who really knows him well, a coach or teammate he trusts."

Williams went on to say, "Some players get hotter than others. Some just can't handle success. When they start going good, they begin to think about statistics, instead of what they have to do to hit the ball well. A lot of hitters stop themselves from having big days, because when they get two hits in the first two tries, they get excited or, in some cases, think they've already had a good day. One way or another, they change their thinking."

Williams remembered, "I had a lot of big days, because I was always the same. I had the same attitude whether I was 0 for 3 — or 3 for 3. I know that when you're concentrating on getting a hit, you won't see the ball as well. But when you're concentrating on seeing the ball, you'll hit it well, and then the hits will take care of themselves."

The hitter's task-oriented goal is always to see the ball.

Take care of the right hitting approach. To most great hitters, the batting cage is a laboratory. We've already spoken of Rusty Staub and Yaz. We also told the story of Tom Seaver and his attitude toward regular and effective bullpen work. Great players use this preparation not only to get loose, but also to keep their fundamental approach sharp and consistent. However, if their preparation results are not sharp, they don't worry or fret. They trust themselves and their approach, and they don't force things to happen.

For example, many a young hitter would get impatient and immediately start to make changes, failing to consider some of the differences between taking batting practice and hitting in games. In batting practice, nothing is really at stake, so his attitude may be subtly — or obviously — different. Emotionally, perhaps. He also knows what pitches are coming in b.p.; the "stuff" on those pitches will be considerably less, etc. Batting practice results don't tell a good hitter when it's time to make an adjustment. His same performance and the quality of his at-bats tell him when to do that. It's an important distinction for a player to make, a good way of avoiding a slump.

An interesting story provides a good illustration of how the ability to maintain "the right approach" can keep a player from being plagued by a slump—the proverbial apple-a-day, keeping the doctor away.

In 1977, Rod Carew was hitting .411 for the Minnesota Twins. It was already July 1. No one hit .400 for an entire season since Ted Williams had hit .406 in 1941. The entire baseball world was excited about Carew's chances. People who didn't usually follow baseball were asking, "What's Rod hitting today?"

In late June and early July, *TIME* magazine was preparing a cover story featuring Carew. They had wanted a special picture for the cover. They hoped to get that shot during some extra batting practice on the morning of July 2. The photographer asked Carew to pull everything he hit to right field. In the photographer's professional judgment, a superior picture would result from this technique.

All season, in batting practice, Carew religiously hit the ball where it had been pitched. But to help out, he pulled everything for almost an hour. In the game that day, Carew began his only slump of the year. In his next 49 at-bats, he had only 13 hits. More significantly, he grounded out to the first and second baseman time and time again. This was not the "real" Rod Carew. This *was* a "real" slump. Carew's approach had been changed.

While trying to figure out where and how all this had gotten started, he remembered that day in Chicago. The batting practice he had taken for the *TIME* photographer "was not Rod Carew batting practice but it had a carry-over effect": Carew had begun to pull everything in his regular batting practice. It was as if someone turned a bright light on in a dark room. Carew knew exactly what he had to do to solve the problem.

He again started taking "Rod Carew batting practice," hitting the ball to all fields," hitting the ball where it was pitched. Within two days he was hitting drives to all corners of the field again. He finished the season with a .388 average, just eight hits short of the .400 mark.

How important is batting practice to preventing and eliminating slumps? Just ask Rod Carew.

Every player has stories to tell. Hitters remember clearly their slump stories. The following is typical: A very productive (unnamed here) player was asked what he thinks about after he swings and misses.

His answer was, "If I'm going good, I don't give it a second thought, but if I'm not going good, I have a check list (mechanics) that I go through."

The next question was, "At what point do you decide to go through your check list? Does it take a few bad days, or what?"

The player replied, "If I swing and miss badly a couple of times, I start checking my mechanics (hands, shoulder, stride, etc.). Sometimes I find the problem and correct it right away. But a lot of times I go a week or 10 days and can't put my finger on the problem. My next move is just to say, 'To hell with it, I'm going to give them 10 at-bats.' I make up my mind to swing easy, concentrate on seeing the ball and hitting it up the middle. That approach always brings me out of a slump. And it's funny, but a lot of the balls I hit the hardest come when I'm doing that."

Why does the player wait 10 days? Why the check list? What would happen if he trusted himself and his swing, if he concentrated on seeing the ball and having an easy swing consistently? Always?

For a player working himself out of a slump, the most important factors are seeing the ball or the target and staying within himself. His visualization skills can serve him well also. By using his imagination, a player can take mental practice, in the batting cage or in the bullpen — or in the field. He can "rerun" his game performance, seeing the pitches or plays that are unsatisfactory, and then make the corrections. As we've said, with skill, he can do that after each pitch. Visualization is a powerful tool, for those who learn to use it. It has helped many players out of slumps — and kept a good number from getting into them often.

Goose Gossage recalled his days with the Chicago White Sox, when Johnny Sain was his pitching coach. "If we were going bad, Sain would tell us to look at our old scrapbooks."

A subtle way of recommending visualization. Read the clippings of how wonderful you were; remember those performances; *see* yourself at that time; reinforce your best approach; get yourself going good again. That, essentially, was the process Sain was advocating. The player's confidence also has a good chance of being restored by his review of past glories.

Superstitions have been woven into the fabric of human beliefs and behavior. Their threads are particularly bright in the baseball world — past and present. Many players (managers, coaches, et.al.) enact superstitions as a way of avoiding bad streaks — slumps. Slumping players, in their desperation, are often willing to employ *any* technique.

These superstitions are based on wishful thinking. Bats that have not produced base hits have been destroyed in moods of religious intensity or just plain anger. Philadelphia broadcaster Richie Ashburn, a former outfielder with the Phillies says, "I've seen guys pour gasoline on their bats and burn them right in the dugout. I took mine to bed, to get to know it a little better. I know that sounds weird, but in a slump a player will do anything."

Not washing "lucky" shirts, wearing the same socks to the ball park — or the opposite approach of destroying "unlucky" shirts, socks, or entire outfits — become the rituals of players who face the uncertainty of each day's performance.

We do not propose these actions as remedial or preventative, but we've already said that people with strong beliefs can very often make happen what they believe will happen. If carrying a particular stone in his pocket helps a player have confidence and faith in himself, he should keep it right there in his pocket.

However, superstitions too often become an immature person's avoidance of his own personal responsibility. They become a player's excuse for "blaming the stars, instead of himself." Stories about superstitious players are always amusing. Sometimes what the player is going through is far from funny, and his remedy is far from effective.

Physical adjustments often can be the solution to the problem of a slump. If the player has gone about examining his approach in a thoughtful, logical way, he can help himself greatly. (The Carew example serves well.) In the late 1950s one of baseball's immortals, Ty Cobb, was living in California. Cobb was a frequent visitor at Candlestick Park in San Francisco. He loved to watch Willie Mays "do his thing" in center field for the Giants.

Bill Rigney was managing the Giants at the time, and he and Cobb spent a lot of time "talking baseball." One conversation concerned slumps. Rigney said, "I don't suppose you had many slumps." He was aware of some of Cobb's enormous achievements: 15 seasons with batting average higher than .350; 11 years with 90 or more runs-batted-in; 12 batting championships; 24-year career average of .367. (And more, of course.)

"You bet I had slumps," Cobb told Rigney.

"Did you have any kind of plan to get out of them?" Rigney questioned.

Cobb responded, "Everyone has to have a plan to get out of a slump. Mine was to get right on top of the plate. You see, when I went into a slump it was because I was chasing pitches out of the strike zone. By moving up in the box and getting closer to the plate, I eliminated my margin of error in judging which pitches were strikes. I knew that if I didn't have to back off [get out of the way] the pitch was over the plate. And if the pitch was away at all, it was a ball." Cobb went on to say, "When I got the strike zone under control again, and I felt comfortable, I would move back to where I usually stood."

Said Rigney years later, "Take a minute and think about the beauty of Cobb's approach. The further away from home plate a hitter stands, the harder it is to judge which pitches are over the corners and which are out of the strike zone. By moving closer to the plate, Cobb improved his judgment and control of the strike zone."

What Cobb did was to make an adjustment to something that was real and sensible. His adjustment was a result of his thought process; it was not an emotional reaction. The term "pressure" had nothing to do with his assessment. Slumps happened because something in his trusted approach had broken down. He made an adjustment and went back to that trusted approach. (Carew again.)

The sooner a player remembers and reactivates the "right" approach, the sooner the slump ends. We have tried to suggest a "right approach" throughout the book. In this chapter, we've tried to recommend a few remedies for those who have strayed, but it always comes down to the player taking responsibility for knowing what approach works best for him.

Obstacle Five: Anger

An angry player is most often a frustrated player. Something has gone wrong for him. A housewife becomes angry when she burns the food for a dinner she's preparing for special guests. A traveler becomes angry when his flight is canceled. The baseball manager becomes angry when a close call goes against him because of what he believes to be an umpire's bad judgment. A player becomes angry after striking out, or throwing a home run pitch, or booting a ground ball in a key situation. A child becomes angry when he doesn't get exactly what he wants.

The frustration of "not having things go our way" can lead to anger—unless we've learned to control our disappointment and express adult judgment, instead of childish emotion. That restraint, followed by constructive behavior, serves as an excellent example of mental discipline. Hard to come by, as all of us know.

Anger *can* act as a motivator, though only for the first few seconds of its life. Many athletes *do* know how to use their anger effectively. Tennis star John McEnroe was a notable example. He and others like him know how to take the energy from it and, through that arousal, rid themselves of the frustration by "taking it out" on their opponents. Football players use that technique with more success than baseball players, not because they have special skills, but because of the nature of the games in which they participate. We won't expound on the differences, which seem clear enough. We will affirm our belief that most athletes allow their anger a life well beyond the first few seconds. The feelings linger and, because frustration and anger are negative emotions, they hinder athletes, rather than help them.

The "Mad Hungarian." Do you remember that nickname? It belonged to former big league reliever Al Hrabosky, who would storm off the back of the mound, turn his back to the waiting batter, and get himself "psyched up" before he threw his next pitch. His "madness" was not anger, as many thought. The antic was invented more to intimidate the batter than to over-arouse the pitcher.

"Once I got mad," said Hrabosky, "I was totally useless. I would feel a surge of power going through my body from the increased adrenaline, but I lost total concentration. All my manager could do was yank me out, 'cause I was useless."

The image of pitching great Sandy Koufax, on the other hand, was one of quiet control. But it wasn't always that way. Early in his career, before he became successful, Koufax did battle with anger and frustration. Koufax said that as a pitching coach in the Dodger organization, he saw "young players getting angry with themselves the way I did, and I wish I could tell them how to curb it."

One piece of advice might be for the player to become aware of anger's effect on his performance. He should look back after an episode of anger and check whether or not he was in control of himself, *during* and *after* the anger. For example, a pitcher who has a ball hit out of the park on him, and who storms around on the mound is readying himself to throw the next pitch while out of control. But if he storms *off* the mound, vents his anger (the resin bag is a common victim of that kind of anger), gathers himself, and *regains his control*, no harm has been done. The next pitch will *not* be a result of the previous one. Any player is capable of examining which of these behaviors he enacts.

Most of the anger expressed by players is a result of failing to execute in the manner they wanted to. Their anger is aimed at themselves. Through severe self-criticism after a poor result, the player punishes himself for his "mistake" or "lack of ability." He thereby shows himself and everyone witnessing his loss of control how much he wanted to do well, how intense a competitor he is. It's a poor show and a poorer strategy.

Joe DiMaggio was an intense competitor. He *played* intensely; he didn't *display* intensely. That famous and filmed kick at the dirt in a World Series, after Dodger outfielder Al Gionfrido robbed him of a home run, is exclusive evidence of the existence of an emotional system in "The Yankee Clipper." That system was *almost always under control.*

Inner intensity is a characteristic of most great athletes. It's applied to their performance in a *positive* way. These outstanding athletes don't punish themselves or put their emotions on parade. They examine what has happened during their performance in a rational way, and they work at improving or fixing it. Anger, they know, makes another mistake more likely, since they will be disstracted by what they just did and not focus on what must be done.

The Heavy Equipment Needed: "Cool"—Channeled Energy

"Cool," the noun. The thing players want when things get hot around them.

Most baseball players, we find, play better when they've learned about all the possible situations that can frustrate and anger them. (Through experience, they also learn that everyone has to deal with such emotions.) As players experience these situations they get to recognize them in advance. They are also, then, more aware of their own reactions to specific situations and, as Koufax eventually was, more able to deal with them effectively, to enact, in players' terms, "Cool."

Players with "Cool" are players with mental discipline. They are the players teammates rely on in clutch situations. They've come to terms with the game, with the situation, with themselves. The *great* ones are not "Cool"; they are "Ice."

Edwin Kiester, Jr., in his article, "The Uses of Anger" (*Psychology Today*, July 1984), quotes Thomas Tutko, co-founder of the Institute of Athletic Motivation. Tutko, speaking of Swedish tennis star Bjorn Borg, said, "When something went wrong, Borg became even more efficient and more intense. He was truly a model who absolutely did not respond to outside provocations. He had the maturity and ego strength to accept the setback and use the emotion to make himself even keener."

Tutko continued, "Jack Nicklaus is similar. Instead of becoming emotional in a situation that might provoke another golfer to anger, he simply concentrates more on the task at hand. Athletes who have learned that do marvelously well under pressure."

Gary Smith wrote about tennis great Ivan Lendl in *Sports Illustrated*. Now famous for his "iron will," Lendl told Smith of the terrible temper he had as a boy.

Lendl's father told the boy, "Emotions don't help you." Lendl's mother scolded her upset son, "If you're going to cry, go home."

Lendl himself told how he hated to lose. "Even playing table soccer against my father, I cried and threw my [toy] player on the table when I lost...I cried so much when I lost points in tennis I couldn't see the ball..."

Lendl's temperament has very obviously changed from a "low boil" to a "high cool." He has seen the ball quite well—as an adult.

Jeromy Burnitz, a rookie outfielder with the New York Mets in 1993, claimed to have won a battle that had raged within him since he was a youngster: a raging ambition accompanied by a hot-headed tendency to punish himself. "Emotional is a decent word for me," Burnitz said. "But I think I came to grips with the fact that I might not ever be what I thought I should be. It's tough being mad at yourself 24 hours a day. It's too hard, and with no benefit."

The cool players have learned, through mental discipline, to control and channel their energy.

An old proverb, heard may years ago: "Anger is a wind that blows out the lamp of the mind."

Great players don't perform in the dark, so they're always able to see the ball or the target.

Obstacle Six: Pain

In his book, *The Ultimate Athlete*, George Leonard writes, "We know very little about pain. It seems mechanical in that it's somehow connected to reflex action, and yet it's highly subjective and can't be easily quantified...The perception of pain is increased by anticipation or dread or tenseness. If you fight it or shrink away from it, that only makes it worse. In some sense, pain is a judgment. It is not a fixed quantity..."

We *do know* about all sorts of drugs that relieve or deaden all sorts of pain. We *do know* that pain is a very individual and personal experience. And we *do know* that feeling pain is a psychological, as well-physiological, experience.

Recent research has found that the brain and the pituitary gland hold hormones previously unknown. These hormones, endorphins by name, are all chemically related. The physiological activity of some of them is much the same as pain-relieving substances such as opium, heroin, morphine—which, while acting on the pain itself, also inhibit emotional responses to the pain. More and more medical researchers are taking the view that mental attitudes affect the body's process of secreting endorphins, which, in turn, affects the "sufferer's" perception of his pain.

Norman Cousins wrote nearly two dozen books, many related to the biochemistry of emotions. His *Anatomy of an Illness* tells the story of his own recovery from a "crippling and supposedly irreversible illness." Since that experience, Cousins has joined the medical faculty at UCLA. *The Healing Heart*, provided "anecdotes to panic and helplessness." One particular anecdote deserves attention here, since its theme relates to pain.

The story deals with one Harry Brink, a man introduced to Cousins at UCLA. Brink was known to one of Cousins' colleagues for his ability to control pain. Cousins met the man and observed a demonstration he gave. The 55-year-old Brink was to lie on a bed of nails. Cousins reported his experience, condensed below.

When Cousins saw...

> ...the white-haired gentleman who had come to UCLA to display his abilities...I thought of the exhibitions I had seen in India. I asked whether I might see the "bed" of nails. Harry produced his board from out of a dirty burlap bag. The board was about two feet by three feet. It contained about 40 to 50 nails, irregularly spaced and extending perhaps an inch and three-quarters above the board. I pressed the palm of my hand against the nails and winced; they were sharp enough to cut...[Harry also wanted to show his ability to control his bleeding.]
>
> Harry lay on the nails for perhaps three or four minutes without apparent pain or discomfort. His eyes were closed and he was breathing deeply and rhythmically. Then he rolled off the board. When he sat up we could see that his back was heavily peppered with red puncture sites. No bleeding—except for one spot on the shoulder where the blood was spurting. We called this fact to Harry's attention. He thanked us and shut if off...
>
> ...Physicians don't need William Shakespeare to inform them that, if human beings are pricked, they bleed. Yet here was a human being who was stuck in 50 places or more and was not bleeding except in one place. What was more startling was that he arrested the flow once he learned of its existence.
>
> What about the pain itself?...
>
> What Harry had done, as the yogis in India had done, was to enable the mind to exert control over the body's autonomic nervous system...

Cousins then discussed the various functions of that system. He referred to each of the functions as "something of a miracle in itself," and pointed out that they go on in their regularity without any knowledge of them on our part. "The very absence of an awareness of the life process," he notes, "gives rise to the notion that we are totally deprived of any control over them. Yet some measure of control is well within our capacity."

Yes, we each have a different capacity, but how far have we ever stretched ourselves in any real attempt to reach it? That's the question we ask throughout this book. That's the test for any human who desires to reach his personal potential. The desire is usually greater in athletes.

Pain can interfere with that desire. It often resides in an athlete's body and surely has interfered with many athletic performances. Even when the source of the pain doesn't weaken them, athletes have been adversely affected in terms of function (running, skiing, throwing, swimming, etc.) and in their ability to concentrate. The problem with the athlete's concentration stems from the fact that he is attending to the pain and not to the performance.

We've occasionally played this little "game" with players. We grab some hairs on the player's arm. He jumps and gives out an "ouch." We then get a handful of hair from his head, and again pull—even harder this time—at the hair on his arm. His attention is redirected—perhaps intensified. He pays no attention to the "pain" in his arm.

A related article appeared in *USA Today* a year or so ago. What was most interesting, we think, was the relationship between the headline and the context. The headline read, "PLAYING VIDEO GAMES EASES PATIENTS' PAIN." The second paragraph of the article read: "A new study finds that playing video games while the dentist fills a tooth significantly lowers a patient's anxiety."

Either the terms "pain" and "anxiety" were confused or they were not differentiated. Dental professor Dr. Sait Seyrek of State University of New York at Buffalo hit the right nerve. He said the video games were "a distraction." The patient transferred his attention from the anxiety/pain to the tasks required by the game. Since the patients paid attention to neither their anxieties nor their pain, they didn't perceive them.

Good pain or bad pain? That's another important distinction for every athlete to make. He should understand the difference between pain that just makes him uncomfortable and pain that can lead to an injury.

The "no pain, no gain" idiom relates to stretching the muscles of the body in order to maximize their use. "Feeling the burn," the weightlifter knows some benefit is accruing from his workout. His tired feeling is a signal that "things are happening" as a result of the workout. He doesn't *quit* when he gets this feeling; he pushes harder. He knows his body needs a little assistance, and his mental discipline provides it.

An athlete—a baseball player—who is not mentally disciplined will sense the discomfort of pain or fatigue and focus on it. He will "give in to it," in this way, paying less attention to his performance and more attention to his pain. Though the pain he feels isn't necessarily a good pain, in that it's there but not physiologically "useful," it still may not be a bad pain, one that will damage his body.

During his first Instructional League after being signed as Oakland's top draft choice in 1984, Mark McGwire felt some pain in his shoulder of his throwing arm. He didn't know whether or not to ask out of the day's game. He was advised to go to the trainer and ask if his arm would be damaged by playing. (He was playing third base at the time.) McGwire reported that the trainer said he would not injure himself. "Then play," he was further advised.

The future American League Rookie of the Year played well in the field and had two extra-base hits in the game. He felt the joy of a good performance, but he felt the greater joy of not allowing pain to be an obstacle in the path of his desire. The pain was neutralized— preempted, in fact—by that desire and changed focus coming from it. That's the choice players need to make *after* they've established the fact that injury will not result from activity.

Tom Seaver said he could force himself to pitch when he was tired, because he *wanted* to. He credited the Marine Corps with teaching him to go on—not give in—where others did.

"Watch Bob Gibson (pitching with the Cardinals at the time), on a hot night in St. Louis, when he's already thrown 150 pitches and feels he can win by continuing where others can't," Seaver said admiringly in *Baseball Is My Life*.

Gibson was a good example. He pitched with a broken leg in a World Series game—because he *wanted* to.

Ray Knight *learned to* at any early age. It can be said that his learning experience was a mental conditioning against pain perception. We first spoke with Knight about the subject of pain in July 1983, when he was playing for Houston. At the time, he was having problems with his Achilles tendon. Small tendons around the main tendon had been torn, and there was talk of an impending operation. When Knight got up in the morning, he had a very bad time getting around, but as the day went on his mobility improved.

"Yes," he admitted, "Some days I can hardly walk." He had developed the injury in spring training, yet here it was four months later and he had missed only two regular season games.

"I missed them not because I wanted to come out, but because Bob Lillis (the Astros manager) made me come out, because I was limping so badly."

Some doctors who had been working with Knight, came up with a taping technique, "borrowed from the West Germans." It helped keep some of the torn tendons from stretching further.

"I should, by all rights, have it operated on now," Knight said. "The only reason I chose not to is, they told me that as long as I could stand the pain, I could play, because they didn't think it was actually going to tear the main Achilles. And I've pretty much in my career had to play through a lot of pain. It's always been something I've been able to do—and do successfully. So I made up my mind that as long as I could run, or walk and be assured by the doctors that I wouldn't have permanent damage—in something that was a career-ending injury—then I would go ahead and play. I took some medication, but you don't get much blood circulating to down there (in the heel), so I've been pretty much on my own. I've scheduled the operation for the day after the season is over."

Knight played in 145 games that season, batting .304. Not-so-incidentally, he had 36 doubles—and four triples.

Back to the early age. We will turn on the tape recorder and allow Knight to give his own personal/historical background of pain tolerance:

> I know why I'm the way I am. So much has been said about my ability to play with pain. It's not that I try to be a macho person, but it does go back definitely to the upbringing I had from my father. My father, when I was a little boy—three or four years old—he never thought of me as a little boy. He always called me his little man.

As an undying attitude of wanting to please my dad, whenever I was hurt I'd never cry.

My daddy was a strict disciplinarian and if I was naughty, he'd spank me. And when I'd cry, he'd continue to spank me until I stopped crying. He was just very tough. Not mean; very loving — but very firm. So I learned at about eight years old that if I didn't cry, I didn't get whipped as long. And I just learned to control the mental aspect of pain. I've learned that everybody hurts, but it doesn't help to cry about it. The big thing was, I felt so good about not showing pain to my father that it was a stimulus for me.

It was a motivator. So, I grew up and played football and all the contact sports. If I got the breath knocked out of me, I got right back up. I never wanted to show hurt. I remember when I was nine years old, I picked up a boat. It fell down and skinned my knee up really badly; really raked it. My dad was there, and I mean it hurt me so badly, and I started whimpering, and he said, "Little men don't cry." And you know, all of a sudden, I didn't even think about it hurting. So I learned if you dwell on hurt, it hurts more and more and more. But if you try to overcome it mentally, you can. I'm not saying everything, of course.

I slid into home plate once against the Braves and had to get 27 stitches. I hit Joe Nolan's shin guards and somehow split open my own shin. I didn't want to come out of the game . . . The reason for that is I love playing baseball. And the overriding effect to everything is I love playing. When I'm sick or got a headache, it would hurt just as much if I'd lie down. More.

I've broken my nose four or five times . . . I've been beaned twice . . . I've got four screws in an ankle I've broken twice. The doctor told me I'd never play any more athletics again. That was my last year in high school.

I remember the night that I broke it; I was playing football. I was the quarterback and I broke my ankle, and I tried to go back to the huddle. I didn't know it was broken; it felt like someone had hit my funny bone. It was a lot of burning sensation and pain, but it was something I didn't worry about. But it wasn't functional, so I kinda limped and tripped going back to the huddle and fell down. They came and took me off the field.

My daddy came to the ambulance with me, and I remember apologizing to him because I was hurt and there was nothing I could do about it.

So I guess you could say I just conditioned myself to pain. I mean I hurt; I hurt just like anybody else—but it's a matter of coping and not giving in to it.

Given what we know about biochemistry and individual differences—as they relate to pain—we can say that Knight most likely *doesn't* "hurt like everybody else." Perhaps he might also have said that there's a difference between what we allow ourselves to feel and what we do not, depending on our desire and our attention.

It doesn't seem appropriate to apologize to someone—anyone—for an injury that came as a result of circumstances beyond our control—nor are we advocating a particular style of "parenting" through the interview with Ray Knight. The point to his story is simply that we all are capable, in whatever way we feel is appropriate, to exert a mental discipline that will affect our body in a number of ways, including the perception and control of pain.

Injury-prone? That was what many people asked about third baseman Chris Brown, when he played for the San Francisco Giants. He became a controversial figure with the team, removing himself from the lineup because of a shoulder injury that management believed was exaggerated by the player. Teammates questioned his attitude.

After he removed himself from the lineup in New York, on Labor Day, 1986, Brown returned to California to have his shoulder examined further. He said at the time, "It just wasn't getting better. It was bothering me mentally, too, because I'm not playing as I'm capable. I just wasn't able to concentrate on what I had to do."

This, then, is a common happening. Players are likely to question the mental toughness of teammates who they believe "give in" to injuries—to pain. Only the person with the pain is truly qualified to know the full extent of it. And often, even he cannot be considered a reliable judge. Still, it is his pain, whatever else is said.

Brown, however, added fuel to the fire made by those who labeled him as a malingerer. During the 1987 spring training, the team trainer sent Brown home because of a sore throat and a mild fever, which developed late in the day. That night, a teammate saw him at an NBA game in Phoenix. Brown had been given permission to attend by the trainer.

Teammate Bob Brenly felt that Brown would only gain the team's respect by playing "when he's obviously hurt." The Giant catcher then added, "The thing is, we don't know if he's ever been hurt."

Brown admitted he had actually been able to finish more games than he did the previous year. The Giants traded him during the 1987 season.

Detroit shortstop Alan Trammell suffered with a shoulder problem that required arthroscopic surgery after the 1984 World Series and he struggled with his performance in 1985. Much of the trouble stemmed from all the attention others were giving his shoulder after the operation. Everyone wanted to know whether he could come back from the injury. Trammell said that his need to tell people, "I'm fine; my arm is fine," got to his head. "My injury was on my mind, and what I needed was for the season to run its course. I know you don't try to make it up [performance level] all at once."

Trammell was second in the balloting for American League MVP in 1987, so he managed to get his mind back where it belonged and "make it up."

Tennis player Jennifer Capriati, at age 16, learned about the power of the sympathetic nervous system during the 1993 Australian Open. Sick and in pain, she and her parents in Melbourne worried about her well-being, to say nothing of what her performance would be like in the quarter-finals. Capriati took her pain and bad feeling onto the court, but once the match was underway she disciplined her mind and focused on the task at hand, "and everything seemed to take care of itself." With some adrenal assistance. She won the match.

"My elbow is killing me," said shortstop Alfredo Griffin, on the day his consecutive game streak stood at 293, when he was playing for the Oakland Athletics. Griffin was asked why he didn't take a day off, which the questioner knew Grifffin hated to do. "A day off would make it worse," the shortstop responded.

"To be a star, you have to play hurt." That's what veteran outfielder Dave Parker told young Eric Davis, when they were teammates in Cincinnati in 1986. Parker gave his view to Davis in August, after Davis had injured his wrist. "With his talent, he can be effective even while playing hurt," Parker said.

Taped up, Davis went on an eight-game hitting streak, hitting .433 with five home runs and 13 RBIs.

No understanding, no mental discipline. Over the long season, baseball players confront pain and fatigue. Stress often is a factor. The more stress a player feels—for whatever reason—the more susceptible he becomes to those feelings. Many times, as a result of excessive pressure, whether from poor performance, personal problems or the like, a player "discovers" a hurt. It might be one he'd normally ignore or not perceive in the first place. His awareness of what's happening to him and his honesty are all he has, if he's to successfully combat his feelings.

We have to be aware of what's truly bothering us; we have to know the enemy, before we can fight back. Knowing the obstacle allows us to know the type of equipment we must use to remove it.

The mental discipline of consistent attitude and consistent approach will help the player grind out consistent performance. Sacrificing comfort for consistency is no sacrifice at all, for those who aspire to personal excellence.

Hall of Famer, former slugger Ralph Kiner, spoke these words to Anthony J. Connor, who recorded them in his book, *Baseball for the Love of It*: "There's no question about it. To star in baseball you have to have some sort of drive that'll motivate you to make the necessary sacrifices. It doesn't come easy, even to the most talented ones. You've got to be able to drive yourself all the time. It's a long season with ups and downs and you've just got to keep grinding it out."

As for pain and discomfort, specifically, the quiet, reserved, dignified, unpretentious Joe DiMaggio had this to say: "You ought to run the hardest when you feel the worst."

The Heavy Equipment Needed: Awareness, a Plan, More Channeled Energy

It's been established that people have individual feelings and reactions to pain. Even more important to us is the suggestion that an individual's own ability to cope with and control pain can be different, depending upon the circumstance and the person's training. A ballplayer who is aware of this and develops strategies for his own use can certainly help himself, since the threat and reality of injuries and pain are his constant companions during each long season.

Pain and pleasure are related. Players who may have suffered with "athlete's foot" can recall scratching the itch with pleasure and feeling "relieved" when the itch disappeared. Pain replaced it. Even a pleasurable activity, overdone, becomes painful. In contrast, pain can be converted to pleasure.

A few years ago a Triple-A pitcher in Tacoma, Washington, was slated to pitch the second game of a doubleheader. The pitcher was troubled by a painful leg, very painful, he said. "This [expletive deleted] is really doin' a number on me," were his [almost] exact words. His limp was real and very apparent. He was favoring the leg, obeying the message his brain had passed on from the body: "Ease my pain."

Nevertheless, the pitcher was going to go out to the mound and take his turn. He did. In the first inning, laboring—in a self-conscious physical sense—he retired the side in order, using few pitches. He considered himself fortunate. He sat in the dugout while his team batted and felt relief from immobility.

He went out for the second inning. Another one-two-three inning. Easy. What luck!

After the third inning, in which he again got three consecutive outs, he sat in the dugout with a seemingly different look. It was a look of anticipation—of wanting to go back out there to the mound. When he did go out, the limp was very indistinct, not very apparent at all. The fourth inning was another fine one. He had a three-run lead by then.

Minor league doubleheaders consist of two seven-inning games, and at the end of the fifth inning, the pitcher had a no-hitter going for himself. He could be taken out of the game at that point and get the "W," the win. The offer was made by the manager, who was aware of the pitcher's no-hitter, but also aware that the player had a painful leg, and appreciative that he had gone out there and given the team's tired pitching staff five innings.

The pitcher would have no part of coming out. He had a no-hitter going!

It remained intact after six innings. The pitcher was now walking almost jauntily to and from the mound. In the top of the seventh, an opposing hitter singled. Then another hitter singled. Then a walk. The starting pitcher was relieved. His team won the game; he gained the victory.

He also gained a great awareness of the relativity of the experience of pain within himself. The next day, he was confronted and asked if it was true that, as the game went on and the performance was so excellent, his perception of the pain became almost a pleasure. Was it true that his perception was one of feeling the pain was responsible for his excellence that night? That he was *using* the pain?

He was amazed by the question, because he didn't know this could happen to other people. "That's weird," he said. "That's *exactly* how I felt."

Hungry animals have been made to turn away from food in laboratory experiments, through the application of mild electric shocks. This is done each time the animal makes an attempt to take some food. The shock is felt in the animal's paws. When the experimental procedure is reversed, so too is the animal's reaction. First, the shock is applied, as a trigger signal to forewarn the animal that food will now be served. The pain is pleasurable, in that it announces pleasure and becomes part of it. The animal digs into the food.

We are motivated to avoid pain each day, as we go through our daily routines. The more physical our activity, the more likely some pain will result. Athletes must learn to deal with the idea and the reality of pain. Their awareness should include the understanding that their *fear* of pain probably is worse than the pain itself. A ballplayer who plays cautiously, who doesn't let it all out, cannot possibly expect to perform on a plane near his potential, and the likelihood of injury may be *increased*. (Case in point: The baserunner who wishes to avoid sliding, then discovers he *must*, oftens injures himself because of his tentativeness.)

The fear of pain seems to be both a natural and an acquired instinct. On one hand, we can be disgusted and run from snakes, depite the fact that we never suffered any pain or unpleasant experience with one. On the other hand, we may be repulsed by a food we once enjoyed, but now make an association with a distinct unpleasant circumstance which we experienced before, during, or after having eaten that food.

What if that Triple-A pitcher had been "smoked" — hit hard — by the opposition in the first two innings? What if he had been knocked out of the game? Would he ever be willing — able — to go out to the mound again with the kind of pain he had that night?

We can be either slaves to or masters of our experience. Professional literature indicates that close to 90% of pain is self-limiting, a result of worry, tension, frustration, fear — and, by the way, abuses to our body such as smoking, excessive drinking, poor diet, etc. That's hardly a statistic indicating control to any significant extent.

A good start in learning to control pain is to destroy the conditioned associations of certain sensations — *to hold back the interpretations and perceptions we have associated with pain in the past.*

Techniques are essential. To begin with, the player should experience the difference in feeling pain sensations. George Leonard presents an easy experiment in *The Ultimate Athlete:*

> Let's start by having [a partner] grasp your forearm with both hands and squeeze it until it hurts. First, let's see what happens when you tense up and struggle to get away . . . OK, now I'm going to ask you to relax and center yourself. Think of yourself as a soft, yielding cloud of energy. Let your arm totally relax, so that it will fall to your side if your partner lets go. Now, ask your partner to squeeze, just as hard as before. Can you notice the difference?

The people most frustrated by pain seem to be athletic trainers. They have to deal daily with numbers of athletes who suffer and complain. A clear physical injury is easy for them to treat; they are trained professionals. Determining the level of pain in each athlete is another matter. The professional baseball trainer feels responsible to "allow the player to go out there, and to know he won't injure himself [further]. And [he] also feels responsible to restrict the player's activity if he'll damage himself by playing." The pressures put on the trainer by players and managers are deeply felt.

So, trainers have an abiding interest in helping players deal with pain. Johnson & Johnson publishes a newsletter for trainers. One issue was passed on to us because of its contents (*Athleticare*, January 1987). It includes what was considered to be a helpful article, particularly for young players, who haven't had the experience of trial-and-error approaches with pain and injury.

The article ("How to Speed up Injury Recovery" by Judy Foster and Kay Porter, Ph.D.) is excerpted below:

A. MENTAL TRAINING

. . . Begin by creating physical healing goals for yourself.

All goals should be set in conjunction with a qualified healthcare professional, such as a Certified Athletic Trainer. For example:

Goal: I want to be strong and able to work out with a healthy body in [determined time, depending on nature of injury].

After writing these goals, write at least five affirmative statements (positive self-statements) for each goal, such as:

1. I am performing pain free.
2. I am strong and healthy.
3. I am healing more and more each day.
4. My body is healthy and pain free.
5. I am healing and nurturing my body.

Read these statements to yourself at least twice a day.

B. VISUALIZATION

. . . Start with relaxation and lead into a visualization. For example:

Relaxation: Breathe deeply several times. Begin to check in with your body to see where you are tense or tight and let go. Relax and breathe. Feel yourself becoming warm and empty, quiet and completely relaxed.

Imagination: Begin to imagine and experience your injured part mending and becoming whole. Send it healing energy and support . . . Experience it becoming stronger and healthier every day. Then imagine yourself performing exactly as you want to perform, well bodied and whole, without pain or weakness.

C. PAIN CONTROL

. . . Directly confront and acknowledge the pain within you. Let go of your anger, frustration and resistance with the pain. Simply acknowledge that it is there. Begin to imagine the injury:

1.   Softening, spreading and becoming defused like butter melting in the sun. Slowly let it dissipate. Bring your attention to your breathing . . .
2.   Becoming a ball or shape and give it size. Put all the pain in the ball or shape giving it a color and feel. Now either throw the ball away or imagine the shape becoming smaller and smaller until it is gone. Bring your attention back to your breathing . . .

By confronting and acknowledging pain through focusing on it rather than fear, anger or anxiety, you release yourself from the intensity of the pain.

As is often the case, someone unfamiliar with a technique or exercise, whether it be concentration, visualization, whatever, is quick to become skeptical. Let the skeptic reread the chapter on learning before making a decision.

It's inevitable that a player who will become successful will have learned to accommodate pain. The player who can effectively use the techniques above and/or can channel attentive energy toward performance and away from pain, as did Ray Knight, comes to terms in his individual way with his very individual pain.

Said Marcus Aurelius, approximately 1800 years ago, "If you are distressed by anything external, the pain is not due to the thing itself but to your own estimate of it; and this you have the power to revoke at any moment."

Said Rod Carew, more recently, "On days when I'm tired, hurting or just not feeling good, when I get in the on-deck circle I start telling myself, 'Boy, I feel strong; I feel great; Gee, I feel good.' And I keep telling myself that again and again. [Review exercises above!] By the time I get to the plate, I've forgot about how bad I feel, and I'm ready to go to work."

Said former Houston pitcher J.R. Richard, "Physical pain can't stop you if your mental outlook is strong."

Physical pain or physical mechanics or external distractions of any type are no match for us if our mental discipline is strong.

After his outstanding performance in the 1993 Ryder Cup golf competition, Chip Beck, after a shaky but victorious performance, stated, "The will to win makes up for bad mechanics."

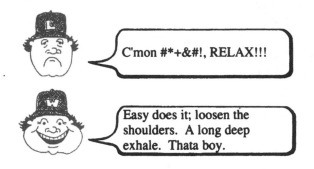

C'mon #*+&#!, RELAX!!!

Easy does it; loosen the shoulders. A long deep exhale. Thata boy.

13
RELAXATION
Tension's Formidable Foe

A paradox is a statement that seems to be contradictory, yet may be true. This paradox *is* true: athletes can *better control* their muscles when they *don't try to*. The tension they create in the *trying* prevents the muscles from being *naturally* loose — *relaxed*.

What happens is that one tension leads to another. Fear, worry, excitement, excessive energy are all considered forms of tension, and tension tightens muscles. Many athletes are unaware of their overaroused state. Even an athlete who recognizes it, may then command himself to relax. (The reason for his being in a state of tension is irrelevant to his muscles.) The tension caused by excessive excitement, let's say, is compounded by the command itself: *"Relax!"*

As a result, the athlete's tightened muscles continue to interfere with performance. The muscles of a baseball player who swings a bat, throws a ball, tries to steal a base or run down a fly ball are muscles working at expanding in order to allow free and effective movement. The player's tension interferes with his muscles' natural fluidity. Steve Sax, *trying* to throw the ball to first base during his "spell" of '83, is one of many such examples.

Increasing numbers of people are attending "relaxation clinics," another indication of the dramatic need people have for relieving

248

stress. Drugs and alcohol are attempted escapes from stress. The mellow feeling, as temporary — and as damaging — as it may be, is a flight away from anxiety and tension.

For a ballplayer, relaxation techniques can be a powerful antidote to anxiety. Every player needs to relax to be effective. But every player also needs to find his *individual arousal level.* As we've said, the football player can generally play at a higher arousal level. The muscles he uses, unless he is in a skill position, do not require such fine control. It's very important for players to find their individual "comfort zone," therefore each player should be discriminating in his use of the relaxation techniques presented later in the chapter. But generalizing from talks with ballplayers — and from reviewing studies of all types of athletes — we find their more common need, in order to perform at or near their peak, is to *lower* arousal, rather than raise it.

A relaxed player is a confident player. Confidence and a positive attitude result in the lowering of anxiety, and thus lessen interference due to antagonistic muscle tension or the loss of ability to direct and control attention.

The toughest advice for a player to follow is the encouragement from coaches and managers at the Little League and big league levels — and all levels in between — to "Relax out there!" "C'mon, loosen up. Nice and easy!" After the next pitch, the player hears, from the same source of encouragement, "C'mon, we need a base hit here." Or, "Aw right, now, big run here at third. Get 'im in!" Or, "Hey, big guy; throw the ball nice and easy; don't walk this guy." The advice is well intended, but it's useless, at best, harmful, at worst. The player, himself, needs to arrive at his appropriate tension level and know how to relax himself.

A degree of muscular tension is required for sitting, standing, and moving. Balance is the key. Excessive tension, as already suggested, has a negative effect on coordination, rhythm, speed, power, and accuracy. Players who play too tight are also susceptible to injury and will usually tire quickly.

For the sake of illustration, let's say that maximum speed and power are achieved when a muscle is contracted from a very slight percentage of tension (10%) to the highest percentage of tension (100%). (Refer to diagram, line A.)

If the starting percentage of tension is 35% (as in line B), the

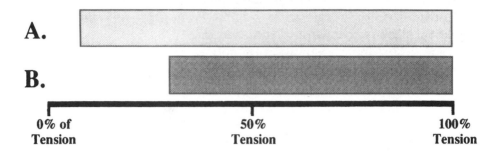

A.

B.

0% of	50%	100%
Tension	Tension	Tension

player conceivably could lose as much as 25% of his speed and power.

Players with a "death grip" on the bat or ball (90% to 100%) will have slow, stiff movements, or they may freeze completely.

Dr. Laurence Morehouse, in his book *Maximum Performance,* talks of the negative effects of tension in another way:

> When you are putting all you have got into an action, some of that force is holding you back. Muscles are grouped around joints in such a way as to oppose each other. While one group acts as accelerators, another acts as brakes. The muscles acting as brakes stabilize the limbs while the accelerating muscles move them . . .
>
> Ideally, both braking and accelerating muscles act in harmony to make the movement smooth and accurate. In order to move at your best, one system must be releasing while the other is hauling. You must feel like you are functioning with only a modest amount of power and effort. [Most baseball players define that amount as about 85%.] In rapid movement it is not the strength of the muscle that is important so much as the ability to relax the antagonistic muscles.

If we make a tight fist and squeeze an object — a bat or ball — we'll find that every muscle in our forearm tenses. Trying to swing or throw with that kind of grip is like trying to drive a car with one foot on the gas pedal and the other on the brakes. The car will move, but not very efficiently, and it will wear out pretty quickly.

Uncontrolled pressures all result in excessive tension. We've discussed many of these pressures, but the pressure we find to be the most prevalent in baseball players of all ages is the desire to always do better. The conscientious player is often driven to "try harder." In the attempt, he's the one to put the "pedal to the metal." The fact is, he puts his foot down just as hard on the brake!

Throwing a baseball and swinging a bat do not require a fast start. The opposite is true; throwing and swinging require a smooth, effortless start. Speed and power pick up as the player moves through the motion, just as a boulder builds momentum as it rolls down a hill.

John Jerome, in *The Sweet Spot in Time*, writes, "A little tension maintains the muscle in a state of preparedness, ready for action. It has been compared to the idling engine of a car. Set the idle too slow (as with a flabby, unfit, toneless muscle), and the engine will stall if you floor the gas suddenly."

A player, then, must know how to set his idle, know what percentage of tension is just right for his start.

Ted Williams recommended "an extremely tight grip" on the bat in his book, *The Science of Hitting*. We asked him when and where he tightened his grip. He responded, "You can't be tight when you start your swing, because you'll never get to the ball. You need that firm grip at contact. Probably I didn't consciously tighten my grip, it just happened."

John Jerome also pointed out the importance of the stretch reflex in getting started: "The stretch reflex means that if you subject a muscle to a pulling force, it contracts reflexively. And, almost every sports motion that requires force has some kind of windup preceding it to enhance its power—the golf swing, the football kick, the sprinter's crouch, the tennis serve. A deliberate elongation of the muscle precedes the contraction, pulling more motor units into play."

His point is particularly significant to the hitter, runner, thrower whose muscles tend to have too much tension during the cocking motion. As a result, the stretch reflex start is not effortless or efficient. Whatever the cause for that muscular tension might be, the player, to become relaxed, must first become aware of his tightness.

The more important a game situation is to a player, the more he needs that awareness. The extent to which he's conscious of his state of muscular tension indicates how effectively he'll be able to control it, keeping it at the level he plays best at — his normal relaxation level.

How relaxed? Every player has a tension level that's right for him, just as he has his own preparation routines and so forth. He may have different tension levels for different functions, finding, for example, that he needs to be more relaxed when hitting than when trying to steal a base.

The best way for a player to establish his appropriate tension/relaxation level is through experimentation. If we use the tension scale referred to earlier, we'll consider 10% very little, 100% the maximum.

> You are the experimenter. You're a hitter. Grip the bat as tightly as you can, 100% tension. Take two or three swings. Remember how it feels. Next, let up your grip a bit — to 90%. Again, take two or three swings while being aware of the feeling now and at 100%. Keep loosening the grip, lowering the tension levels about 10% each time, swinging, feeling, comparing — until you get the loosest grip possible.
>
> Next, start back *up* the scale — until you arrive at the tension level you feel is just right, as if you're fine tuning a radio, to get the station clarity just right. Fine tune your tension level by going a little beyond and then back.

It has been our experience that players have found 10% to 20% to be the level just right for them when starting a motion — a movement. But a scale only establishes ranges. Each player establishes his own relaxed start.

Awareness Before Relaxation

The player who cannot relax during his performance should certainly identify the source of his anxiety, as we've suggested. That is a problem. But he should also be able to recognize the symptoms. Identifying them enables him to more effectively focus his relaxation techniques.

A list of ballplayers' most common "tension tendencies" would include:

Squeezing the ball or bat
A tightening of the legs
Breathing irregularly
Clenching jaw
Grinding teeth
Forced swallowing
Dryness in mouth
Tightened buttocks
Knotted or queasy feeling in stomach
Twitching

Our muscles are easier to deal with than our minds. "Getting our heads straight" can take a considerable amount of time. Getting our muscles "straight" can be a speedier process. Once a player feels what's happening to him—through his awareness—he has a chance to effectively treat the symptom, at least. Away from the field, he can focus on the problem. Usually, relaxed muscles help "gentle the mind," which is a fringe benefit.

Relaxation Techniques

Even the great clutch players can get too keyed up, too tense, just before the action. The difference between the "clutch player" and the "choke player" is that the clutch player gets his state of relaxation under control *before* the action. He has a method. He knows that just telling himself to relax—or being told—won't get it done.

During his time, Reggie Jackson was one of the best clutch performers in sport. It seemed as if everyone knew of "Reggie," because it seemed he always came through in big moments, in key situations. Even when he "failed," he was considered to be great. He left the fans thinking, "They were lucky to get him out this time, but I feel sorry for the pitcher if he gets another chance."

There's no doubt that Jackson was at his best in those big situations, when he was challenged (not threatened), when the spotlight was on him, which he loved. At those times, observers could see the excitement build in him; he was like a caged animal. But on those occasions, he took much more time than usual before he would step into the batter's box.

Opposing fans and players would think, "Reggie's show-boating again." But he wasn't putting on a show then; he was *preparing* himself for the challenge, getting himself *relaxed* and *under control.* Over the years, he had found out what helped, which mind games to play when it was "game time."

The best competitors get "keyed up," but they know that excessive excitement leads to excess tension. "Keying down"—relaxing— becomes the more immediate process to preceed performance.

Again, the first step in controlling your state of excitement— your state of relaxation—is awareness. Be aware of the level of excitement or tension. Be aware of whether you have to "get it up" or "key down." Experiment in order to get to your own appropriate level.

Major league players have told us they use a variety of techniques for relaxation during the game. Following is a composite list:

1. *Get away from the source of pressure.* Take a break. Get off the mound or out of the batter's box or smooth some dirt with your foot, etc.

2. *Talk out loud to yourself.* Many players can be seen mumbling to themselves on the mound or in the batter's box, quite often as they're getting away from the source of the pressure. Juan Marichal is one of many. Said the Hall of Fame pitcher, "When I got in a tough spot, I would walk around behind the mound and have a meeting with myself. I talked out loud. That seemed to help more than just talking in my head."

Catchers in the American League said that, "When Reggie Jackson started mumbling, look out, he was going to do some damage." Yogi Berra and Pete Rose talked to the catchers and umpires to stay relaxed. Both said they didn't pay attention to what they said or what was said back to them. Former Detroit pitcher Mark Fidrych was always talking aloud before readying himself for the next pitch.

How a player talks to himself—whether in his head or aloud—can have a very strong effect on his state of excitement. The speed and tone of the player's "voice" is as important as what he says. A rapid speed and harsh tonality, for example, will tighten the muscles, overpowering an otherwise effective message. You can also talk yourself to sleep, if the cadence and tone are too slow and too gentle.

Experiment. Try something like this and feel the effect: "Get it geared up now," in a *slow, gentle* way. Then, *rapidly* and *angrily*, tell yourself, "Just relax now, calm down!" You may be able to feel, and therefore understand, that *how* you delivered the message had a greater effect than *what* the message was.

3. *Use movement.* When players get too "keyed up," their movements will tend to be faster and stiffer than usual, sometimes jerky. In an extreme cases, they almost freeze up. To relax yourself, make your movements looser, longer and slower. Keep your body language the same as it is when you're at your best.

4. *Stretch.* A good way to relax muscles is by stretching. Stretch slowly, as you do when you yawn. By thinking about how it feels as you're stretching, you'll also help clear the mind.

Billy Williams told us, "Slowly rolling my shoulders forward, stretching those muscles a couple of times always relaxed me."

That isn't surprising, since tension in any part of the body will also be felt in the muscles at the base of the neck. Many players are aware of excessive tension there and in the area of the upper back. They can be seen trying to relieve it by jerking and flopping their head around. That's fine—if it works. But they may find they can get better results with a gentler, smoother stretch.

5. *Visualize.* Many players have a favorite spot they like to think about: a beach where they lie near the ocean or a stream in a quiet, wooded area. Others like to think about a song that relaxes them.

Von Hayes told us he has a room where he likes to sit and relax while listening to music. He said, "When I get too keyed up in a game, all I have to do is think about that and it relaxes me, brings me right back to where I want to be . . . "

Incidentally, in 1981 the Phillies built a six-foot by eight-foot "box" that is ventilated, sound-proofed, and set up with an audio system. Many players have used it for relaxation and other purposes. Relaxation tapes are available (as are tapes on concentration, confidence building, etc.).

"Close your eyes. We are ready to go on our journey. Picture yourself at the seashore. It is early in the morning . . ." That's a sampling of one of the relaxation tapes heard in the Phillies' "B-Room." ("B," as in "breakthrough.") More? "Take a deep breath. Exhale slowly. Visualize a rainbow. . . . "

6. *Tense your muscles for a few seconds, and then let go, completely relaxing*. Remember how Gary Ward got the "tension level" he wanted by squeezing his bat as tightly as he could and then relaxing his hands a few seconds before the pitcher delivered? Others do the same.

7. *Focus your eyes, concentrating on a blade of grass or a pebble for about five or six seconds*. This technique is good for clearing the mind by shifting concentration from inner thoughts to something outside your body.

8. *Relax the muscles around your eyes, mouth, and jaw*. Tightening is commonly felt in these areas, and players relax these areas often after stepping out of the batter's box or off the mound.

9. *Control your breathing*. Consistent performance cannot be achieved without consistent breathing patterns. Informed people know the relationship between breathing and relaxation, but few people consider the impact breathing has on physical function. The amount of air a person has in his lungs while inhaling, exhaling, or holding his breath has a dynamic effect on balance, coordination, timing, speed, power, and accuracy.

Anthony Robbins, in his book *Unlimited Power*, writes, "If you have a healthy circulation system, you're going to live a long healthy life. The environment is the bloodstream. What is in control of that system? Breathing. It's

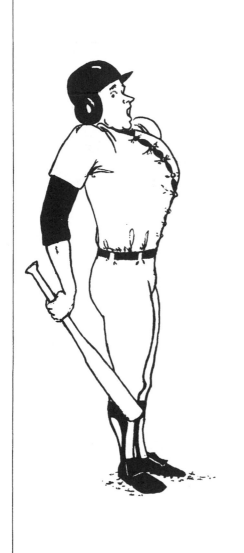

A long, deep exhale always helps.

the way to fully oxygenate the body and stimulate the electrical process of each and every cell."

Robbins further discusses the reliance of the lymph system on deep breathing, and he recommends " . . . ten deep breaths . . . at least three times a day," as a "first key to healthy living." The importance of effective breathing is overlooked by many people. Athletes should not be guilty of such an oversight.

Those familiar with martial arts, power sports, and speed sports know how the effectiveness of their performance diminishes when their breathing is "out of sync." Elite marksmen found that to be consistently accurate, they must time the squeezing of the trigger with their breathing. Shooters exhale fully, then take a small inhale, then hold their breath for two or three seconds, then squeeze off between heartbeats.

An athlete's breathing pattern should correspond with his movements — flow with them. Usually, if a ballplayer is breathing in a relaxed manner when he finishes his preparation, his breathing will be good; it will flow while he executes his movements. Players run into trouble when their breathing is stifled or otherwise erratic just before the action. That happens when they're concentrating intently on their body or the situation. In trying to give as much energy as possible to the brain, they hold their breath longer and breathe shallower.

Research indicates that our minds are at peak efficiency when, after breathing in a relaxed manner, we have a slight intake of air and then hold our breath for between two and four seconds. If we get to six seconds, we become susceptible to distraction, through our own thoughts or because of something that's going on around us.

It was not, then, surprising to find that most players exhale as they finish their preparation. Pitchers, particularly out of a stretch position, coordinate their breathing with their motion in coming set, inhaling as they raise their hands, exhaling as they bring the hands down. Patterns are more varied for pitchers out of their windups, but they're still coordinated to movement, whatever the individual approach. Hitters tend to exhale after the last practice swing, just as they come set with their hands. Fielders, as they come set. The breathing is part of the set-up. When the players begin to concentrate, they inhale very sightly, then hold their breath.

A number of players have learned to control their breathing through the martial arts. Some, like Goose Gossage, learned from playing basketball—shooting foul shots. When Gossage became "too worked up," he just told himself to "do [his] thing, like setting up to shoot a free throw." The majority of players haven't been taught about breathing; they've discovered on their own, through trial and error, how to help themselves. Some, of course, haven't made the discovery yet.

Following are some suggestions about breathing that might be helpful:

1. Simply being aware of your breathing can help relax you, because it takes your mind away from the thought that is causing the tension problem. It's then easier to switch your concentration to the task at hand.

2. Breathe the way you normally breathe when you are relaxed.

3. Breathe in slowly until your lungs are full. Don't force it or raise your shoulders with the inhale. Hold it for a couple of seconds. Let the air slowly, completely, fall out at its own rate—without forcing it. Prolong the exhale just a bit, letting your shoulders fall with the exhale. Keep in mind: *It is the exhale that relaxes.* If you cut that short, the benefit will be reduced.

When a person sighs after concentrating or worrying about something, he has gone through the same process without being aware of it. However, he has probably held his breath too long.

This is what frequently happens in movie theaters during a suspenseful or moving part of the film. The audience, which has been holding its collective breath too long, lets out a sigh—or gasp—of relief after the climax of the scene.

Singing, humming, and whistling can be effective in helping to reduce anxiety, according to the late Hans Selya, father of modern stress research and author of many books on the subject, including *Stress Without Distress* and *The Stress of Life*. Selya pointed out that singing, humming, and whistling all are done while exhaling.

Two notable examples can be used from the 1988 World Series. Pitcher Brian Holton, coming in as a reliever for the Los Angeles Dodgers, sang a song to himself as he walked from the bullpen to the mound before his first World Series appearance. It was a song, his mother reminded him on the phone the next day, that his father had sung to him when he was a child — a child in need of some comfort and assurance.

A national television audience watched Series MVP Orel Hershiser sitting in the Dodger dugout between innings of Game 5, the final game of the '88 World Series. His head was leaning back, his eyes were closed, his lips were moving.

Hershiser explained, "I was too excited (at that time) about (the thought of) being in a World Series and winning, so I relaxed and sang hymns to myself." It had a calming effect, and that approach led to the desired result.

From time to time we hear about a ballplayer who is good for a team because he keeps everybody loose; he makes them laugh. Laughter is a fine relaxation tool. Selya considers a good belly laugh to be the most effective relief for distress. A nervous laugh, which most of us have experienced, is "nature's way" of trying to relieve some of our stress.

We don't recommend that a player start laughing after making the last out of a big game. Or that a pitcher belly-laughs himself to the clubhouse after having given up a game-winning hit. Such behavior would probably cause considerable stress for the coach or manager and, shortly thereafter, for the player. There is an appropriate time and place for everything, and it its proper setting, the "light touch" of laughter is a remedy for heavy hearts and tight muscles.

"Our minds need relaxation and give way
unless we mix with work a little play."

— Moliere

Be "psyched up," not "tied up."

I've Got It, Now!

14
THE WINNING WAY
A State and Statement of Mind — In Summary

Vince Lombardi is remembered as the coach who led his Green Bay Packers to five NFL championships in seven years and consecutive victories in Super Bowls I and II. He's remembered even more as the man who spoke these words: "Winning is not everything. It is the only thing."

The words are often quoted — and more often misinterpreted. People incorrectly believe Lombardi meant that winning — the *result* of a game or season — was the only thing that mattered, that losing was a failure. Not so.

Lombardi didn't hate to lose. He *hated* the *idea* of *losing*. Obviously then, he *loved* the *idea* of winning.

The striving for excellence is the enactment of a player's idea of winning. It is first a state of mind, then a state of being. Sport — and history — show us that the idea of winning, put into action, will lead to winning.

The right results come from the right approach.

"Winning is not a sometime thing," Lombardi told his players. "It is an all-the-time thing. You don't win once in a while. You don't do things right once in a while. You do them right all the time."

You do them right all the time!

"Of all the lessons I learned from Lombardi, from all his sermons on commitment and integrity and the work ethic, that one hit home the hardest," former Packer great Jerry Kramer told *Sports Illustrated*. "I've found in business, in my life after football, that only 15 to 20 percent of the people do things right all the time. The other 80 or 85 percent are taking short cuts, looking for the easy way, either stealing from others or cheating themselves. I've got an edge on them because whenever I'm tempted to cut corners, I hear that raspy voice saying: 'This is the right way to do it. Which way are you going to do it, mister?' I don't have any choice. I have to play to win."

Well, we all have a choice, Kramer included. What he meant to say—and what we will say—is this: *When you know the right way, and you know you want to go that way, there is no acceptable reason to make any other choice.*

There are plenty of excuses, certainly, but none that should be accepted by the player—by *you*. If you want success, you prepare for success. You expect success. And in your pursuit, you are winning!

I Only Talk Winning. That's the title of a book written by Angelo Dundee, who was the trainer of Muhammed Ali and Sugar Ray Leonard. In the book's final paragraph, the author tried to explain why he came up with that particular title. He wrote, "In life there are positive and negative thoughts. And hey, it doesn't cost you a cent more to think positively. *I Only Talk Winning* stands for 'Don't be afraid of losing.' Losing is nothing. There is no such thing as failure, only learning how."

There *is* such a thing as failure, we believe. Failure is wanting without working: the desire for success without the desire to do what it takes to attain it. Having goals without making the commitment to achieving them. That's failure. That's a losing way.

The winner is the one who makes every possible effort—*all the time*—to win. Pete Rose knew "there were games that meant nothing, games when you might not feel like hitting, but you have to make those at-bats just as important to you." Then, any "failure" that may result is, as Angelo Dundee suggests, only learning how to make a more effective effort next time.

Learning means change, and no improvement is made without it. Winners know that. They make the choice to find out what can help them reach their goal, and then they dedicate themselves to whatever makes them more effective as a player — and as a person. Learning is only one step in the process of winning. Many people know *what* to do. The winner chooses to *do it — all the time!*

Winners make the choice:

> To get something out of all situations, rather than complain about them.

> To hustle, rather than dog it.

> To be prepared, rather than just show up.

> To be consistent, rather than occasional.

> To be early, rather than just on time — or late.

> To want to learn, rather than want to explain or excuse.

> To do more, rather than just enough — or less.

> To be mentally tough, rather than mentally lazy or intimidated.

> To concentrate on what to do, rather than what may result.

> To be aggressive, rather than passive — or submissive.

> To know their limitations, rather than try to do more than they're capable of.

> To think about solutions, rather than worry about problems.

> To accept adversity as part of the game — and of life, rather than magnify the adverse conditions and seek sympathy.

> To share with and help others, rather than be selfish.

> To think and act positively, rather than negatively.

"A SCOREBOARD FOR A WINNER" is the heading of a sheet we saw posted on a locker room bulletin board at Yavapai College, in Prescott, Arizona. We appreciated it. In a different way, it says a number of things about winners that have been said above and throughout this book. It also has some additional definitions of a "Winner." It enhances our summary and definition of "A Winning Way," though not every statement is entirely acceptable to us. Nevertheless, we felt it worthy of inclusion. The "author" was not identified on the paper.

SCOREBOARD FOR A WINNER

A Winner takes big risks when he has much to gain. A Loser takes big risks when he has little to gain and much to lose.

A Winner focuses. A Loser sprays.

A Winner says, "Let's find out!" A Loser says, "Nobody knows!"

When a Winner makes a mistake, he says, "I was wrong." When a Loser makes a mistake, he says, "It wasn't my fault!"

A Winner isn't nearly as afraid of losing as the Loser is secretly afraid of winning.

The Winner works harder than the Loser and has more time. A Loser is always too busy to do what is necessary.

A Winner takes a big problem and separates it into smaller parts, so that it can be more easily manipulated. A Loser takes a lot of little problems and rolls them together until they are unsolvable.

A Winner goes through a problem. A Loser goes around it and never gets past it.

A Winner makes commitments. A Loser makes promises.

A Winner shows he's sorry by making up for it. A Loser says, "I'm sorry," but he does the same thing the next time.

A Winner knows what to fight for and what to compromise on. A Loser compromises on what he shouldn't and fights for what isn't worthwhile fighting about.

A Winner learns from his mistakes. A Loser learns only not to make mistakes by not trying anything differently.

A Winner says, "I'm good, but I'm not as good as I ought to be." A Loser says, "I'm not as bad as a lot of other people."

A Winner tries never to hurt people, and does so only rarely. A Loser never wants to hurt people intentionally, but he does so all the time without even knowing it.

A Winner listens. A Loser just waits until it's his turn to talk.

A Winner would rather be respected than liked, although he would prefer both. A Loser would rather be liked than respected, and is even willing to pay the price of mild contempt for it.

A Winner is sensitive to the atmosphere around him. A Loser is sensitive only to his own feelings.

A Winner feels strong enough to be gentle. A Loser is never gentle. He's either weak or a petty tyrant by turns.

A Winner respects those who are superior to him and tries to learn something from them. A Loser resents those who are superior and tries to find kinks in their armor.

A Winner explains, and a Loser explains away.

The Winner feels responsible for more than his job. A Loser says, "I only work here!"

A Winner says, "There ought to be a better way to do it!" A Loser says, "That's the way it's always been done!"

A Winner paces himself. A Loser has only two speeds, hysterical and sluggish.

A Winner knows that the verb "to be" must preceed the verb "to have." A Loser thinks that enough of the verb "to have" is what makes a verb "to be."

[That is a] fatal mistake in the grammar of existence.

Many other winning attitudes can be identified. They reveal themselves in our daily lives. The more committed we are to being a "Winner," the more apparent these attitudes seem to become. Our purpose in this book has been to present a practical, philosophical guide for excellence on and off the ball field, using as models the strategies and behaviors of players recognized and respected for their approach and achievement. They are acknowledged Winners. They are outstanding models.

Their strategies, to sum up:

Goals

Winners don't become winners by accident. They set goals: long-term, intermediate-term, and short-term. As Don Sutton said, "Without goals we bounce around like ships without rudders."

Result goals may be to win 20 games during a season or to bat .300, but a player has to figure out how he can help himself reach those long-term goals.

He does this by focusing on *daily, functional goals*: goals of attitude and behavior. *Goals* of *approach* — to hitting, pitching, all dimensions of his game.

He has *control* of these goals! It is very helpful to put them in writing and refer to them each day. Persistence is the key. (A list of functional goals can be found in the Appendix of this book.)

Expectations

Simply, a player must be able to distinguish between these specific *task-oriented goals* and the "goals" — *expectations* — others have for him. First, these expectations address the needs of people other than the player himself: his family and friends, fans, people of the media. Second, they are too broad and tend to put pressure on him and distract him from what he *must do* in order to be successful. Third, they work to undercut the player's own feeling of control.

Dedication

"The difference between the possible and the impossible lies in the man's determination," says Tom Lasorda. Determination and commitment are common values and uncommon practices. Goals without a determination to achieve them are useless. They may sound good, but it doesn't take the player past "wanting without working." Goals are reached through a commitment to them.

Players have to decide what price they're willing to pay. As Jerry Kramer said, most people won't pay the price. The "average guy" doesn't fit our definition of *Winner*. But professional baseball players aren't "average guys" to begin with. If they act as if they are, they most likely won't be professionals for long. They certainly won't be Winners.

What they do off the field is as important as what they do on the field. Their lifestyles will affect their careers. They have to make choices about activities, leisure time, diet, etc. It takes a lot of *mental discipline* to tell family, friends, media, or teammates, "No; I have to get my rest." Or, "I have to get some work in now." Or, "I need some time alone." Winners also have to say "no" to their own desires.

Some players may talk about this as a sacrifice, but a highly committed player doesn't look at it as a choice that involves sacrifice. *He's glad to do whatever he feels can help him get what he wants.*

Said Ty Cobb: "If I hadn't been determined to outdo the other fellow at all cost, I doubt I would've hit [even] .320. In other words, my lifetime batting average has been increased at least fifty points by qualities that I'd call purely mental."

The earlier a player dedicates himself truly to peak performance, the more likely he is to achieve it.

Responsibility

A player's *responsibility* begins with a willingness to acknowledge who he is and what he is—and what he wishes to become. He's responsible when he is accountable for what he does or does not do.

Excuses do not serve a player's sense of responsibility. The more a Winner takes, the more he wants. Responsibility leads to a sense of control. An irresponsible person is either lazy, insecure, fearful, or ignorant. Those are not the traits of a Winner.

Attitude

Everyone has an *attitude*. It's actually a state of mind. It indicates how we're viewing the world; how we're viewing others; *how we're viewing ourselves!*

Awareness is crucial. Knowing that attitudes affect behavior and performance is crucial. Understanding that attitudes can be changed is just as crucial.

A sensible, optimistic, energetic attitude is crucial.

If we know what attitude we'd like to have, and we know it's possible to change our attitude, then a *commitment* to that goal is crucial! A worthwhile commitment for all of us, since none of us has a *perfect* attitude.

Confidence

The basis for true confidence is not performance. We may lack confidence in a particular situation, but we can still retain a confidence in ourselves. That self is served by our sense of purpose, responsibility, and attitude, meaning that "building confidence" is an expression of what we do to improve our *real* self, as well as our *perception* of ourself.

The more we *dedicate* ourselves to achieving specific goals, and the more we work effectively with these "building blocks," the more confident we become. It's an easy formula to mix; a hard one to swallow — for the "average guy."

Learning

"They know enough, who know how to learn." Henry Adams mouthed those words.

"I am always looking for a better way. I am never satisfied." Carl Yastrzemski said that, near the end of his career, at that.

Everyone learns, even those who don't try. But great people and great performers go beyond that. They are *intentional learners*. They are *seekers*. They want to know more. They want to find a better way.

They are Winners, in that their goal is to get as close to perfection as possible. They don't know how far that journey is, but they want to learn — so they take it! Every day.

Preparation

Winners know that hard work alone is not enough. A plow horse can work hard. To be Winners, we must work hard "intelligently." That means:

Making an honest assessment of strengths and weaknesses.

Formulating a plan for improvement (remembering that strengths, as well as weaknesses, need attention).

Working on all phases of the game, including the mental: knowing defenses, reading hits, getting signs, understanding situations — what is required; what should be anticipated.

Understanding that quantity without quality is a waste of time. *The quality of the effort identifies a Winner.* He knows how to get the job done when he's tired and not feeling 100%. He *learns* to do this in practice—after the Losers have given in and headed for the shower. A Winner spends time practicing his mental approach off the field, as well as on it.

His preparation is an indicator of his dedication.

Visualization, concentration, and relaxation require time, effort, and technique. Many techniques have been provided earlier, in the specific chapters. The Winner takes the responsibility for the time and effort. He chooses and uses those techniques which best suit him. With conscientious use comes familiarity—and, we believe, improvement in each area.

Mental Discipline

How to "sum up" *mental discipline*. We spent many pages trying to convey the many aspects of it: control, balance, and so on. Definition of the term is, once again, critical. The ability to focus on the task at hand, without regard to any possible external or internal factors that might distract from that task: *That*, we feel, is a working definition of mental discipline. The mind is focused on the "immediate do-able."

Pressure, pain, and resultant anxiety are preempted by strong concentration skills—and by strong mental resolve.

The best way to sum up would be to get back to Vince Lombardi, who believed that mental discipline—mental toughness—was prerequisite to success of any kind in any field.

"Mental toughness," Lombardi said, "is many things and rather difficult to explain. . . . Most importantly, . . . a perfectly disciplined will that refuses to give in. It's a state of mind—you could call it character in action."

In Conclusion: The Power of Positive Thinking

The state of mind, the character that Lombardi mentions is tremendously influenced by what a person says.

Certainly, what one person says may sometimes affect another person. But what he says *always—and dramatically—affects him.* Whether he speaks to others or to himself, his words will have an impact on how he continues to think and act.

So you've heard plenty about "the power of positive thinking." Most people have by now. But people don't come close to understanding how much power positivism really has. And they don't come close to thinking and acting in a consistently positive way. The more they — *we* — can do that, the more likely *we* are to be Winners.

Winners think of problems, negative factors, or obstacles as challenges to overcome—or as something too insignificant with which to be concerned. The attitude is actually not as hard to develop as it would seem, once we start paying attention to our words—and deeds.

Positivism is the essential characteristic of a Winner. And even Winners underestimate the power of it. That power should be known—and put to use.

Let's conclude with some contrasting examples of Winners and Losers, their thoughts, their words on a baseball diamond. The results for these players are usually predictable:

Winners think: "I can; I want to; I will; We will; We'll find a way; I'll adjust."

Losers think: "I can't; I have to; I hope; I want to avoid (embarrassment, failure, etc.)."

A Winner is pitching on a bad mound. He says, "I'll get used to it." Or, "I'll find a way." Or, "I've been good on worse."

A Loser says, "How do they expect me to pitch here?" Or, "I can't push off." Or, "No way anyone can pitch on this mound." Or, "It's not my fault if I get lit out here."

A Winner who gets off to a bad start says, "I'll get it going." Or, "I'll make an adjustment." Or, "There's a long way to go yet."

A Loser says, "Damn, another bad day." Or, "I can't get anything going today." Or, "I just don't have it today." Or, "What's wrong with me?"

A Winner who has not previously done well in a particular ball park will say, "I know what it takes to pitch effectively here. All I want to do is concentrate on doing my thing—the things I can control and know how to control." Or, "This park is no factor."

The Loser says, "This park is impossible to pitch in." Or, "This place is a jinx. I always have bad luck here." Or, "There's something bad about this place. I can't get it done here for some reason."

The game is on the line. The Winner says, "I love it. This is what it's all about. Let me be the one."

The Loser says, "What's gonna happen if I blow it?" Or, "Why me in this situation? It always happens when I'm not going good." Or, "I hope I don't embarrass myself."

The opponent is known to be tough. The Winner says, "All I need to do is what I know how to do. I'm prepared." Or, "It's just me and the ball."

The Loser says, "This guy's too much for me." Or, "I hope I'm not overmatched." Or, "I wish I didn't have to face this guy."

The field conditions are poor. The Winner says, "I can't change the conditions, so I'll adjust to them and just play my game." Or, "Another challenge to meet!"

The Loser says, "How can I be expected to play under these conditions?"

Sound familiar? We're capable of going either way. It's our decision and choice as to which way we go.

Pitcher Jose DeLeon struggled with the Pittsburgh Pirates in 1985, to understate what he went through. Talking about the ordeal of facing each new game, DeLeon said simply, "I just don't ever expect to win." His record for the year was 2–19. We can say it's hard to maintain a positive attitude under such trying circumstances, or we can say that those circumstances were, to a great extent, the *result* of a *negative attitude*. What we say indicates what we believe. What would *you* say? That's what matters.

Tug McGraw said, "You gotta believe!" Believing goes along with saying. Just saying the right things isn't enough. Remember. *Believe what you say. Then do it!* If you do, you'll not only enjoy the performance — you'll enjoy the feeling.

"To put your ideas into action is the most difficult thing in the world," wrote Goethe.

That is the challenge to everyone who would be exceptional.

"Try?" said Yoda, in *The Empire Strikes Back*. "There is no try. There is only do or not do."

Winners are exceptional because they meet the challenge — they DO!

Part Two

INTRODUCTION

Part One of *The Mental Game of Baseball* has presented a philosophical, theoretical, and practical foundation for achieving excellence in baseball. Also provided, through anecdote and specific exercises, are the routines that players establish, the problems they face, and the possible solutions available to them, insofar as their mental approach to the game is concerned.

Part Two of the book now addresses the individual elements of the game. It treats "mental fundamentals" in specific chapters on hitting, pitching, fielding, and base running.

An Appendix is to be found following those chapters. It lists the task-specific goals players should set for themselves as they work at enhancing their performance—and establishing a personal standard of excellence.

15
HITTING

"A bat at its widest is 3 3/4 inches in diameter; some pitchers throw the ball more than 90 miles an hour; and the distance from the pitching rubber to home plate is 60 feet, 6 inches. This means the batter has two-thirds of a second in which to uncoil and get good wood and full body into the pitch. And not all pitches come straight in — they dip, float, soar, and drop."

— *Rod Carew*

A 90-MPH fastball should reach the plate 0.4 second after the pitcher lets it go. The batter has about 0.1 second to pick up the incoming pitch visually and "recognize" it — discern whether it is a fastball, a curve, or slider and where it is likely to be headed in relation to the strike zone. (During that tenth of a second the pitch travels almost one-third the distance home.)

The batter has another 0.15 second in which to decide whether or not to swing (or whether to get out of the way of a wild pitch). He loses sight of the ball thereafter — it is almost two-thirds of the way home — but he has another 0.15 second in which to start his swing and guide it to the spot where he thinks the ball is headed. To hit a fair ball he has to meet the ball within about 15 degrees to either side of a dead right angle to the direction the pitch is traveling, which means within about 14 inches of the ball's total travel. That means he has to have the bat there during the time the ball is passing that 2-foot arc. This passage takes 0.013 second. One study indicates that if the batter does not have the heel of his forward foot raised by the time the ball leaves the pitcher's hand, he's already missed the pitch.

— from *The Sweet Spot in Time*, by John Leonard

"See the ball; hit the ball."
— *Pete Rose*

The explanation of the process of hitting can be made to sound complex or simple. The fact remains: children hit baseballs well at an early age with little or no direction. Pete Rose claimed he was far from being a genius, but he knew how to see a ball and hit it. His talent, by his own admission, was not exceptional. His approach was.

Your eyes are your guidance system, therefore seeing the ball is, by far, the most important aspect of hitting. A hitter can use his eyes more effectively by training himself to respond to what he sees. His eye discipline is much more important than whether he has 20/20 vision or wears corrective lenses.

Why is seeing the ball as well as possible so difficult for a batter? Why does a baseball look as big as a volleyball when the coach tells you to take a pitch, and, on the next pitch when you're allowed to hit, it looks like a white pea or seed?

The following is a review of possible answers to the question:

1. THE EFFECTS OF FEAR, ANXIETY, TENSION

Muscular tightness and poor breathing patterns result from these feelings. Concentration is also affected, which means the eyes may then react to irrelevant cues.

2. THE HITTER FORCING HIMSELF TO HIT

This is the attitude of the "I gotta/I'm gonna" syndrome. The message of self-talk spoken while a player is in this state tightens his muscles *and* interferes with the message of the hitter's guidance system (his eyes).

3. DIVIDED ATTENTION

Thinking is an internal function.

Seeing is an external function.

Hitting is a physical function.

When a hitter tries to handle more than one function at a time, he is dividing his attention. The message from his eyes will not be clear. His guidance system needs a clear channel to do its job.

4. IMPROPER USE OF EYES

Good hitters have consistent eye patterns. Their eye patterns include: where they look, when they look, the type of focus they have. The type of focus is often referred to as "broad" and "fine" focus. Looking at an interviewer and seeing *all* of him is *broad focus*. "Zeroing in" on his eyes would indicate a *fine focus*.

Many young hitters are taught to look just at the release area (where the pitcher releases the ball). The hitter ends up staring into an area where nothing is happening. Consequently, he sees a background and/or his eyes dart from one place to another. Eyes are attracted to movement; they do not stay still very long unless the person is in some form of trance. (Steve Garvey told us, "When I got my eyes to the release area too soon, I didn't see the ball as well, as often.")

Many good hitters are not as consciously aware as Garvey and others like him, but they unconsciously discover that getting their eyes to the release area is very important. If they are too early or too late, they don't see the ball well. A hitter can only maintain his focus for a short period of time before there is a break in concentration. Most of the time, a broad focus can be held four to five seconds; a fine focus for two or three seconds. Hitters who keep their broad or fine focus too long may find themselves distracted, and they will lose that sharp picture of the ball.

Hitters find there is a rhythm and pattern for their eyes that is just right for them, and that moving from broad to fine focus is more effective than just tuning right in to a fine focus. The process of discovering and discipline is a mental one.

5. TENDENCY OF EYES TO MOVE AHEAD OF OBJECTS THEY ARE TRACKING

A. Hitters often experience this when they don't see the ball out of the pitcher's hand, but pick up the ball three or four yards after the release.

B. Then their eyes jump to the hitting area, the result being that they don't track the ball in the middle of the zone.

C. Every hitter has been aware of not seeing the ball in the hitting area, because his eyes have moved to where he thought his drive was going.

6. OVERSWINGING

When a hitter swings too hard, or when he muscles up to swing, the muscles in his neck tighten, and his head moves with his shoulder out of the hitting area.

A few years ago, A. Terry Bahill (University of Arizona) and Tim LaRitz (Carnegie Mellon University) did research on tracking a baseball. Their findings suggest that those who track the ball best track it with their eyes and their head. This confirms what veteran baseball players know: "If your head doesn't follow the ball from the pitcher's hand into the hitting zone [and if an infielder's head doesn't follow the ball into the glove], you're not seeing the ball as long as you can."

It's often easy to tell when a person is working at seeing an object well. His posture gives him away; he moves his head forward and sticks his chin out. We suggest that a hitter who moves his chin toward the ball is helping himself to see it better.

FUNDAMENTALS FOR SEEING THE BALL

PREPARATION

1. *Preparation for seeing the ball is achieved through visualization.* Many hitter's accomplish this simply by remembering a pitcher's pitches. As Willie Stargell said, "The night before the game I think about every pitch he might throw me, and then, after I've seen that pitch once the next day, my picture of that pitch is so strong, if he made any kind of mistake I would do some damage."

When visualizing, see the ball the way you want to see it — looking as big as a volleyball, seeing the release, the spin, the movement. See it through the entire 60 feet, 6 inches; see the ball hit the bat (even though, in reality, you don't).

Visualize the strike zone as a "cone," beginning at the point of release, then having the zone change into a rectangle as the zone moves into your own rectangular strike zone at home plate.

1. Visualize the pitches starting inside the cone and staying in it all the way. (Refer to diagram A, p. 282.)
2. Visualize breaking balls starting in your cone and then breaking outside. (Refer to diagram B, p. 282.)
3. Visualize breaking pitches starting outside your cone and coming into it. (Refer to diagram C, p. 282.)

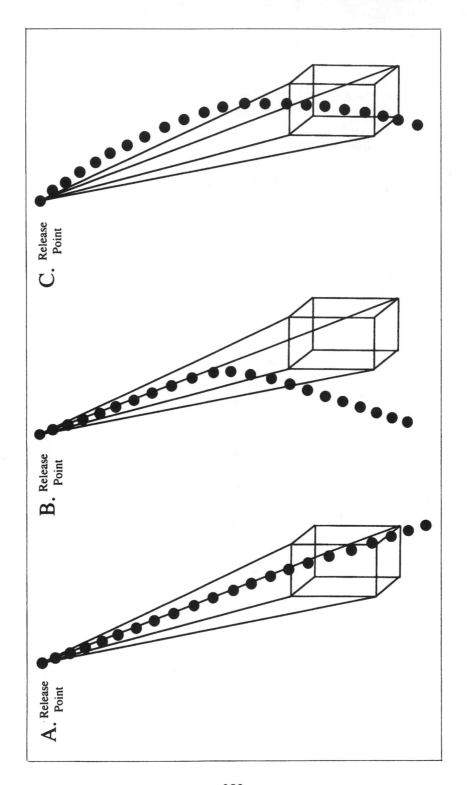

2. *Let your eyes take control.*
A. Get thinking, analyzing, and planning (your internal work) out of the way before you step into the batter's box.
B. Relax and clear your mind (possibly repeating a key word or phrase).
C. Become unconscious of your body, putting it on "automatic pilot."

3. *Establish consistent eye patterns.*
A. Avoid concentrating too soon.
B. As the pitcher begins his windup or goes into his stretch, put your eyes on him, using a broad focus.

Examples of where hitters have their eyes when in broad focus:
George Brett — Letter on the cap.
Steve Garvey — Pitcher's face (not looking for anything).
Ted Williams — "Just kind of the whole thing" (in reference to the pitcher's upper body).
C. About the time the pitcher's hands separate, move your eyes to the release area and fine focus.

4. *See the release.*
Train yourself to see the ball come right out of the pitcher's hand. Bob Watson said he could see the pitcher's hand on the side of the ball when a curve was being thrown. "Many times as the pitcher released the pitch, I knew what the pitch was. I didn't know how or why I knew, but I knew, and that was all that mattered."

This isn't surprising, since many times our eyes will see things that don't register on our consciousness. Still, we can react unconsciously to what is seen.

5. *Track the ball.*
Think of the 60-foot, 6-inch flight of the ball from the pitcher's hand to the hitting area as going through three zones.

ZONE #1 is the area from release to half the distance to the plate. Hitters who have trouble in ZONE #1 usually don't pick up the release. When a hitter doesn't see the release, but first sees the ball about six feet out of the pitcher's hand, he is figuratively allowing the pitcher to "cheat" him by delivering the ball from six feet in front of the rubber. (Refer to diagram, p. 284.)

ZONE #2 starts at the half-way point and ends two yards from the batter. This area is very important, since it is where the movement of the ball begins. It's where a hitter can first see the spin on

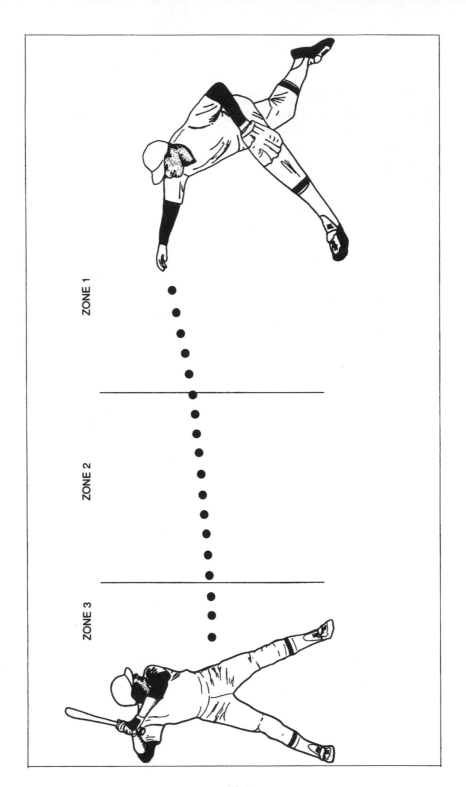

ZONE 1

ZONE 2

ZONE 3

the ball. Some hitters say they don't see spin, but it is there to see if you look for it. It's easier to see the spin on a breaking ball. On a four-seam fastball, the ball just looks white. On a two-seamer, the hitter can see a red seam. For those who do not see spin while at bat, we recommend standing behind or on the side of the batting practice catcher and watching the spin. Then, step into the batter's box and take some pitches while concentrating on seeing the spin.

ZONE #3 is most troublesome for hitters. In batting practice, against mediocre pitching, it's possible to hit decently even when not tracking the ball all the way to the bat. Hitters are fooled into thinking "all's well that ends well" in b.p. But if they aren't seeing the ball well in ZONE #3, hitters will not have any consistency against good pitching. Good pitchers have good movement in this area. We suggest hitters take a lesson from Steve Garvey and develop the habit of keeping the head down until an instant after contact.

Only the best hitters consistently see the ball well in all three areas. Most hitters see it well in two of the three zones. For example, they may not pick the ball up out of the pitcher's hand, but they do see it well the rest of the way. Or, others may concentrate on the release and contact, but they don't see the ball well in the middle zone. Still others may get good looks in ZONE #1 and ZONE #2, but come off the ball in ZONE #3, as they start their swing.

Most players feel they are seeing the ball *well* when, actually, they're not. When a hitter is having trouble, someone will usually ask him, "Are you seeing the ball well?" The answer is usually, "Yes, I'm seeing it okay, but I'm doing something wrong." However, if the hitter is asked if he has ever seen the ball better, he invariably will respond, "Oh sure," then tell about the times when the baseball looked like a grapefruit or volleyball.

We believe *the hitter is in complete control of how well he sees the ball*. Therefore, it is his responsibility to overcome the many interferences and excuses that exist, which keep him from having his "best look"—seeing the ball as well as possible—*on every pitch*.

CHECK YOURSELF: *How well are you seeing the ball?*

l. A good habit to get into is questioning yourself, "Have I ever seen the ball better?" If you have (the answer will usually be, "Yes"), remember when, where and the pitches you saw.

2. Many players find it helpful to take two or three pitches at the beginning of an at-bat, just to see how well they are seeing the ball.

3. Many players evaluate how well they see every pitch. They find that their use of a grading system makes them more aware of how well they're seeing the ball. Give a grade of 1 for your best look, a 5 for your poorest. If, for example, you grade your view of a pitch with a 3, the next step in the process would be to determine in which zone or zones you didn't see the ball well. Getting this specific information will help you fine-tune your "look," your focus. It certainly establishes your awareness, to begin with.

Hitters often ask themselves, "How did I miss that pitch?" They then answer themselves, "I must have opened my shoulder too soon," or "I jumped out at that pitch."

When an experienced hitter has a pitch to hit, and he swings and misses, the mechanical problems he may discover are a result of: A) *not getting his #1 look at the ball;* B) *overswinging.*

Overswinging is not just a result of trying to hit the ball too hard; it also results from seeing the ball late or making the decision to swing too late. When that happens, the hitter's body unconsciously tries to compensate by getting the bat through faster, to catch up with the ball.

The attitude most hitters take into a game is, "I'm going to get a good pitch to hit, then I'll hit it." We don't believe this to be a good approach, because the hitter is programming himself to see the ball, decide if it's a good pitch, and then decide whether or not to swing.

We recommend the attitude Al Oliver took to the plate. He said to himself, "I know this pitch is going to be right down the middle, and I'm going to hit it. If I see it's not [down the middle], I'll stop, unless I have two strikes or it looks too big to take." He emphasized to himself, "I am not *looking* for the ball down the middle; *I know it's going to be down the middle.*"

The essential element of Oliver's approach is, "I'm swinging until I see it's a pitch I don't want, then I'll decide to stop." After seeing the ball, most hitters make a decision to swing. Al Oliver went up to swing. He made a decision when he wanted to take the pitch.

There is another benefit derived from Oliver's approach. When a hitter "knows" pitches are going to be down the middle of the plate, more pitches appear as if they actually are.

During our conversation with Ted Williams, he confirmed the merit of Oliver's philosophy. Williams said, "When a pitcher has a great fastball, you can't wait until you see the ball to get started. You have to anticipate what area the pitch is going to be in and approach that area. You can adjust some after you see the ball, and you can stop if it isn't close to where you anticipate."

Williams went on to talk about how a hitter should adjust in a game. He said, "When someone had a good fastball and I was late on it, I'd tell myself to start earlier. If I fouled a couple of pitches back, I'd tell myself to raise my sights. I wouldn't analyze my swing; hell, I trusted my swing. And why should you change your swing when you just missed?"

He then brought up an excellent analogy. Every time a hitter changes his swing — his mechanics — it is the same as a marksman changing rifles. The marksman doesn't change rifles every time he misses the target, because he wouldn't learn how to set the sights, or know what adjustments to make unless he had the opportunity to fire two or three rounds with the gun.

Another Williams — Billy — had this to tell us about adjustments he made at the plate after swinging and missing: "Hey, when you swing and miss, you're either swinging under the ball or over it. Most of the time, under it. If you're late, you are on your fists. If you're early, you're on the end. So there isn't really much to think about."

The simplicity of that answer should make every player stop and consider, "This really is a kid's game."

Basically, the adjustments a hitter makes during an at-bat are: 1) Fine-tuning his look at the ball; 2) Adjusting his sights; 3) Adjusting his timing. *All thoughts about stance and mechanics must be left outside the batter's box!*

In the batter's box, be easy; see the ball.

Hitter's should never give away an at-bat because they aren't ready mentally. (He will be ready physically if he's ready mentally.) Hitters must be aware of their state of readiness. And if a hitter isn't ready, *he must take control: call time, and fix himself, so as to be ready.*

THOUGHT PATTERNS FOR AN AT-BAT

Based on Bob Nideffer's model for concentration, we recommend the following process. The hitter's sequence of thoughts may vary slightly, but he should establish a consistent pattern.

1. *Looking at the situations on the field*
   Broad External Focus
2. *Looking for the signs*
   Narrow External Focus
3. *Analyzing situation*
   Broad Internal Focus
4. *Planning, visualizing what is to be done*
   Narrow Internal Focus
5. *Stepping into the batter's box and getting comfortable*
   A Mental Break
6. *Monitoring breathing and tension level*
   Narrow Internal Focus
7. *Turning control over to "automatic guidance system" (eyes)*
   Narrow External Focus

After the pitch:
8. *Analyzing, evaluating what happened*
   Broad Internal Focus
9. *Visualizing adjustments in approach*
   Narrow Internal Focus

Go back to Step 1.

Keep in mind hitting is an external function; thinking is an internal function. Remember also, Yogi had it right; you can't think and hit at the same time.

OUTLINE FOR AN AT-BAT

1. *Initial preparation*
   A. Discipline conditioning and batting practice routines. (Review Staub's in Chapter 4.)
   B. Know your opposition.
   C. Study the pitcher's release and the movement on every pitch.
   D. Visualize new pitches coming in, "hitting" them the way you want to hit them.

2. *In the on-deck circle*
   A. Analyze the situation and set your plan.
   B. Get loose and relaxed.
   C. Self-coach yourself with reminders about mechanics, if necessary.
   D. Get emotions under control; set appropriate tension level.

3. *In the batter's box*
   A. Relax. (For some, control breathing, then forget about it.)
   B. Put yourself on "automatic system," using trigger word, if needed to keep mind clear.
   C. Allow the eyes to take control.
   D. "Let it flow."

4. *After a pitch has been thrown*
   (If something wasn't right, or you were dissatisfied about anything, get out of the box, and . . .)
   A. Get the "garbage"—whatever made you unhappy—out of your mind.
   B. Visualize the adjustment you want to make.
   C. Start over again: visualize what you're going to get and how you're going to hit it. Relax.

Don't rush your thinking. *Keep a normal, steady pace.*

See the ball. Hit the ball.

16
PITCHING

"If you don't know the difference between good hitting and bad pitching, you are heading for stormy waters. We have all seen pitchers with the greatest stuff in the world who never seem to rise above the mediocrity of a .500 record. They pitch, as the phrase goes, 'just well enough to lose.'

"They lack the ability to distinguish between their mistakes and good pitches well hit. They overestimate how well they are pitching on a given day, and when they are tagged, they lose confidence. Instead of battling back with their best stuff, they become defensive and hesitate on the mound."

— Tom Seaver

"It is better to throw a theoretically poorer pitch whole-heartedly, than to throw the so-called right pitch with feeling of doubt — doubt that it's right, or doubt that you can make it behave well at

that moment. You've got to feel sure you're doing the right thing—
sure you want to throw the pitch you're going to throw."

—*Sandy Koufax,* in *A Thinking Man's Guide To Baseball* by
Leonard Koppett.

"I don't ever doubt myself. I don't feel any pressure . . . I just
try to stay calm, follow my game plan and not overthrow."

—*Dwight Gooden*

Pete Rose's "See-the-ball; hit-the-ball" approach is a reduction
to lowest terms of what a hitter finally must do, after all his philoso-
phizing and theorizing about the art of hitting. We refer to the
words of Tom Seaver, Sandy Koufax, and Dwight Gooden in an attempt to reduce pitching to its own lowest common denominator.
Basically, the message is: know your capabilities; have a plan; believe in that plan *and* in your ability to throw the ball where you
want to, the way you want; assess the results objectively—and keep
yourself in control.

Capabilities may change from game to game—inning to inning.
The plan may change from pitch to pitch. Adjustments, certainly,
are called for. But all that is reduced when the pitcher finally steps
on the rubber and takes the sign from the catcher. Selection. Location. Or, as Rose might say if he were a pitcher, "See the sign; see
the target; throw the ball." That simple—at that moment.

No single belief or behavior is exclusively responsible for making a
pitcher successful or "great." Philosophies and strategies vary. For example, Steve Carlton reduced pitching to "an elevated game of catch"
between the pitcher and the catcher, without regard to the batter.
Catcher Rick Cerone would tell his pitchers, "Hey, there's just you and
me; there's no hitter out here." In contrast, Hall of Fame pitcher Jim
Palmer gave elaborate attention to the study of opposing hitters, to his
own fielders' strengths and weaknesses—and to wind currents. Many
fine major league pitchers could conduct seminars on the art and

craft of pitching. Differences in approach would be evident. Simiarities would be more evident.

But how a pitcher applies the theoretical and the physical is the key to successful pitching. Knowing what to do is a start. Bringing it "across the white lines" is a second step for the pitcher. Up on the mound, the *doing* is his true measure.

"Pitching is a game within a game," said Tommy John. "To fool the batter on a pitch, you have to think. Every pitch will dictate what the next pitch is."

We will not make an attempt to deal with the "dictation" of strategy here, since the "game within the game" develops uniquely for the pitcher as he pitches. We do wish to address John's reference to the importance of thinking—functional thinking. That is, what the pitcher wants to do and how he wants to do it. It is *not* thinking about consequences, statistics, and so on. John is talking about the winning mind games of intellectualizing pitching.

But there even may be danger for acknowledged intellectuals. Pitcher Mike Flanagan was said to pitch intelligently, unless his competitive "stubbornness" got in the way of his brain. There was a time when Ron Darling was described by his manager as a pitcher who was highly intelligent, but lacking in "common sense" when on the mound.

The commonality of sense and approach that successful pitchers share is a useful guide. Despite the extreme difference in pitching style, and a clear difference in pitching philosophy, Jim Palmer and Sandy Koufax, as examples, had an essential approach in common.

Palmer's goal on the mound was "to make the batter hit the ball—except when you absolutely can't afford to." Koufax said, "I became a good pitcher when I stopped trying to make them miss the ball and started trying to make them hit it." (That from a pitcher with 2396 strikeouts in 2324 innings pitched.)

"You have to learn to throw before you can learn to pitch," Koufax also said. There are basic—common—fundamentals that must be mastered before a pitcher can get his "best stuff" in the strike zone. Many pitchers master the physical aspects of baseball and have great stuff, but they don't become big winners, because they fail to develop the mental part of their game.

Again, Tom Seaver: "The difference between those who win and those who lose is mental. It is the effort winners give, and their mental alertness, that keeps them from making mental mistakes . . . Dedication and concentration are the deciding factors between who wins and who loses."

Players who don't have God-given ability often accomplish more than those who do. Tommy John is an excellent illustration. His remarkable success and longevity — after a tendon transplant in his forearm — were achieved despite the fact that he was throwing the ball just over 80 miles per hour.

The dedication Seaver spoke of has been documented and discussed earlier in the book. One doesn't become a great pitcher by accident. There are fundamental steps to climb, as we've said in Part One of this book. We broadly restate a few here:

A REVIEW OF "MENTAL FUNDAMENTALS"

1. *Know yourself physically and mentally.* Know your strengths and weaknesses. You must be able to "play" to your strengths and improve your weaknesses.

2. *Establish self-control.* This is a result of mental discipline. You must be able to control your thoughts, emotions, and actions. You're either in control, or are being controlled by situations and distractions. Remember, the pitcher is the only player on the "defensive" field who is actually an *offensive* player. He acts; the batter reacts. The pitcher starts with that control.

3. *Understand and deal with the issue of pressure.* Being at your best in so-called "pressure situations" is the ultimate challenge in sport, the most demanding test of self-control. The proper philosophy and mental approach allows pressure situations to be welcomed opportunities, rather than dreaded threats.

4. *Define and use failures.* Remember, *you* are not a failure when you fail to reach a goal. Be sure to take responsibility for your actions. Don't alibi or look for some place to lay blame for mistakes or failures in performance. That's a big step up the ladder of learning and improving. Mistakes that you learn from are rungs in that ladder.

5. *Learn how to manage success.* This is a final step to excellence. It's one step that many major league players fail to take. After reaching the goal of playing in the big leagues and having some success, they become self-satisfied. Many believe, "I've proven I belong, that I can play here. I know what it takes and what I have to do." The great players, despite their success, have a different attitude. They are always trying to learn more, always trying to find a better way. They're never self-satisfied.

"Don't mistake activity for achievement." John Wooden knew that the difference was based on the quality of a team's or player's preparation. A pitcher's preparation is an on-going process. Concentration cannot be turned on a few minutes before it's time to pitch. A starting pitcher begins his mental preparation a few days before his next turn. (Many pitchers keep notebooks on their performances and/or the "habits" of opposing hitters.)

You are the pitcher. You begin by thinking about a game plan. Your next step is to consider the hitters and possible situations you will be facing; how you'll pitch to them; how you'll approach each different situation.

As a pitcher, your level of respect and desire to win may vary, according to the opponent. You must often play mind games to get yourself in the right frame of mind. Pitchers who are big winners year in and year out—the great competitors—*look at every game, every pitch as important.* They don't become preoccupied with the opposition's ability or previous accomplishments. They focus on how they're going to do their job.

As a pitcher, you will have times when you feel that you're going to have a good day. You get up feeling strong and confident. Your mind is clear. When that happens, you can't wait to get to the ball park and begin pitching.

At other times, you wake up feeling, "This isn't going to be my day. I wish I didn't have to pitch today." You cannot give in to those feelings. Negative feelings can and should be stopped—and changed through positive thoughts.

These positive thoughts focus on how you are going to pitch certain counts to certain hitters; on how you pitched well in the past when you woke up feeling the same way; on how you are mentally tough enough to approach your performance in a controlled and commanding way, knowing that what matters is how you *act*, not how you *feel*.

Patterns and routines are important. For consideration as part of your routine:

> *The night before* — What you do. What you eat and drink. What time you go to sleep.
> *Amount of sleep* — Too much sleep may cause lethargy. Too little may cause weakness or edginess.
> *Diet* — What you eat and when you eat.
> *Activities* — The control of what you do during the day. Distractions can affect your emotions and use up energy.
> *Departure time* — When you leave for the ball park. Allow enough time for relaxed preparation. Don't leave so early that the time spent at the park is aimless. The idle time of anticipation can cause edginess or, worse still, anxiety.

At the ball park, the routine continues. You want everything to be the same as the last time (unless you're making an adjustment you feel is an improvement). On game day, you do not want to be rushed. You avoid the usual horse-play or other activity that uses physical and mental energy. You avoid pre-game interviews, telephone calls, and conversations, because they can trigger thoughts which you do not want to entertain before getting ready to pitch.

A relief pitcher's approach to getting ready is different from that of a starting pitcher. As a relief pitcher, you must be ready almost every day. Consequently, your day is similar to that of a regular player. You do not normally begin to get ready for a game until after infield practice. Mental preparations must not begin too soon for relief pitchers.

As is the case with every player, a relief pitcher will establish his own comfortable routine. As an example, however, we refer to the routine of Mike Marshall, winner of the 1974 Cy Young Award. Marshall liked to take a warm whirlpool for five minutes before the game started. Early in the game, he studied the opposing hitters and was aware of the flow of the game. As the game moved toward the late innings, he would begin to anticipate which hitters he might be brought in to face and how he would pitch them. When he got the call to get loose, he was "in the game" — he was already mentally prepared.

Any number of times, relief pitchers have told us they anticipated *not* being called into a game, and when surprised by the call, they found themselves unprepared. The results, they said, "were not pretty." A relief pitcher should anticipate being called. No call; no harm.

Warming up

"Warming up — getting loose" — should be taken literally. Warm muscles are stronger and will stretch more. When you are warmed up, everything moves easier and comes easier. Getting the muscles warm is accomplished by the increase of the blood flow. As Satchel Paige said, "Gettin' the juices goin'." You must get loose before you can get your timing and rhythm.

As you warm up, mentally try to fine-tune your concentration. You can imagine you are pitching to certain hitters. Many successful pitchers are even more specific; they imagine counts (0-2; 3-1; etc.) and situations (runner on third base, George Bell hitting). The successful pitchers have found that their bodies respond to plans developed before the action. Steve Carlton even concentrated on location *before* his warm-up for every start. He sat in the training room with his eyes shut and concentrated on "the lanes of the plate." (He divided the plate into three sections, the outside width of the ball, the inside width of the ball, and the fat middle part. He visualized himself hitting the outside and inside sections.)

When you feel good about your warm-up, you can't wait to get into the game. However, a poor warm-up can be devastating to an inexperienced pitcher. Every pitcher runs into days when nothing seems to go well in the bullpen. Sometimes the pitcher finds it impossible to understand why. Following are some reasons why you may warm up poorly — and some thoughts about how you might be able to get back on the right track:

1. Getting loose too fast becomes a physical problem, but starts as a mental one. The pitcher "can't wait to get going." You don't have to wait, if you follow a defined

and sensible schedule. When you start throwing too hard too soon, your muscles often rebel by contracting (trying to protect themselves). When that happens, you can't seem to get the stiffness out of your arm. Some "macho-types" are proud of being able to get ready fast. On occasion, they *force* their bodies to get ready, thus increasing the possibility of an arm injury.

Pitching coaches advise pitchers to give themselves plenty of time to get ready physically. "Don't force it. Control your mind and let your arm and body tell you how fast to move along."

2. Believing that if you warm up poorly you will pitch poorly can only hurt, not help, your performance. It can hurt you in two ways. First, you will press, in order to be "razor sharp." Second, expecting to pitch poorly, you will pitch to that expectation. Your head fails you before your arm has a chance to show you what it can do.

Veteran pitchers know they can be "ragged" in the pen and great in the game. They know they can get hitters out when they aren't sharp. They don't panic if they're wild, or if a certain pitch isn't working. They don't fight the situation. When they aren't sharp, they stay relaxed, throw easier and work at getting "the feel" they want. Experienced pitchers are confident they will find the groove in the game, if not in the bullpen, so long as they remain patient.

3. Analyzing what is wrong often dominates a pitcher's thinking when he's struggling in the bullpen. The dominant thought in your mind acts as a guiding system and is the major factor in controlling performance. The last thought preceding performance carries a lot of weight, but it isn't necessarily the dominant thought. The strength and duration of previous thoughts may be too much to overcome, so keep *all* your thoughts on what you want to do, rather than analyzing whatever is going wrong.

Experienced pitchers think ahead; they are concerned about what they're going to do next, about corrections and adjustments they're preparing to make. It's as simple as the difference between thinking, "I'm dropping my arm" (analysis), and "Get your arm up" (command to act).

In athletics, the persistent analysis of what is wrong can become a form of negative thinking, if the thoughts dwell on errors and substandard performance. You can save time and mental effort, and assure a better performance, by thinking of what you want to *do*, rather than what you *don't* want to do.

4. Getting frustrated and angry when things aren't falling into place right away is a common bullpen behavior. This doesn't change the fact that it is usually counterproductive. Sometimes, anger can serve to motivate the pitcher and intensify his concentration. What he concentrates on becomes the issue in such cases. Most often, the frustration itself is getting the focus. "I can't get the ball down." Or, "The breaking ball is a foot short." Again, the negative aspect gains the spotlight. Getting mad either works in the first few seconds, or it doesn't work at all. Irrational thinking, which frequently accompanies anger, must be stopped immediately, or it will lead to irrational behavior and poor performance.

Holding anger inside also will work against you, because it becomes a distraction. It is all right to get mad — but make it short, if not sweet.

Oakland's Rick Langford, while pitching 28 complete games in 1980, 19 of them victories, said, "There are lots of times I get mad at myself and get on myself after making a bad pitch, but I always take the time to do some rational thinking about what I'm going to do *now*. I have to forget the past, before I make the next pitch."

That practice should start in the bullpen.

Crossing the Foul Line

The great pitchers, the Carltons and the Seavers, the Koufaxes, the Bob Gibsons, the Whitey Fords, were at their best between the foul lines. However, many pitchers leave their best stuff in the bullpen.

What is it that can happen to a pitcher during his walk from the bullpen to the mound? What happens when he crosses the foul line?

Baseball people call a pitcher "gutless" when he consistently leaves his best stuff in the bullpen. But the problem is usually *not* one of courage. It is a problem of *thinking*. Note some of the factors that may affect a pitcher's thinking:

In the bullpen—No risk. No chance to fail.
In the game—Chance of a bad day. Possibility of failure and embarrassment.

In the bullpen—No concern for impressing or pleasing others.
In the game—Desire to please and impress others.

In the bullpen—No judgment or criticism given by others.
In the game—Concern/worry about what others are thinking, saying about the pitcher and his performance. Booing by fans.

In the bullpen—Easy to concentrate; very few distractions.
In the game—Many distractions. Thoughts about opponents' intentions and abilities. Thoughts about the expectations of others. Coaches, teammates, fans shouting at pitcher (even encouragement).

In the bullpen—Just "a game of catch." Easy to think about what and where to throw the ball.
In the game—Thoughts about the damage the hitter can do and what he may do now. Thoughts of consequences. Trying to decide what is the "right pitch."

In the bullpen—Thoughts only about "the here and the now": the next pitch.
In the game—Thoughts about a previous bad pitch or play behind the pitcher or umpire's bad call.

Essentially, there are only two factors preventing you, the pitcher, from throwing as well in games as you do in the bullpen. First, you *lose concentration* because of additional and disorganized thoughts. Second, you change your thinking through your desire (conscious or subconscious) to throw better than you did in the bullpen, which results in an increase of tension level. Your head, then, affects your arm—and your entire body.

Breathing and Tension Levels—An Important Review

Your breathing, remember, is affected by *what* and *how* you think. Every time you focus your mind, you have a small intake of air and breathing either stops or becomes very shallow. Rapid and disorganized thinking usually leads to hyperventilation (shortness of breath). Hyperventilation increases muscular tension throughout the body.

Consistent breathing patterns accompany consistent athletic performance. A pitcher's breathing will affect:

*coordination
*timing
*balance
*range of motion
*tension level
*accuracy
*power

Each pitcher must determine the breathing pattern that is right for him. Young players should experiment until they find a pattern that is comfortable, natural—and seems to work well.

The Mental Wind-up

Naturally, as a pitcher, you will have plenty to think about during a game. You must know what's happening in the game, so that you can anticipate possibilities and plan accordingly.

The content, timing, and "delivery" of those thoughts are critical. You must have a consistent mental approach—a disciplined mental wind-up.

A mental wind-up is a step-by-step thinking process that is organized and controlled. An airline pilot has a procedure for checking his instrument panel; a pitcher should have his own procedure of thinking his way from one step to the next. After you develop and practice a good mental wind-up, it will become as automatic as your delivery to the plate. You won't have to think about it or work at it. Your mental wind-up, from habitual use, will become integrated into your entire pitching approach.

The following are elements of a pitcher's mental wind-up:

Off the mound

Complete all thoughts about previous pitch, play, and/ or call. Immediately, following any performance, you have a tendency to look back (consciously or subconsciously) and evaluate what has happened and what you've done. When evaluations are positive, thoughts are completed rapidly, and you get right on with your thinking about the next pitch. When the evaluations are negative — when you don't like the way things turned out — you have a difficult time forgetting the event. Many times you're still thinking about what went wrong on the previous pitch or play, as you're beginning to throw the next pitch.

You should be certain that thoughts about adjustments and intentions have time to sink in, that they dominate thoughts related to what went wrong. This is difficult to do effectively on the mound. *Step off* — "separate your environment." Turn your back to home plate. Gather yourself. Vent any anger quickly; clear the frustration. Make the necessary mental adjustments (target, delivery, thoughts, tension level). Be clear and definite about what you want to do on the next pitch. *What*: fastball, curve; *Where*: target; *How*: "smooth and easy." Do as much of this thinking as possible with mental pictures. Anticipate possible plays — what to do with all types of balls that you may have to field; how to hold runners.

Step back on the rubber, ready for business: *The next pitch.*

On the rubber

Look for the sign from the catcher. *Relax.* Inhale and exhale with a slow, prolonged breath. *Visualize.* Include how you want to feel emotionally and how you want your delivery to feel. When all is going well, everything "flows."

You can keep it going just by continuing the good tempo you've established. *Let the ball throw itself.* When you know what you want the ball to do and it's happening, it's as if the ball has a will of its own. Let it happen. Check any runners — and pitch.

Ideally, you shouldn't have to think that much between pitches. You need only think about making necessary adjustments, anticipating, planning, and relaxing. When your thinking is orderly, this process takes only a few seconds. You must get into a mental "groove," before it's possible to establish a pitching "groove." You must learn what your business is (the next pitch) and discipline yourself to focus on that business without distraction. That allows you to settle comfortably into both "grooves."

What happens when you slip out of that groove? When your rhythm and timing are off? When you feel as if you have nothing on the ball?

You must learn to interpret discomfort as a message from your body that says, "Make an adjustment." Instead of being frustrated or giving in, check your keys:

1. Are you overthrowing?
2. Are you trying to be perfect?
3. Have you strayed from your normal breathing patterns?
4. Are you trying to do more than one thing at a time?
5. Are you tensing up?
6. Are you thinking about getting outs, or getting the inning/game over with, instead of dealing with one pitch at a time?
7. Are you being impatient?

When things are not going well, you may have a tendency to let your ego take over. You then start to think about what's happening to you, instead of what you want to make happen. Remember to get off the mound as you consider these possibilities. Take a break. Have a meeting with yourself:

Relax for a moment. Use controlled breathing. Stretch. Roll your shoulders.

Talk out loud slowly, calmly, You may remind yourself:
"One pitch at a time."
"No hurry; be patient."
"Smooth and easy."
"Nice and loose."

"Trust yourself; you know how to throw."
"Just let it happen."
"Just keep pitching."
"Good, low strikes; see the target and let it go."

Remember the last time you felt real good out there. Recall it with as much detail as possible. Get the scene, the hitters, your tempo, your feelings. How easy and effortlessly you were throwing—and anything else you may want to remember. Take your time; enjoy the image.

It may be helpful to change your tempo when you're struggling during the game. (Remember, "struggling" doesn't mean that base hits are falling in, or that hitters are hitting your best pitches. It means your mental and/or physical approach has broken down. Be certain to make the distinction between approach and results!) Most often, when things aren't going well, a pitcher slows himself down. But you have to be careful about your tempo. It has definite effects. If you work slowly over a prolonged period of time, taking a lot of time between pitches, you are likely to get caught in the trap of "thinking too much." Too much thinking—trying to think of "everything"—leads to divided attention. The focus of attention—concentration—becomes less intense, widening, slipping away.

The same breaking down of concentration becomes a problem for the defensive players playing behind the pitcher who always works slowly. When they're forced to wait over a long period of time between pitches, a defensive player's attention tends to wander, making it difficult for him to perform at his best. The difference in a defensive player's alertness can be seen, when there is a pitcher who goes right at his business or a pitcher who dawdles on and around the mound.

You must use your time and tempo appropriately when you "fix" yourself. Slow it down, but don't put yourself and everyone else to sleep. Get after business. The "fixing process" takes only a few moments. If it's done right, it doesn't have to be done continually.

Pitching When Tired

During a baseball season, the daily grind of the schedule can take its toll. You'll be asked to pitch when you are tired, ill, or having nagging pains. *To be a consistent winner, you must be able to pitch effectively when you're tired or not feeling well.*

Not many pitchers have the will, the skill, and the commitment to maintain concentration under those adverse circumstances. Fatigue, as Vince Lombardi suggested, can "make cowards of us all."

You can take the easy way out. You can tell yourself, "I've done my job; I shouldn't be pitching, the way I feel; they're asking too much of me; they can't expect me to be at my best, as much as I've been pitching."

One way or another, you can set yourself up for failure by not expecting to get the job done, making excuses (even though they may be legitimate "reasons"), or feeling sorry for yourself. Thoughts about "self" become a preoccupation and a distraction from thoughts about the job to be done.

Great competitors do not give in when they're tired. But they can have trouble getting outs, because they try to compensate with more effort. Their desire works against them, because the extra effort causes them to lose their smooth, effortless delivery and rhythm. Their competitive nature may also lead to their taking chances they wouldn't normally take if they felt strong and confident.

The "big winners" have the mental toughness, the mental discipline, to continue to do what they are supposed to do and stay within themselves. They know how to pitch when they're tired; they know how to get the job done when they don't feel well. *They trust themselves.* Satchel Paige probably pitched more innings than any other man. He was often tired. But he kept a steadfast philosophy. "The more tired I get, the looser I get," Paige said. "You can't fight it. You've got to roll with it, and take one pitch at a time."

The "big winners" know how to pitch when being hit hard or when all the breaks seem to go against them. It isn't easy, but, again, that's where mental discipline must be applied.

Even the Tom Seavers of baseball have had to fight the battle. Remember what he told *Sports Illustrated* writer Pat Jordan? "You want to quit. You feel it is all hopeless. You have to force yourself to forget and start over as if it (getting 'ripped') never happened. Some guys can't do that. They are always fighting things beyond their control."

And all kinds of control are required of successful pitchers.

Throwing Strikes

Many young pitchers make the mistake of going into a game *hoping* to throw strikes, instead of *being determined* to throw strikes. (Better yet, *knowing* they'll throw strikes.) As we mentioned before, there's a great distinction between hope and determination.

When Joe Sambito made his major league debut for the Houston Astros against the Pittsburgh Pirates in 1976, he was uncharacteristically wild. Sambito said the reason was, "I was just *hoping* to throw strikes. I kept telling myself, 'Just throw strikes,' but I couldn't. Later, I realized what I'd done to myself. I didn't have a target. I didn't even think about where I wanted to throw the ball. I was just hoping the ball would go into the strike zone."

Some pitchers "nibble," aiming for the corners until the count is 2 or 3 balls and no strikes. "Nibblers" don't like to aim for the middle of the plate at any time. There are two types of "nibblers."

One is "afraid" of the hitter. He gives the hitter too much credit, thinking that every time he makes a bad pitch, he'll be 'ripped.' The other "nibbler" has read in the newspaper or heard from other pitchers about "hitting the black" on the plate. This type becomes convinced that going for the corners is the way to pitch. No one can tell him otherwise, because he is behind in the count most of the time, and when he does come into the strike zone, he gets hit. Both types are victims of their own thinking.

Major league pitching coaches can be heard telling pitchers again and again, "Go after the hitter; be aggressive; challenge the hitter." They are trying to tell the pitcher to throw the ball for the middle of the plate, knee high. Aiming for corners leaves no margin for error on one side of the target. In other words, if the target is on the corner of the plate, and you throw a pitch one inch from your target, it may be a ball. Jim Palmer said, "I always aimed for the middle of the plate. I knew the ball wasn't going to be there anyway."

After pitching to several hitters, you can refine your target. For instance, if your control is good, you may decide to aim for the inside or outside third of the plate. If your stuff is so poor that you must make *perfect pitches all the time*, consider playing another position. Having to be perfect all the time is an unattainable goal.

Getting Ahead of the Hitter and Finishing Him

The batting average of hitters who hit the first pitch is less than .190. You should take advantage of this statistic and throw the first pitch for a strike. There are pitchers who do not want to. They argue, "He's a first-ball hitter." If a hitter *is* a first-ball hitter, the following questions should be considered by the pitcher:

*Does the batter get hits on the first pitch?
*Does he chase pitches out of the strike zone?
Should I let him make an out on the first pitch?

Most first-ball hitters want to hit fastballs, but they usually chase breaking balls also. Keep in mind that first-ball hitters make outs more than four out of every five times they put the first pitch into play.

When you throw the first pitch for a strike, and then stay ahead of the hitter, he does not know what you will throw. He may guess, but there will be doubt. Look at the effect different counts have on hitters:

1 BALL and 2 STRIKES: The hitter knows you can throw any pitch you have, including pitches you don't control well, because you do not have to throw a strike. You should take advantage of the hitter's doubt. *Go right after him.*

2 BALLS and 2 STRIKES: The hitter "feels" he has an idea about what you'll throw, and he has had a chance to look at (and time) more pitches. His confidence grows. You and the hitter are even — *you've lost your advantage.*

3 BALLS and 2 STRIKES: The hitter thinks, "I know what he's going to throw now." Whether he's right or wrong, he is confident. *Any time a hitter has three balls in the count, he has an advantage.* He has the margin for error; he can be fooled and foul it off. You have no such margin.

Many times, you get two strikes on a hitter, but cannot "finish him." Sometimes the problem is as simple as trying to do too much —

trying to throw too hard (not staying within yourself). You may have trouble finishing hitters, because you try to make perfect pitches. You get too fine and you don't throw the ball over the plate. As a result, you lose the advantage of having two strikes on the hitter — and often lose the hitter. You should keep in mind that good hitters become tougher with every pitch they see, because they see movement, get the pitches timed, and even recognize it sooner.

With a count of no balls and two strikes on a hitter, you try to get the hitter guessing about your intentions or try to move his eyes away from the area you will throw your next pitch—the *out* pitch. Hitters like to see consecutive pitches in the same area.

Some pitchers make the mistake of not having good stuff on the 0-2 pitch, and then, even though it may be out of the strike zone, it gets hit hard.

Young pitchers try to "finish" hitters by getting them to chase outside pitches. Experienced pitchers know that hitters are more likely to chase low pitches than outside pitches. They try to pitch lower and lower, even bouncing curves to hitters who tend to chase them.

Another consideration after getting two strikes on a hitter: pitches on the corners that were called strikes early in the count are often called balls, because some umpires—at all levels—are reluctant to call experienced hitters out on strikes.

Finally, this inexcusable circumstance. Pitchers who have a tendency to let a hitter get away after they've had the hitter 0-2 or 1-2 have often found that they "relaxed" at that point in the count. What they actually did was take the hitter and the situation for granted. They thought "this hitter is history." As a result, the pitchers lost their concentration—their intensity—and ended up losing the hitter.

To extend that problem a bit, pitchers often pitch great to get out of trouble or to get a tough hitter, then lose their edge—intensity and concentration—on the next hitter or in the next inning, and the "roof falls in." Focus and determination must be consistent—consistently good.

It's much more difficult for a pitcher to protect a lead than it is for him to work effectively when his team is losing. Many pitchers have asked us why it is they "give up two or three runs at the get-go, then pitch great after that." After the opposition has scored early, the burden — the responsibility, "the pressure" — is on the hitters to score runs. The pitcher "settles down," when he feels himself relieved of pressure and relaxes. Performance is always enhanced by relaxation.

On the other hand, when a pitcher is in a tie ball game or protecting a one-run lead, he tends "to feel more pressure as [he] gets closer to the end of the game."

The greatest pressure many major league pitchers claim to feel comes when they're working at getting the last out, while protecting a one-run lead in an important game. The pressure is there because the pitcher doesn't want the win to slip away, and he knows that one pitch can get in the way of that goal.

It is a supreme challenge for you, whenever you may be in that situation. But the challenge doesn't come from the hitter. It is *your* challenge to master *your* self-control and maintain *your* mental discipline. Only those who can do that will win the challenge and get the "big outs" with any degree of consistency.

There may be those times when you'll "sail along," pitching very effectively, until you take a lead into the late innings. Then everything falls apart. You lose four miles on your fastball and can't throw a strike. It's easy to understand how that happens. Even as a Little Leaguer, when it came down to the last inning, with the chance to "wrap up a victory," you heard people who hadn't said anything all game suddenly giving advice and encouragement:

> "Don't give 'em anything to hit."
> "Don't make a mistake; you have the game in the bag."
> "Don't walk anyone."
> "You only have to get three more outs."
> "Let's see you really finish strong."

These thoughts — most often negative, at that — will stay with you and automatically come into your mind over and over again in that situation, year after year, unless you become aware of what's happening, and of the fact that as it is happening, *the situation is controlling your thinking*. Since thoughts control actions, *you must take control of your thoughts* and of the situation. Apply the mental strategies you know — the thinking strategies and the behavioral ones.

Being able to get the out you need — the "last out" — is a special talent, one you want to be aware of — and one you want to develop.

The Relief Pitcher's "Last Out"

The relief pitcher's job is to save games — to get that "last out." He must have particularly strong mental discipline to be successful in this role. He cannot "give in." Relief pitchers who enter a game with the attitude, "Hey, I'm only human; I may fail," are not cut out for the job of pitching when the game is on the line. When called into the game, the relief pitcher should feel and *believe*, "I'm the best man for the job. I'm going to get the job done."

Often, when a young pitcher sees his best can be beaten, he tends to "fold." Relievers must understand their "humanness," but they must also be able to recover, with strength and confidence, from the failures of a bad outing — or from one pitch to the next. They must rationally know that it's impossible to get everyone out, or get the job done everyday. But they must go at that job as if they're invincible.

When Joe Sambito was one of the top relief pitchers in the major leagues, he said, "If I come into a game in the bottom of the ninth to protect a one-run lead, and I give up hits to the first two hitters, I'm not going to give in. I'm not going to worry about what happened. What I'm going to do is keep thinking the same, always. 'What will I do with the ball hit back to me? Where will I go if there's a hit? Where am I going to throw this pitch?' I take it one step at a time."

Pitching Inside

To be successful, you have to be able to get outs on the outside of the plate, because the majority of your pitches are there. You want to keep most breaking pitches away from hitters; and a majority of fastballs are also thrown outside. Experienced pitching coaches tell young pitchers to pitch the outside of the plate, so that when someone does hit the ball well, he'll be hitting it to the longest part of the field, center field.

But it's also understood that if you throw pitch after pitch on the outside part of the plate, you'll run into problems The hitter will start guessing — correctly — that pitches will be in that area. *You must pitch inside to keep hitters honest.*

For you to be effective against good hitters, *you must pitch both sides of the plate.*

After you've pitched inside with good stuff, some doubt enters the hitter's mind. He begins to wonder, "Was he giving me a message, or was he trying to break my [wooden] bat?" The hitter may then worry about getting started a little sooner, "getting out front." Once you have him thinking about "getting jammed, opening up sooner or pulling the ball," the outside part of the plate is yours.

However, many pitchers do not like to pitch close to hitters. Some don't want to hurt anyone; others don't want the hitters to think they're being thrown at. The pitcher wants to be "Mr. Nice Guy." Consequently, when he does pitch inside, he does so tentatively, without throwing his best stuff. Either he gets "ripped" or the pitch has no effect on the batter.

The results, of course, "prove" that he cannot pitch inside. This, then, becomes the claim he makes, when he refuses to do so.

When you *are* pitching inside — trying to keep the hitter honest by keeping him off the plate — you do not want to hit him, thereby giving him a free pass to first base. The best place to throw the pitch is in the area of the belt. Hitters can usually get out of the way of pitches in that area, but the message is loud and clear.

Many pitchers have difficulty understanding that there is a conflict between "being a winner" and "being a nice guy" on the ball field. The winners know they can't have it both ways. Tom Seaver told Larry Merchant of the *New York Post*, "I had to choose between a nice-guy image and a losing-guy image. I found I had to brush hitters back on occasion. I threw a message pitch. The message was, 'Don't dig in on me, or I will brush you back.'"

Said Seaver, "I don't consider throwing a brushback pitch unethical. There is fine line between good, hard baseball and dirty baseball; between gaining respect and using fear."

Many hitters acknowledge that they feel more comfortable hitting against pitchers they know personally. Some major league hitters even make it a point to get to know a rookie pitcher who looks as if he's going to be around for a long while. The hitter works some mind games, trying to shape a "Mr.-Nice-Guy pitcher," who plays right into the hitter's hands — and zone.

Everyone wants to be liked, but you must decide what is most important to you. Winners can be well liked. They frequently are. *But they are always respected.* They play the game clean — and *hard*.

The Pitcher's Scheme

The best pitchers all identify and review their approach — the scheme of things — that has helped them prepare for their success:

> *Stay in shape.
> *Be ready when called on.
> *Know the opposition.
> *Master the mechanics.
> *Master the pitches.
> *Have a consistent mental wind-up.
> *Maintain focus without distraction.
> *Deal with one pitch at a time, always.
> *When things go poorly, think about the solution, not
> the problem.

Not every pitcher can throw the ball 90 miles an hour. But every pitcher is capable of controlling the ball, his thoughts, emotions, and tension levels — *his behavior*: how he acts and how he reacts. Every pitcher can learn to think and behave the way that will get the most out his natural talent — in every situation.

17
FIELDING

"I don't like them fellas who drive in two runs and let in three."

—*Casey Stengel*

"We should remember that with everything there is in the game of baseball, the thing there's most of are outs. That makes it pretty important to catch the ball and know what to do with it after you've caught it."

—*Bill Rigney*, former second baseman

"I'm awake out there."

—*Frank White*, another "heady" second baseman

What should be said about the mental approach to fielding? That the fielder should be awake? That he should concentrate? That he should be alert?

Anticipation and attentiveness are absolute requirements for the defensive player who aspires to excellence. But there's more. A quick review of the table of contents of Part One of this book might provide some further insight.

Goals

Kansas City second baseman Frank White has won a number of Gold Gloves. Over his long career, White, who accasionally hit fourth in the batting order, has demonstrated great pride in his fielding. He was attentive to his fielding. It was his goal to be an outstanding fielder, and like Ozzie Smith (see Chapter 9), his work ethic was constructed to help him attain that goal. He has.

Third baseman Graig Nettles and Boston's Wade Boggs came to the major leagues without the "talent" for fielding that the Whites and the Brooks Robinsons were acknowledged to have. Their apparent goal was respectability in the field. They went beyond being just "respectable" third basemen. These "natural" hitters are immensely proud of the attainment of their goals as defensive players.

> Assess your needs as a defensive player. Set up specific goals to work on in order to improve yourself. (See Appendix.) Pick a goal or two to work on each day. Add on at regular intervals. Monitor your improvement.

Expectations

Just using Nettles and Boggs as two of many examples, let it be said that many baseball scouts, coaches, and managers have limited expectations for players who are not adequate or superior fielders in high school, college, or the minor leagues.

> Once again, the player shouldn't concern himself with what others expect of him. If he sets his goal to become

a fine defensive player, he won't be affected by the limitations others have tried to project on him.

Dedication

A commitment to hard work after a goal has been set is the requirement for excellence. Playing defense is no exception. The quality of a player's practice habits is the tip-off as to whether or not he's truly made the commitment. Again, refer to Ozzie Smith's words in Chapter 9. Anyone can "take balls off the bat" and call it practice. The extent of the player's mental and physical commitment to fielding *each* ball hit to him indicates the extent to which the player is dedicated to becoming as good a defensive player as possible. Remember, it's more "fun" for most players to work on their strengths; more "fun" to hit. Outstanding first baseman Keith Hernandez admits that hitting is more fun for him than fielding. But he has worked diligently to become the great fielder he is. It's tougher to dedicate yourself to something that isn't your favorite activity.

> *Practice.*
> *Practice the right way.*
> *Practice the right way every day.*

Responsibility

It's always *your choice*, remember. Even the great Ted Williams and Ty Cobb were reluctant to dedicate themselves to defensive excellence. Their choice. Maximizing *all* your talents, enhancing *all* the dimensions of your game leads to *total excellence.* That would be *our* goal for a player who aspires to greatness, but it is *your responsibility* to make your choice.

Excuses? They don't work for defensive players either.

> If the sun gets in your eyes, you're responsible for figuring out a way to shield the sun.
> If you threw to the wrong base because a teammate told you there was one out and there were two, it remains your responsibility to have known how many outs there were.

A bad hop? "There's no such thing as a bad hop," said Leo Durocher. "It's the way you played it."

Take the responsibility, and you'll get the control.

Attitude

How do you feel about working on your fielding to begin with? How do you feel about the importance of defense? Where did these attitudes come from? Do they help your game — or do they help you feel comfortable about your behavior? Examine the answers carefully. Adjust your attitude accordingly.

Confidence

You're not likely to be confident if you haven't done anything to improve what might be your deficiency, in this case fielding skills.

Follow through on your commitment to improvement, and an improved level of confidence will also result.

Confidence is a state of mind. Believe in what you're doing and you'll believe in who you are.

Set task-specific defensive goals. You will build your confidence as you achieve each goal.

Learning

Third baseman Mike Schmidt, speaking to David Whitford of *Sport* (July 1986): " . . . In the first third of a game, I think you should do everything you can to prevent the opposition from getting an easy run . . . As a defensive player, anything I can do to prevent that is important to my ballclub.

"Most guys would never even consider guarding the line in the first third of a ballgame. But if he hits a double, then one hit can score him. If he hits a single, it takes two hits or a home run to score him.

"Now, let's take it a step further. Let's say I don't want to give up the lead in the first third of the ballgame . . .

" . . . I get accused of thinking too much . . .

"Baseball is a game that needs to be studied in order to be appreciated."

In order to be *played*, we would add to Schmidt's assessment.

> Study the game and you'll learn the game.
>
> Learn your own strengths and weaknesses as a defensive player. Then you can make the adjustments, the compensations. Do you go better to your right? Then "cheat" a bit to the left. Do you come in on a fly ball better than you go back? Then play a tad deeper.
>
> Be aware of what you can do and do it aggressively.

Preparation

Learning leads to preparation. Having understood what can happen, you prepare yourself for those possibilities.

First baseman Keith Hernandez, described by writer Craig Wolff (*Sport*, June 1987): "[Hernandez] knows which way the wind is blowing at Shea Stadium by the directon in which the planes are landing at LaGuardia Airport. He has taken the time to study their takeoff and landing patterns, because he knows that the flags atop Shea are an unreliable gauge of wind direction. This helps him determine which way to hit and also helps him judge pop flies. He knows the infield around the National League by heart. Backman swears that he once heard Hernadez talk for two hours in a restaurant about each National League stadium...He has faith in Wrigley Field. San Diego has improved. He likes Candlestick Park, but only early in the game. Later, he says, after they spray, the dirt and the wind picks up, clumps form in front of him..."

Hernandez spoke about scooping throws out of the dirt: "To make my glove fit just so, I soak the four fingers in warm water until the leather is saturated. I play catch with it for three or four days. Then I put two balls into the pocket and fold the four fingers in. I tape the glove..."

Preparation has many dimensions. Each one has a purpose: to be at your best, always.

Take ground balls or fly balls off the bat with the same mental attentiveness called for in a game. That is the way the best prepare themselves.

Habits form easily. Develop good habits through consistently good preparation.

Continue to assess the style and substance of your daily preparation. Are you practicing the way you want to play?

The pitcher who "waltzes" through fielding drills in spring training is preparing himself for what? See how many "routine" plays pitchers mess up. But their performance usually results from the "routine" they practiced most—a waltz. In that sense, they too "prepared" themselves.

Visualization

Perfect practice makes perfect. There is no easier way to be perfect than by practicing through mental pictures.

Run the pictures over in your mind, projecting how you want to take your position/stance. Start your movements, focus in, make the play.

Run it over and over. It helps. And you don't need a field to do it on. (Review Chapter 10 for specific techniques.)

Concentration

Willie Stargell, in *Out of Left Field*, (by Adelman & Hall): " . . . Outfield is the hardest position to play. It takes great concentration. Balls don't come to you often, but you must tell yourself that every pitch that is thrown is going to be hit to you."

In a sense, outfielders do have it toughest, in that they're most responsible for disciplining their concentration on every pitch. A catcher knows the ball is headed toward him on every pitch, and every infielder understands the distinct possibility of the ball being hit his way. Also, the infielder is closer to the hitter than the outfielder is. That alone keeps him "on his toes."

As Stargell said, the ball isn't hit to an outfielder as often, so he must control his concentration in the face of the fact that he can often "get away with" having his mind wander. Ah, but what of that *one* bad jump he gets on a fly ball? The one that loses a big game? A big series?

The great players never want to be caught by surprise. They have control of their concentration. An outfielder must sometimes use "tricks" to keep his mind in the game. These devices, however, serve him the better to be prepared.

Stargell again: "Keep watching the wind, moving with the [other] players, noticing whether the surface is wet or dry, if the grass is tall or short. How far are you from the fence? What is the fence made of? Can you be daring?"

Use self-talk to direct yourself with relevant cues. That will keep your concentration directed. Use the cues that are appropriate for the position you're playing on defense. Stargell's are for an outfielder, of course. Catchers and infielders will have different cues, but the approach will be the same.

Keep your attention on business before every pitch. See the ball. Be ready for it.

Mental Discipline

Ozzie Smith pointed out the extreme need for a defensive player's mental discipline. "You know, having to concentrate on every pitch *is* a form of mental discipline. But do you realize that as a hitter, you only have to concentrate on, say, 25 pitches a game. As a fielder, you have to discipline your mind to be prepared about 150 times a game. That's tough. It takes work. That's why taking [practice] ground balls as if you were in a game helps you get that discipline for the game. For game after game, over a long season. Yes, it's tough."

Because a ball isn't coming at a fielder in the immediate and urgent sense it does to a hitter, the mental discipline Smith speaks of must be more controlled by the player. The situation *allows* for more distraction (as in the case of outfielders).

A hitter has a bad at-bat. He takes that bad at bat into the field with him. He dwells on the results of that at-bat — or he might even be making a wise adjustment for his next at-bat. The timing and setting of the adjustment is inappropriate. As a fielder, he shows no mental discipline.

> Be aware of your thoughts. Know whether the obstacle to concentration is a bad at-bat, a previous error, pain in your leg, etc. Listen to that thought.
>
> Catch yourself and stop the thought. Tell yourself what your business is.
>
> Trigger your concentration by smoothing the infield dirt, pounding your glove, checking the other fielders, etc.
>
> Establish a routine for disciplining your mind in the field. Distractions always present themselves. As Ozzie Smith said, "It's tough." But necessary.

Relaxation

Ozzie Smith also recalled his early days as a major leaguer. He remembered having to go into games as a late-inning defensive replacement at shortstop. "You know," Smith said, "It was hard to relax in those situations. I mean, when a pinch hitter is used at the end of a game, not that much is expected. He may get a hit, but there's a good chance he won't. But when a player is put in for defense with the game on the line, he'd *better* make the play on a ball hit to him. I felt that pressure those days."

We dealt with a minor league player in the Cleveland organization who said he could handle ground balls at first base just fine, with two outs in the ninth inning — and his team winning, or losing, by 10 runs. "But let the score be 3-2, and I'm knotted when that thing is hit to me."

A fielder can't have soft hands in that state. Relaxation techniques are in order if you suffer from a similar malady.

> After rereading Chapter 13, apply specifically appropriate techniques during your fielding drills or practice sessions. Consciously make it part of your approach, until it is naturally integrated.
>
> Review your "philosophy." Why are you tight? What's

at stake? What are the catastrophic consequences of an error?

Relax your mind and your body will follow suit.

Fielders should make their practice sessions as important to them as their batting practice is. The opportunities for fielding practice will often have to be initiated by the player himself, whereas batting practice is a more regular part of every day's game preparation. Find a time; find a place. Get after achieving the goals you've set for your defensive improvement.

A FIELDER'S MENTAL GUIDE FOR GAMES

Know the physical conditions (surface, fences, contours, wind, weather, etc.)

Know the game situation (score, outs, position of other fielders, identity and tendencies of the hitter, count, type of pitch to be thrown, etc.) and position yourself accordingly.

Know what you want to do with the ball if it's hit to you. Anticipate what a baserunner might do. Know what alternatives exist for making a specific play.

Follow the routine you have developed for readying yourself before each pitch. Include a breathing pattern (slow exhale), a key for getting your attention focused, a set time to get your eyes to the hitter and/or the ball, a physical stance, an anticipated movement.

Be soft; be easy; be ready; be quick; be aggressive.

18
BASERUNNING

"The accomplishment that gave me the most pride was stealing 104 bases in 1962 for a major-league record. This surpassed Ty Cobb's record of 96 stolen bases, which had stood since 1915 and was generally considered to have been written in concrete . . . To acquire that record, I endured a lot of pain and anguish. Stealing those bases was a hard-bought record."

— *Maury Wills*, in *How to Steal a Pennant*

"Casey Stengel, when he was a young player, came up to me one night and asked, 'Ty, on outfield hits, how do you manage to take that extra base so often? You don't look that fast to me.'

"'I'm not,' I told Casey. 'Rounding first, I look to see which hand the guy has used to field that ball. If he's right-handed, and the ball's in his left hand, it means he has to cross over his body and turn to make the throw. That's my edge, and I take it without hesitating.'"

— *Ty Cobb*, in *My Life in Baseball*

"Johnny Bench was considered slow afoot. He didn't steal bases. But he was an outstanding baserunner. He always knew what he was doing on the base paths. He cut a sharp corner around second when he was going from first to third. That saved him time and helped make up for his lack of speed. Not many people notice things like that, because not many people pay attention to baserunning. They say baseball is a game of inches. Well, there are plenty of inches you can gain on the base paths if you know where to find them."

— *Ron Plaza*, former Cincinnati Reds coach

Knowing what to do and doing it, we've said any number of times, are two different things. Well, insofar as baserunning is concerned, we'll change our old tune a bit. Speed has usually been considered the prerequisite for being a great baserunner. But having speed — and knowing what to do with it — are two different things. There are many who are swift of foot, but slow of a mind to use that speed effectively. Not that they are mentally unable. Rather, they are mentally *unwilling* — unwilling to use their skills. Some players, of course, are simply unaware of the importance of being an excellent baserunner. Perhaps Ron Plaza's words have already opened a few such minds.

Every baseball player has the ability to run. The distinction for a basestealer is that he can run very quickly. But the player who is an outstanding basestealer has also learned to use his mental equipment well. He has studied and refined his art.

Even players who are slow afoot are capable of study. These players aren't great basestealers, but they can be (and many are) great baserunners. They get around the bases safely — and aggressively, taking advantage of opportunities that they have *anticipated*. They rarely get doubled off base. They somehow manage to take the extra base when it's there for the taking.

How do they do this? There's not that much to say in response to the question. But those who apply the simple answer become exceptions to the rule. Baserunning, you see, is not really a *lost* art. It is a *neglected* one.

We believe there are a number of reasons for this being the case. The most significant one is the mistaken belief that only the speedy runner can be an outstanding baserunner. The young position player who lacks speed plays his way onto a team by showing, and taking pride in, his hitting and/or fielding prowess. Because he's slow, his first coaches—Little League, high school—paid little attention to his baserunning, unless it was to tell him, "When I time you to first base, I use a calendar." Or to call him "Clyde," as in Clydesdale. So there is no perception on the player's part of running as a useful tool for him. It's a liability he carries around with him. Slowly.

Anyone who has had this happen to him needs an immediate change of attitude. So do those who move swiftly—but ineffectually. Others may require an attitude where none previously existed.

As is the case with all facets of baseball, effective baserunning requires a positive attitude and an effective mental approach.

Dave Nelson, when he was an infielder for the Texas Rangers in the mid-'70s, once stole second, third, and home in the same inning. Quite a feat. Currently, Nelson works with Cleveland's baserunners. Nelson's lessons include four mental prerequisites for effective baserunning (not just base*stealing*):

1. **A will to be a complete player**
2. **A pride in learning and preparedness**
3. **A competitive aggressiveness**
4. **Good judgment**

Those four attitudes can be found in all maximum achievers who play the game. Let's examine each, as it relates to baserunning.

The will to be a complete player is simply a drive to seek one's personal potential without being self-limiting. Johnny Bench's arm and bat were enough to get him into the Hall of Fame. But he did not allow his legs to be self-limiting. His heart and brain gave them the necessary support, so that he gained recognition, from those who watched him play every day, as a fine baserunner.

Many players take their limitations as final statements; many others take their talent for granted. The will Nelson speaks of is the same will we have advocated throughout this book.

A big, young catcher currently in the Oakland minor league system has high grades for his arm and power at bat; a low grade for his running speed. During 1987 Instructional League play, the player was told about Bench. The minor leaguer began to work diligently and effectively at compensating for his lack of speed. Approaching first base on a hit to the outfield, he *slowed down*, thus being able to get as right an angle as possible on the turn. The same at second. And at third. He had learned that by doing this, he would save more *distance* than he lost in *time*. Valuable inches!

The player's concentrated dedication to self-improvement became the insignia of his running. He had previously worn a "badge of shame" for his slowness afoot.

If all players worked as hard at baserunning as this catcher had, they would become more complete—and more threatening to the opposition. The threat of a baserunner is proportionate to his speed—and his ability to use it fully and intelligently.

Learning and preparation are powerful factors in the achievement of athletic excellence. (Review Chapters 8 and 9.) One of the problems related to baserunning and learning is that many coaches of young players, and the players themselves, feel baserunning is basestealing, period. Consequently, players without speed feel that whatever there is to be learned does not pertain to them.

This, of course, is not the case. Every ballplayer has the ability to be an effective baserunner, if he values learning and preparation.

There is knowledge a baserunner should have, as there is knowledge a fielder should have—or a hitter, or a pitcher. It's as important for a baserunner to know about the "texture" of the base paths as it is for Keith Hernandez to know about it as a first baseman. It's as important for a baserunner to know the condition of the outfield grass or turf as it is for the outfielder. Will a base hit to the outfield shoot into the gap, or slow up on wet grass? It's as important for a runner on base to know the strength and accuracy of the outfielder's throwing arm as it is for the outfielder to know the runner's speed and tendencies.

Clearly, it's important for the batter-runner and the baserunner to know and be attentive to everything possible. Certainly, this can't be taught in a complete fashion on these pages, but the runner can seek out teammates, coaches — anyone who can help him learn and be more prepared. There will be a number of different philosophies, but again, the player must find what works best for him and for his team.

After information there is the application. First, in practice. We have seen very few players use a standard baserunning routine effectively during their batting practice. Usually, after a player has had his last hit in his b.p. round, he ambles down to first. Sometimes, he makes a perfunctory stop there; sometimes he keeps ambling around the bases. Is he practicing taking a *good* lead off first? Is he watching the b.p. pitcher's shoulder as he practices? Though this isn't an ideally realistic practice, the player can get some value from it. Does he try to read the balls coming off the bat while he's on each base? Though pitchers are usually shagging balls in the outfield, the practice still can be helpful to the runner. Does the runner use the opportunity? *Any* opportunity?

At the end of the 1986 season, Chicago White Sox manager Jim Fregosi was upset with many of his players because they weren't preparing themselves as they played the game. He decided to hold "spring training" in September, shortly after two baserunning errors resulted in a loss of a game to Kansas City.

"A lot of players when they get on base would rather talk to the opposing player than see where the people are positioned," Fregosi said. "They should be thinking about the things that should be done . . . They don't understand game situations."

Dave Nelson teaches players how to work at getting jumps and reinforcing their learning by practicing on their own. Only the exceptionally motivated players manage to find the time. It is a familiar truth.

Players are taught to use their own judgment when going from first to third, but good judgment is a result of previous knowledge, and the average player — the mediocre baserunner — seems to find it easier to rely on someone else.

Far from being a mediocre baserunner, Ty Cobb once knocked

down his third base coach, as he rounded the base on his way home, after the coach had given him the "hold-up" sign. The coach apologized for getting in Cobb's way, adding, "But I could see the ball and you couldn't and I figured . . . "

Cobb told him he *could* see the ball. "The secret," Cobb explained in his book, *My Life in Baseball*, "was that I'd been practicing for hours running full speed while training myself to look over my right shoulder, and keeping tabs on the whereabouts of the ball. I see big leaguers do this only rarely any more. They run blindly and depend on coaching signals, often misunderstood, instead of depending on the fact that the human neck is built on a swivel, and it only takes a lot of hard practice to make it your most dependable base of observation."

The physical practicing of turns, the looking back, getting leads, sliding properly, etc., all enhance performance on the base paths. But there is also the mental practice.

Baserunners are always told to anticipate all possibilities. They must be prepared for hits to all parts of the field, line drives that are catchable, bunts, ground balls, swings and misses, fielding errors of all types, pick-off attempts by pitchers or catchers. This can be done effectively through visualization. The baserunner might tell himself to watch for a line drive, but his words alone do not adequately prepare him for the appropriate action. The play should flash in his mind, along with his proper response.

How many times have we seen runners doubled off a base on a line drive, just after hearing the warning from a coach to "get back on a line drive"? Many times.

For young players (including major leaguers), the toughest judgment play in baseball is what's referred to as "reading base hits." This does not only involve reading and getting a jump on the hit. The runner must also anticipate and know when to stay put.

Players who excel at this always know where the defensive players are positioned. They locate them before the first pitch to the batter, and they continue to check them every pitch or two thereafter, because defenses often will move as the count changes. Once the baserunner has a mental image of the defensive positioning, his mind games continue. He then imagines the defensive players' range, arm strength, and accuracy and hits to all parts of the field that are particularly difficult to read. He also imagines balls that can be caught. This "imaging" allows him to recognize quickly the hits and possible outs.

Baserunners also have snap decisions to make on many ground balls. For example, a runner on second base or third base with less than two out often has to read the ball to determine whether to go or stay. In order to make a quick and correct decision, he must anticipate (visualize) different types of ground balls and his response to each of them. This is an essential mental preparation for those who wish to be outstanding baserunners.

Ty Cobb was as devoted to his movement around the bases as he was to his movement from station to station, when he stole a base. He watched pitchers' movements: shoulders, hips, knees, elbows. Nowadays, pitchers and catchers are timed. Does a baserunner know the opposing pitcher's time to the plate? Does he know the catcher's time to second base? Does he know the pitcher's physical and behavioral tendencies? Does he throw over to first twice, and then deliver to home plate—always? Valuable knowledge can be converted into valuable inches—into the valuable edge that every great competitor works at getting.

Competitive aggressiveness is a trait of every outstanding athlete. It has nothing to do with what a player says. It has everything to do with what he does. Some people call it "arrogance," and they don't mean it to be complimentary. Frequently, an intimidated player tries to demean an opponent with that label. But great players take the term as a compliment, regardless of how it was intended.

"To be a star and stay a star," said Joe Morgan, "I think you've got to have a certain air of arrogance about you, a cockiness, a swagger on the field that says, 'I can do this and you can't stop me.' I know that I play[ed] baseball with this air of arrogance, but I think it's lacking in a lot of guys who have the potential to be stars."

"Baserunning arrogance is just like pitching arrogance or hitting arrogance," Lou Brock told Hal Bodley (*USA Today*), shortly before Brock's induction into the Hall of Fame. "You are a force and you have to instill you are a force to the opposition. Don Drysdale and Sal Maglie would throw a ball close to the hitter to let you know they were out there. That's pitching arrogance because now he's coming at you. He's just driven you to your very best. And he wants to challenge that.

"Baserunning is the same thing, with one exception. The runner gets to first base and stands out there nine or ten feet off the base. The question then becomes, 'How do I act? How do I respond? Do I challenge them or do I back away?' If you're arrogant, you are presenting a presence that tells the opposition, 'I am ready for the test.'"

We remember the great Jackie Robinson's arrogance—all the more remarkable in the context of his battle to fight racial prejudice as he played. On the base paths, he seemed to go beyond Brock's "I am ready for the test." Robinson's arrogance seemed to take the initiative of asking the opponent, "Are *you* ready for the test, because I am always going to be testing you?"

Cardinals announcer Jack Buck, sympathizing with opposing teams, said about outfielder Vince Coleman's aggressiveness on the bases, "He'll get in your brain. When he's running around in your brain wearing spikes, it's terrible."

Don Mattingly doesn't feel all that sorry for opponents who have to deal with the Yankees Rickey Henderson. "Basically," says Mattingly, "Rickey terrorizes an entire team. It's kind of neat to watch."

Jackie Robinson, Rickey Henderson, Tim Raines, Coleman, Brock, Marquis Grissom, Delino DeShields, et. al., could cause "massive brain damage," perhaps. But any aggressive runner, regardless of speed, can cause enough minor damage to win ball games. You do not have to be intimidating to be a good baserunner; you do not have to forfeit an edge because you are not swift.

Case in point: Jim Fregosi spoke further about his team's baserunning in '86. "They take horrible leads. They don't fight to get good leads."

Fight. That's the aggressiveness *any* runner can have. Fight for what you are capable of getting. You can't get Coleman's nine or 10 feet off the bag? What can you get? Do you test to see your limit?

Does it vary from pitcher to pitcher? When you reach your limit, do you stay at it—or retreat from it? Are you thinking more about getting back to the base safely, than getting off it to get the edge— the valuable inches?

When you get a hit to the outfield, are you always thinking of taking the extra base, or are you satisfied to get comfortably into first or second? Are you assuming the outfielder will mishandle the ball, or are you assuming he will handle it? The answer to all these questions tells much about your effectiveness as an aggressive baserunner.

The aggressive competitor is running to take the extra base, then holding up when he sees he can be stopped. The non-aggressive, passive — lazy — baserunner runs and assumes he will stop. He then becomes surprised by an outfielder's blunder. Often, he's thrown out trying to take advantage of the blunder, because he's lost his inches *before* he reacted and accelerated. More often, he just holds up, because it's clearly too late to take advantage of the misplay.

Do you remember Al Oliver's approach to hitting? He went up there swinging, and then decided when not to, rather than going up to take, and then deciding when to swing. Aggressive.

Do you remember Willie Stargell's advice to fielders? Assume the ball will be hit to you, rather than assuming it won't be hit to you. Mentally aggressive. Prepared.

The competitive edge can be gained everywhere on the field, by anyone. Even by slow runners, on the base paths. Take the sharp, deep turn; cause the outfielder to take his eye off the ball and muff it. Don't let the defensive players be comfortable. Be aggressive; do some damage.

Good judgment is the final ingredient in our mix for the baserunner. You may have the heart of a hunter and all the equipment, but you'd better have a good aim when the lion appears. As a baserunner, aggressiveness and knowledge are put to proper use through good judgment — knowing when, where, and why to run. Knowing the degree of risk and the extent of consequences. Putting into action the do's and don'ts of baserunning, as set down by your coaches and managers, and as learned by you (e.g., not making the third out of an inning by being thrown out at third base).

Judgment is simply the application of the knowledge and understanding you have. A player who doesn't know what is called for on the base paths isn't using bad judgment; he's just ignorant — unaware. Lack of learning is hard to tolerate. Mistakes in judgment can be tolerated, so long as they aren't continually repeated. If a baserunner adopts the attitude that every mistake he makes will be fatal, he'll focus more on his judgment than on the situation and task. And he'll then lose his aggressiveness. Good judgment comes with experience.

Aggressive play leads to risk. Every great athlete takes risks, but only when he believes the odds are in his favor. Look for the right moment; know what you want to accomplish; be prepared; be attentive.

A football player may run with "reckless abandon." A baseball player runs with good judgment.

If you now know what to do — do it. You know you can if you make the commitment.

We conclude on this, by now, very familiar note.

APPENDIX
Task-Specific Goals

The following pages list some task-specific goals to serve players on a daily basis. They relate to both the physical and the mental—the behavioral and the attitudinal.

Setting specific goals helps the player to focus on his own strengths and weaknesses. it gives him purpose and direction. It reinforces the basic tenet of every exceptional athlete: focus on the job to be done. For baseball players, that translates into a focus that is always on the situation and the next pitch, and the mental and physical preparation for it.

Similarly, you can only focus on one goal at a time, therefore you have to determine what your priorities are and what the right times are to work on them.

A true dedication to the attainment of the goals that follow results in the "perfect practice" habits of elite athletes—and in consistently fine performances.

Also found in this Appendix are player self-evaluation forms, utilized to monitor behavior during competition. Many players have used them effectively, and have correlated excellent performance on the field with high scores on their evaluation form. These forms may be photocopied and used from week to week for practice and regular season games. Players may add specific entries to the list, according to individual behavioral goals and needs.

HITTING

Practice Goals

Disciplined batting practice (staying within self)

Seeing the ball as well as possible

Controlling the bat and the ball

    Situation hitting (hit & run, hit it hard on the ground, opposite field hitting, etc.)

Game Goals

Pre-game plan

On-deck circle to batter's box

Use of self-talk and relaxation techniques

Staying within yourself (letting it happen)

Concentration/focus—Seeing the ball (putting on "automatic pilot"), letting eyes take over

    Gathering between pitches

    Being mentally ready on every pitch, in every situation

    Every at-bat a good, tough a.b.

    Being the intimidator, rather than the intimidated

    Establishing strike zone through discipline

Anticipate swinging on every pitch (See it; time it; stop if you see it's not a pitch to swing at—depending on situation)

Other Individual Goals

BUNTING

Sacrifice

Technique

Practice results

Game attempts/successes (monitor ratio)

Good location

Took pitch for a strike (wanting to bunt)

Missed or fouled ball off

For a Hit

Technique

Practice results

Game attempts/successes

Concentration Level

Knowing what's to be done

Seeing ball well

Other Individual Goals

PITCHING

First-pitch strikes

Effective 0-2 pitches

Finishing hitters

Ball-strike ratio

Getting outs before three-ball count

Good location (down vs. up)

Good fielding

Holding runners

Unloading time to the plate

Backing up bases

Sound mechanics

Preparation (selection/location/commitment to pitch)

Concentration (focus on next pitch and target)

Relaxation (breathing patterns)

Establishing good tempo

Gathering self after difficulty (self-talk off mound)

Handling clutch situations and/or difficulty (mental discipline)

Other Individual Goals

CATCHING

Anticipation

Taking charge of game

Throwing accurately in infield practice

Setting up and giving targets

Mechanics

    Catching balls

    Blocking balls

    Throwing

        Getting rid of the ball

        Throwing "strikes"

Pop-ups

Tag plays

Pitch Selection

    Getting ahead

    Getting outs early in the count

Communication with pitcher

    Knowing his abilities, tendencies, and needs

    Before game

    During game

Tempo

Concentration/Alertness

    Knowing game situation

    Knowing batter's strength/weakness/previous at-bats

    Knowing batter's/runner's speed

Other Individual Goals

INFIELD PLAY

Throwing Mechanics

   Concentration

   Release

   Accuracy

Ground Balls

   Preparation

   Concentration

   Mechanics

   Consistency

      Routine plays

      Difficult plays

   Coming in on balls

   Going to right/left

Pop-ups

Movement on every pitch

Jumps (anticipation)

Other Individual Goals

OUTFIELD PLAY

Knowing playing conditions (every pitch)

Knowing situation

Anticipation

Communication

Movement on every pitch

Seeing ball off bat

Getting good jumps (first two steps)

Charging balls on the ground

Taking good routes

Backing up plays

Catching mechanics

Throwing mechanics

    Footwork

    Release

Throwing accuracy

Hitting cut-off man (consistency)

Other Individual Goals

MENTAL KEYS FOR FIELDERS

Date: ☐

PREPARATION
(Appropriate postioning for each hitter)

☐☐☐☐☐☐☐

CONCENTRATION
(Consistence readiness on each pitch)

☐☐☐☐☐☐☐

ANTICIPATION
(What to do **when** [not if] ball is hit to me)

☐☐☐☐☐☐☐

RELAXATION
(Breathing; coming set 'easy')

☐☐☐☐☐☐☐

AGGRESSIVENESS
(Making play vs. letting ball play me;
on toes, not heels)

☐☐☐☐☐☐☐

POISE
(Controlled responses to errors/bad plays,
i.e. body language, self-talk)

☐☐☐☐☐☐☐

CONSISTENCY
(Thought process; positioning)

☐☐☐☐☐☐☐

VISUALIZATION
(Seeing myself making the plays)

☐☐☐☐☐☐☐

Excellent =4
Good =3
Fair =2
Poor =1

MENTAL KEYS FOR PITCHERS   **Date:** [   ]

AGGRESSIVE APPROACH [| | | | | |]
(Forcing contact; challenging hitters)

INTENSITY LEVEL [| | | | | |]
(Heat & Light; not flickering, not burning the house down)

CONFIDENCE [| | | | | |]
(Trusting stuff)

FOCUS/CONCENTRATION [| | | | | |]
(Selection, location, **target**)

TEMPO [| | | | | |]
(Get the ball back & be ready to go;
slow for necessary adjustments)

RELAXATION [| | | | | |]
(Breathing; appropriate thinking patterns)

SELF-COACHING [| | | | | |]
(Positive, task-oriented self-talk)

POISE [| | | | | |]
(Body language, consistent behavior on rubber)

VISUALIZATION [| | | | | |]
(Off the rubber)

Excellent =4
Good   =3
Fair   =2
Poor   =1

MENTAL KEYS FOR HITTERS

Date: [   ]

ON-DECK PREPARATION
(Knowing game situation and performance keys) [ ][ ][ ][ ][ ][ ][ ][ ]

AGGRESSIVE MENTALITY
(Ready to swing!) [ ][ ][ ][ ][ ][ ][ ][ ]

FOCUS/CONCENTRATION
(Clear head, seeing the ball) [ ][ ][ ][ ][ ][ ][ ][ ]

ABILITY TO MAKE ADJUSTMENTS
(Pitch-to-pitch, between at-bats) [ ][ ][ ][ ][ ][ ][ ][ ]

SELF-TALK
(Positive self-talk; focus on function) [ ][ ][ ][ ][ ][ ][ ][ ]

POISE
(Relaxation/Breathing, Body language) [ ][ ][ ][ ][ ][ ][ ][ ]

CONSISTENCY
(Thought process, Trusting swing) [ ][ ][ ][ ][ ][ ][ ][ ]

VISUALIZATION
(On-deck circle) [ ][ ][ ][ ][ ][ ][ ][ ]

Excellent =4
Good =3
Fair =2
Poor =1